Why Wait For Detroit?

Drive An Electric Car Today!

Articles on electric cars by
Bob Batson, Robert Beaumont, Paul Brasch,
Mike Brown, Scott Cornell, Fred Daniel, Lester Embree,
David Goldstein, Michael Hackleman, Jay Harris, John Hoke,
Ken Koch, Joseph LaStella, Kevin McDonald, Shari Prange,
Joe Stevenson, Jim Tervort, Jim Treacy, Bill Williams,
Bill Yerkes, and other pioneers

General Moto

Edi

The nei
will s

So

Second Edition, Printing No. (read last number): 5 4 3 2 1
ISBN Number 1-879857-02-2, published through the Gutenberg Project, c/o Michael Hart, 217-344-0367, 405 West Elm Street, Urbana, IL 61801. Directory of EV Resources is updated on an electronic bulletin board: 301-422-8704. Send updates to C. Harrison, 301-495-7113 (work), 301-422-8704 (home). New England EAA has established an EV database. Contact Jan Dolansky, EAA database administrator 508-374-8291. Compuserve has an EV computer bulletin board: sign up at 800-848-8199, Operator 190. You can gain access by calling Compuserve with a modem.

Acknowledgements

This book began with a question: "What is the basic information needed by the first-time owner of an electric car?" From the avalanche of articles and suggestions sent by EV advocates emerged these pages, with a promise for a larger book in the future. This project would not have been nearly as informative or attractive without the proofreading, feedback and criticism of the contributing authors, members of electric car organizations, and everyone else who volunteered time to read the first draft. Special thanks to Michael Hackleman, Doug Cobb, Bob Adams, Bob Batson, John Newell, Ruth MacDougall, Lew Gulick, Beatrice Vornle, Raymond Merz, J.R., Larry Alexander and Shari Prange.

Special gratitude to Glenn Barr, M.J. Marvin-Matthews, and the public relations people at the Big Three and VW. To Seventh Generation mail-order catalog company: thank you for re-introducing us to the wisdom of the first North Americans, who believed, *"In our every deliberation, we must consider the impact of our decisions on the next seven generations."* May our car purchases today have a benign impact on the world of the great-grandchildren of our great-grandchildren. Cover design: Kevin Keegan and J.M. Kayman (first edition), Jim Treacy (second edition) of IST, 1508 Swan Street, Washington, D.C., 20036, tel. 202-483-1855, fax 202-483-0073.

Printed in the U.S.A. by Printing Corporation of the Americas, 620 S.W. 12th Ave., Pompano Beach, FL 33060, 305-781-8100. Photo preparation by SBS Graphics, Oakland Park, FL; J. Verdeguer's crew (305-568-9444) and American Litho, Fort Lauderdale, FL; Lithograpics, 1716 Eye St., N.W., Washington, DC; D. Yuzenas, Margate, Florida.

With much gratitude to J.K. and A.C.P.: May you one day find an electric car that makes you feel comfortable, so that you, too, can enjoy zero-emissions driving.

Photo by Shari Prange.

Three-wheeled EVs like this Vortex are considered motorcycles and can often cost less to insure and maintain than a converted EV.

Contents

Dedication

To the hundreds of EV pioneers
who are working to offer an alternative to
the internal combustion engine,

to the Electric Auto Association,
founded in 1967 and celebrating 25 years of
providing information about EVs to the public,

to the thousands of EV owners
who daily express their commitment to
cleaner air and a secure energy future,

to Leo Schatzl, Vic Jager, Frank Flowers,
Don Wilson, Walter Laski, Dean Kopp, G. Rogers Porter,
Keith Cronk and other visionaries
whose batteries gave out
before their work was finished, and

to everyone who will live in the post-petroleum era,
especially Stephanie, Kristen, Marina, Alexandra, Nicholas, Jessica, Olivia, R.K.,
Elisabeth, Zoë, Richard, Wendy, BBB (Sibyl), Faith, Dick, Chuck, Fawlty, the
Chesnut boys, Deepak, Rohit, Shruti, Micah, Jacob, Scott, Jeffrey, Brett, Webster,
the Bohnsack kids, Sol (Chi-Chi), Luna, Seba, Elisa, the Patterson kids, David,
Asha, Ayesha, Shoki, Bob, Shadeux, Barney,
and the next seven generations.

**We must get rid of the infernal combustion engine,
or it will get rid of us!**

Leo Schatzl
who commuted to work in an EV for 20 years
*and appeared on **Fight Back!***
(the public television show for activist consumers)
1919-1989

Preface to the Second Edition

To the Reader: The first edition of *Why Wait For Detroit?* contained the essence of two books: 1) a general introduction to electric vehicles (EVs), the basics for the new EV owner and a list of resources for EV components and supplies; and 2) technical information and in-depth information on electric cars, including an extensive chapter honoring today's EV pioneers. **Book A** is presented here in its second edition. **Book B** is scheduled for release in December 1993, and will cover 400 pages of the most comprehensive material ever collected on electric cars. *It will celebrate all types of alternative-fuel vehicles and anyone who owns an electric car.* **If you own an electric car, send a photo. You'll be listed as an environmental and balance-of-trade patriot. If you were driving electric cars before the Exxon Valdez oil spill of March 1989, you're an EV pioneer, and you should send a short biography** for inclusion in the "Big Book."

Book B ("the Big Book") will cover every conceivable aspect of owning an electric car; it will be called *The EV Encyclopedia: A Guide to Electric Vehicles,* retailing for $19.95 (add $1.00 for postage if ordering directly from SFEAA). Net proceeds from the sale of all books published by the South Florida Electric Auto Association are supporting the public education programs of electric car organizations.

There is no deadline for being included in "the Big Book" because a supplement will be assembled annually to keep the EV Encyclopedia up-to-date.

A Word About This Book

Thanks to the volunteered suggestions of a number of manuscript readers, this revised version of *Why Wait For Detroit?* has an improved structure, making it more accessible to the casual reader.

The editors made every effort to keep the pace entertaining, eye-appealing, and lively, while stuffing each page with useful information. While we did not aim to produce a comprehensive directory of every organization concerned with the environment, many groups that are not usually associated with electric cars have been included to suggest two things: 1) the need for EV enthusiasts to expand their focus and note the impact of their EVs on the environment, and 2) the need for a coalition of utilities, environmentalists, nuclear energy supporters, clean coal lobbyists, renewable energy advocates and natural gas suppliers to work together to support electric cars. EVs are not the only answer, but they are part of the solution. Getting ten percent or twenty percent of vehicles converted to battery power is just the beginning. We gain nothing if the highways remain congested (our EVs won't pollute, but we'll still waste time). The EV coalition should support efforts by groups like the Association for Commuter Transportation and the U.S. Department of Transportation to remove incentives that encourage single-occupant commuting. Let's work to reduce the supply of employer-subsidized parking.

The graph on the inside cover of this book comes from a book called *Beyond Oil: The Threat to Food and Fuel in the Coming Decades.* Published in 1986, the book has been reissued and is available through Carrying Capacity Network, 1325 G Street, Suite 1003, Washington, D.C. 20005, 202-879-3045. The philosophy of looking at the big picture, which is the central purpose of Carrying Capacity, is part of the philosophy behind *Why Wait For Detroit?* Where it makes sense to recycle existing cars, we advocate conversion to electric. Where it makes sense to wait for vehicles designed from the ground up, we suggest that you wait for Detroit to produce the car you are seeking. In certain regions, it makes sense to purchase a natural gas or methanol vehicle, so we don't argue against these "alternatives" to EVs. Our common foe is the imported barrel of crude oil. We are looking "beyond oil," and you are invited to join us in making the transition to the post-petroleum era.

Steve McCrea (Ft. Lauderdale, Fla.) and Richard Minner (Sacramento, Calif.)

May 6, Clean Air Day: Join us in celebrating May 6 as the anniversary of the Los Angeles Initiative, proposed by Councilman Marvin Braude and adopted by the Los Angeles City Council on May 6, 1988. The following is extracted from the City Council's minutes:

Widespread use of electric vehicles can contribute significantly to the improvement of air quality in Southern California. Because these vehicles use a clean and easily transportable source of energy — electricity — they can provide mobility without the resulting byproducts of combustion.

It is important that the City of Los Angeles take all possible steps to ensure the prompt development of a Southern California market for electric vehicles. Attainment of the federal air quality standards is one of our most pressing environmental problems and it is one which requires aggressive and innovative solutions.

The need for cleaner air and the pending leap in electric vehicle technology come together at a very opportune time. The City of Los Angeles, in cooperation with the region's major electric utilities and the private sector, can guarantee a large and stable market for electric vehicles. This market can result in even greater advances in electric car technology and cleaner air.

September 27: The End of the ICE Age Day: The California Air Resources Board adopted emissions standards on September 27, 1990, requiring 2% of new car sales in California to be zero-emission vehicles in 1998. The CARB standards have been adopted by a number of states, ensuring the widespread return of electric vehicles before the end of the 20th Century. *Named by Wendy Brawer, New York, N.Y.*

A note of caution from the editors

What does it cost to own a practical, "guilt-free" zero-emissions automobile? Let's be candid: in most cases, **this book advocates that you switch to a slower, heavier and more expensive vehicle that can't travel as far as your current car.** *Why? Because protecting the environment and our lungs, reducing oil imports and investing in a sustainable future all demand a shift in our priorities and values away from high-performance cars powered by inexpensive gasoline. Sure, EVs require less maintenance than conventional cars, most of our trips by car are well within the range of most EVs, and you'll read in Chapter 11 about why it's cheaper to pay five cents per kilowatt-hour instead of $1.30 per gallon. However, the editors encourage you to get a balanced view of the car of the future.*

Most people are not willing to learn how to build their own EVs, so the initial cost of future EVs will be somewhat greater than many of the costs quoted in this book. Most consumers want an easy-to-use vehicle that doesn't need an engineer to calculate the miles left to travel, and that costs between $10,000 (for a used car converted to battery power by a trained mechanic) to around $25,000 (for a hybrid EV with a computer to monitor battery levels). The most affordable EV, a conversion, costs three times more than the typical family's second car, which averages four to six years old and can be replaced for under $3,000. Never mind that the maintenance and fuel costs are usually more for the internal combustion engine, or that the life-cycle cost of an EV is sometimes less than the ICE car. **The critical obstacle to widespread acceptance of EVs remains the initial purchase price.** *To reduce air pollution and the need for oil imports, public policy should either tax gasoline to encourage the use of sustainable fuels or provide subsidies to individuals who switch to cars powered by alternative fuels.*

Throughout these pages the contributing authors repeatedly point to the benefits of battery power. Even if your utility makes electricity from fuel oil, you are still reducing the demand for gasoline, which is the principal reason for the industrial world's dependence on imported petroleum. To determine the real costs and benefits of driving a less-polluting vehicle would require us to agree to assign a higher value to gasoline and all petroleum products (somewhere between $100 and $200 to replace a barrel of crude oil with sustainable substitutes like ethanol and other wood derivatives). This is not going to happen in this century, so we salute anyone who trades several thousand dollars (what you could spend on a new TV and a trip to Europe) to hasten the day when EVs are commonplace. Once a certain critical number of EVs are on the road, public perception will change from **someday** *to* **today.**

Foreword

By Marvin Braude
Los Angeles City Commission

Southern California has the worst air quality in the United States. By far, the biggest source of that pollution is the motor vehicle.

Yet Southern Californians are heavily dependent on their cars, because of the sprawling nature of the Los Angeles area and because it lacks a comprehensive mass transit system.

Unless something revolutionary was tried, it seemed clear to me, back in the spring of 1988, that our air quality problems would continue to get worse. If that happened, the federal government would make good on its threat to impose strict penalties on Southern California. Though this might improve our air quality, it would certainly damage our economy.

The answer was here all along — the electric vehicle. EVs are clean and quiet. They can be made competitive with gasoline-fueled cars, and they can be accepted by the motoring public if they are built with the full range of amenities. Yet for reasons of their own, American auto manufacturers were not willing to put the needed resources into making EVs readily available to the motoring public.

To help break this logjam, I proposed an international competition among auto makers for 10,000 EVs for Los Angeles' lucrative market. Business, industry, private citizens and government agencies alike could buy these vehicles and make a contribution to cleaning up our air while driving a clean, reliable and comfortable vehicle.

My proposal came to be known in the auto industry as the Los Angeles initiative. This initiative is, I believe, a bold step toward bringing the economic potential of the electric vehicle to fruition. By stepping in to be the catalyst for the development of

at least 10,000 EVs for the drivers of Los Angeles, our City Council has played a pivotal role in what may be the largest, and certainly the most significant, transportation pilot project in California's history.

If EVs win wide public acceptance in Southern California — and I believe they will — we can finally begin to reverse the trend toward dirtier and dirtier air, a trend in which the automobile has been the chief culprit.

For any metropolitan area, in any country, where auto-generated pollution looms as a health risk and a damper on the local economy, the EV can be an important part of the solution. We in Los Angeles are happy to be showing the way.

Commissioner Marvin Braude

Introduction

Why wait for Detroit? It is not a rhetorical question. We know that one day millions of electric cars will be sold each year, and those cars will be coming from big assembly lines. The major auto makers -- both U.S. and abroad -- have already begun to prepare for the inevitable. But they are big, conservative, and therefore tend to move slowly. We need not wait for them to lead the way.

This book is born of the conviction that for electric cars, the question is not "if" but "when?" And the answer is: the sooner the better. Although electrics are not yet direct replacements for gasoline-powered cars, for many uses they have been practical for years and their applicability is ever increasing. This book shows you why and how electrics are the future, why and how they are ready today, and gives you what you need to show others.

The first section of the book provides general information for educating the public about electric vehicles. It concludes with a list of things you can do. Of course, the very best way to spread the word is to join the pioneers who drive electrics today; the second section tells you how to do just that. Driving an electric is very effective because people invariably find the clean and quiet electric car appealing, if only they get a chance to see one. Finally, the last section lists all the various resources you may need.

Over two dozen EV experts contributed articles and comments to the various stages of the manuscript. To give the reader a feeling of this collegial and cooperative environment, the notes introducing the comments have been italicized. As with any emerging technology, there are numerous points of uncertainty and disagreement, and the editors believe that airing all sides of a particular issue will assist the reader in identifying essential information. The three most significant points of disagreement are 1) **safety issues,** such as the 30-mph crash test and the number of safety fuses that should be required; 2) **"now or later,"** whether government should intervene to support commercialization of current technology or focus on development of more advanced technologies; and 3) **the most feasible drive system,** alternating current (which is more efficient and likely to drop in cost in the future) or direct current (DC, which is more widely available today).

We present the viewpoints of three Citicar owners (Jim Treacy, John Hoke and Lester Embree) to demonstrate the power of giving consumers the opportunity to drive a smaller vehicle. It would take another book to share the hundreds of other testimonials that we could have collected from satisfied Citicar drivers, and the message would be the same: owning and using a small battery-powered "runabout" feels right. It brings a sense of adventure to everyday errands and commuting: EV owners are not contributing to the importing of oil and the smaller car is easier to park. These pioneers join others who have converted conventional cars to battery power in spreading the EV gospel: electric vehicles are enjoyable. Compared with gasoline cars, the maintenance is easy and fun: no oil changes, no toxic fumes while refueling, and no guilty feeling when the television reports another oil spill. As Lester Embree has observed, *"One drives within nature, not against her."*

Whatever you do -- from telling friends and neighbors about EVs to buying your own electric car -- it will help bring the electric future that much closer, to the benefit of us all. The future of the electric car is tied to the future of mankind. The city air we taint and the pollutants we send to erode the ozone layer affect current and future generations. Stemming oil consumption will be an economic boon to all oil-importing countries, and will conserve one of the world's great natural resources. We invite you to join in this movement for a better future for all.

Richard Minner (Sacramento, Calif.) and Steve McCrea (Ft. Lauderdale, Fla.)

Portions of this book previously appeared in the Electric Vehicle News, edited by Lew Gulick, 1911 N. Ft. Myer Drive, Arlington, VA 22209. Subscriptions: $30/year for 11 issues.

Good Bye, Gasoline! Electric Cars Are Here

By John A. (Jay) Harris

The gasoline age is almost over: if you don't agree, look at the graph on the inside front cover of this book. Fortunately, the basic technologies for electric, solar and hybrid cars are already here. However, most car owners don't know that these alternative-power cars offer a long-term, sustainable solution to the pollution and supply problems of the internal combustion engine. Incentives and inducements are therefore needed to encourage the private sector to begin the process of enabling the public to purchase these cares in large quantities.

Although the achievement of the current goals of the environmental movement for CAFE standards of 45 miles per gallon for autos and 35 mpg for light trucks by the year 2000 will do much to conserve fuel and to reduce unfavorable impacts on the environment, *these minimal goals are not a long-term solution.* Even the widespread use of prototypes already completed by many of the major auto companies (attaining 70 to over 100 miles per gallon) cannot be sustained, since petroleum supplies are finite.

Electric vehicles are one long-term alternative to the challenge of providing personal transportation that doesn't depend on imported oil. According to California's South Coast Air Quality Management District, EVs cause 97 percent less pollution than gasoline cars, even when emissions from their power plants (the primary source of electricity for charging batteries) are considered. They are also far quieter, more energy-efficient, and cost less than half as much to operate as internal combustion cars. And, most importantly, their fuel can be derived from renewable sources of energy.

International public-private cooperation is helping to bring EVs to the mass market. A study funded by the Swiss government concluded that electric cars offer so many advantages that their introduction should be encouraged by official measures and policies. Volkswagen is fabricating 50 diesel/electric hybrids designed around their Golf model with support from the Swiss government. VW has also formed a joint venture with the Swiss watchmaker best known for its Swatch trademark) to build inexpensive EVs.

In the U.S., a number of companies offer kits to convert existing cars to battery power. These firms are ready to tap a potential annual market of hundreds of thousands of cars that still have many years to serve after their original gasoline engines wear out.

It is becoming increasingly apparent to those working for a sustainable future that the sooner we can convert from fossil-fueled engines to electric, solar and hybrid car production (and hydrogen fuel cells), the better the chances of our avoiding a chaotic, unhealthy, far more polluted and possibly bankrupt world less than two decades from now.

This article was condensed from a longer article prepared for the Center for Sustainable Transportation, 1130 17th Street, #630, Washington, D.C. 20036. The author is an environmental activist, grant maker, investor in electric/solar car companies, and an owner of a solar-assisted electric car.

The Sacramento Municipal Utility District's EV Pioneers project is part of a long-term effort to convert much of the transportation sector to electricity. Vehicles like this electric G-Van are loaned to local businesses to offer every person in Sacramento a ride in an EV. *Photo courtesy of SMUD.*

The EV Experience
Why Don't All of Us Drive EVs?
By Jim Treacy, EV Pioneer

I've been driving an electric vehicle in Washington, D.C. for upwards of eight years. Almost everyday I'm stopped and asked, "What is that?" and "Do you work for NASA or something?" and "How far, how fast, how much?" Shortly after I accommodate their questions I'm inevitably told, "That's the car of the future!" It never fails to turn their heads when I explain, "Actually my car was built in 1976!"

Why don't all of us drive EVs? My answer to this question is simpler than one might expect. **The average person finds it too difficult.** Whether this is because of a problem of access, or difficulty in justifying the cost, or just plain ignorance about EVs and not having the time to learn isn't really the issue. These concerns will inevitably iron out as the demand for EVs increases.

It is my belief that if consumers discover that the EV will improve their quality of life, then a strong demand for EVs will emerge. My marketing background tells me that where there is a strong demand, a realistic market will evolve, and hence money will be made. Once people see that money can be made in the EV market there is no telling where it will go! It is my hope that as I describe my experiences driving an EV in a major metropolitan city for eight years, others will understand that an EV can improve their quality of life as well as the environment.

I distinctly remember my wife's face as my broken-down Citicar was towed in front of our house. It was something between "what the hell is that?" and "what the hell is wrong with you?" With the theme song from *Chitty Chitty Bang Bang* ringing through my head, I explained that this was the perfect car for use in the city. It goes 40 mph, with a range of about 45 miles on a seven-hour charge; it costs about a penny a mile. She must have sensed my sincere determination because she stated simply, "That's nice, dear," turned and retreated into the house.

Shortly after the tow truck cleared and my wife was gone, I was alone looking at my newly acquired Electric Vehicle. Actually, I was alone with every 8-to-10-year-old from about a full square mile, looking on. I realized then that I didn't know the first thing about this car! By now I'm sure you've figured it out: no, I don't work for NASA. In fact, I own a company which markets computer training. Regardless of my inexperience, I was determined to get this baby running.

With a manual which I borrowed from an EV enthusiast, I gathered my lifetime-guarantee Craftsman wrenches: I was ready to work. I looked at the diagrams, I looked at the tangled, burned-out web of wires, I – – – – knocked on my physicist neighbor's door (he's a *theoretical* physicist, but I won't go into that)! He explained basic circuitry and once again I was off and running. I untangled, retangled, and connected each wire to its mate and soon enough I was ready for the infamous test run. I collected my wife and my neighbor. The 8-to-10-year-olds never really left. I was ready to declare victory. With the *Chitty Chitty Bang Bang* theme once again soaring through my head, I proudly held up the key. I sat behind the wheel. I slid the key into the "ignition." I turned it...nothing happened. I quickly shook and wiggled every primary wire and turned the key again. Nothing. Ready to accept defeat, I turned to get out of the car and mistakenly tapped the power pedal. The car moved! Immediately my brain registered – it's an *electric* car, it's *supposed* to be quiet. When you're stopped, the motor is essentially off.

So the test runs soon turned into trips to the grocery. The car immediately took the lead role in city driving. People were stunned at the unexpected acceleration of the car. In this small lightweight car I could easily pull in front of its prehistoric colleagues at stop lights. Not only that, when it came to parking there was always just enough space to fit a car such as mine. There was a distinct moment when I realized the car had finally earned the approval of my wife. We had a dinner engagement in the often-crowded Georgetown area, where normally there would be no chance of a free parking space. There is nothing like pulling in to a half-size space and parking within feet of your expected destination. My wife's smile reflected her surprise and pleasure.[1]

I continued to enjoy daily use of the car. However, I was soon ever so politely reminded by a ticket from one of our ever so friendly DC policemen that it was time to get the car inspected. To say the least, I was not particularly excited about the prospect of an inspection. I had already experienced the caustic charm of the DC inspectors with my gas powered car. Nevertheless I arrived at the station in my freshly washed, fully charged, legal down to the 1/4-inch tire tread, electric Citicar. At 10 a.m. the line was no more than 20 cars, so I was feeling lucky. Like ducks in a row, the line slowly etched[2] on towards the large garage door fixed with a red/green light.

Finally I was next. I caught the attendant's eye. I smiled. Without the slightest hint of expression he turned away and flicked on the green light. Like a soldier ready for battle I entered the station. The inspector in SOP form[3] started the routine. "Headlights, tail lights, brakes..." I couldn't believe everything was so calm and methodical. I thought to myself, "Hey, this is no big deal – maybe they see EVs all the time." Then I pulled up to the emission booth. The inspector circled behind the car. I thought, "Should I say something?" Everything was so solemnly quiet. I stepped out of the car and walked up to the inspector. He looked up.

"Where's the pipe on this thing?"

"It's electric," I answered, "there is no tail pipe." I was nervous, trying not to sound the least bit condescending; I felt like I was in grade school, telling my father I got a D– in history.

"Where's the engine?"

"Down there," I pointed, "but it's off when the car's stopped. Besides, it's electric, it emits nothing."

He had a job to do and nothing short of the earth's end would stop him. He told me to drive a little bit and he would hold the emission wand around the electric motor. So there we were: me in the car and the inspector jogging behind with his wand strategically fixed near my motor. I didn't reveal so much as an inkling of laughter until the official green sticker – a medal of honor – was placed victoriously on the bottom left corner of my windshield. On my way home I laughed so hard that tears dropped from my eyes!

While I would like to say, "From then on I drove off into the sunset without a problem," I didn't. For the first year the car frequently broke down. Amazingly, however, everything was simple to fix. If the motor broke I could take it out in minutes and have it rebuilt for about the cost of a gas car's tune-up. In eight years, I've had this done once. *Just a quick side note: disconnect the power first before removing the motor or you might arc-weld a wrench. Believe it or not, after more than a second glance, a somewhat reluctant sales manager honored my lifetime Craftsman guarantee.* Even after upgrading power cables, reinforcing axles, and a few

---

[1] Before the Georgetown triumph, my wife would grumble, "We never see each other! You don't spend enough time with me, you're always working on that car! I'm never driving in *that* thing!" Now she suggests that we take the EV rather than its gasoline-powered cousin because we can park so much more easily.

[2] I felt like I was etching a groove in the cement, it was taking so long. I was digging in deeper, getting lower and lower, grinding into the pavement as we crept forward!

[3] Standard Operating Procedure, which is Naval jargon for *going by the book* and *being a bureaucrat.*

other augmentations, the car's maintenance is still minimal compared to the gas powered car I've owned during the same eight years.

It soon became apparent that the key to the success of this car is that it's in a class of its own. It is cheap, quick, small and efficient. Not only that, but there's an extra: no exhaust. A note to the "Big Three": if you want to compete in the electric car market,

> 1) don't try to compete with the gas powered car (the EV is in a separate class),
> 2) don't expect anyone to buy a car simply because it doesn't pollute (that's an extra),
> 3) don't listen to anyone who says it can't be done (call me, it can!).

Jim Treacy admits that he wastes energy because he rarely walks anywhere – he takes his EV. "People tell me that I'll never find parking, but it's never a problem." He describes himself as a "real-world EV expert" since he has been driving an electric car daily since 1984. "I influence people because they see me driving my car. They want to buy one and they wonder why I don't produce electric cars. I'm in marketing, I'm not an engineer! But at least it gets them thinking: why don't all of us drive EVs?" Treacy owns a marketing firm in Washington, D.C. which specializes in computer training.

Jim Treacy with his trusty steed. Note the warning labels, installed to keep curious people away from the car. The two passenger CitiCar is one of 2,200 made by Sebring-Vanguard between May 1974 and December 1975.

Safer than a motorcycle, smaller than a Geo Metro

Why is the Citicar eight feet long? Word-of-mouth among the admirers of micro EVs assumed, "To make it easy to park head-in on the street. That's the width of a parking space." Answer: the typical metered parking space is seven feet wide; the Citicar was built to fit across the width of a standard car trailer.

But this raises the question: **What's the best size for an easy-to-park car?** We asked an experienced urban EV driver, Jim Treacy, who observed, "Eight feet long is perfect. It's about half the size of a regular car and if it were any longer it wouldn't fit in the spaces I'm always finding. If it were shorter, I'd feel cramped." He added that it's difficult to document the size of these spaces on streets without metered parking.

"If everyone drove an 18-wheeler, a Cadillac would be the perfect car for parking, since the spaces between each truck would be just right. One reason why I have such an easy time parking my car is that nobody else is driving a Citicar, so there are all these half-sized spaces along the street."

The typical parking space equipped with a meter is somewhere between 21 and 23 feet long and seven feet wide. While not suited for parking perpendicular to the road, one could imagine cooperative minicar owners parking at one end of the space, leaving 12 feet for the next eight-foot minicar to slip in front. The smallest cars currently sold in the U.S. are 50% longer than the Citicar.

Here's a plea from city dwellers to entrepreneurs looking for a niche in the car market: Make an easy-to-park EV, and we'll buy it!

Know Your Air

By Richard Minner

Vehicle emissions account for roughly half to two thirds of many air pollutants: one of the primary benefits of electric cars and other alternative fuels is cleaner air. To assess these benefits, it helps to know something about the pollutants involved. This primer gives brief explanations of the primary air pollutants and is aimed at those who don't know their VOC from their NMOG and ROG. Bear in mind that air pollution is complex and there are many unsettled areas. One particular complication is that not all pollutants are emitted directly into the air in their final forms: many result when "precursors" react in the atmosphere.

Criteria Pollutants

In the United States, the Environmental Protection Agency (EPA) and the California Air Resources Board (CARB) have regulatory authority over sources of air pollution. California is the only state that can set its own air quality standards, because it was the only state doing so before the EPA began setting them. Other states can adopt either the EPA or the CARB regulations. Pollutants for which the EPA or the CARB have set ambient air quality standards are known as Criteria Pollutants. Note that the list changes as new regulations are adopted.

Particulates (TSP, PM10): This pollutant category comprises dust, soot, smoke, and other suspended matter. Particulates are respiratory irritants and contribute to acid rain formation. Total Suspended Particulates (TSP) refers to all particulates, whereas PM10 refers to particulate matter smaller than 10 microns. These smaller particles are the primary health concern because of their ability to reach the lower regions of the respiratory tract. PM10 has largely replaced TSP as a measure of particulates. Diesel vehicles contribute nearly one fifth of the more than 7 million tons of particulates released each year in the United States, while gasoline vehicles contribute less than 1 percent.

Hydrocarbons (HC, VOC, ROG, NMHC, NMOG et al.): This is a broad class of pollutants comprising hundreds of specific compounds containing the elements carbon and hydrogen. Hydrocarbons can react to form ozone, but all hydrocarbons are not created equal. In particular, methane (the smallest HC) is essentially non-reactive and is usually considered separately from other hydrocarbons. There is little agreement on the best acronym for the remaining "reactive hydrocarbons" and all of the following are used: VOG, VOC, ROG, ROC, NMHC, NMOG (V = Volatile, R = Reactive, OG = Organic Gases, OC = Organic Compounds, NM = Non-Methane). To a chemist there may be subtle differences between these, but they are used more or less interchangeably; VOC and NMOG appear to be the 1992 favorites. With the NMOG it is important to consider the "evaporative emissions," which emanate directly from vehicle fuel systems and from fuel handling. These can contribute a significant portion of the total vehicle NMOG, particularly in warmer weather. More than 20 million tons of hydrocarbons are released in the United States annually, with nearly half from highway vehicles.

Reactivity Factor: Different fuels tend to produce different HC mixtures. To account for the variable reactivities of the different HC species, the CARB has defined the concept of an overall Reactivity Factor for each fuel/vehicle combination. The reactivity factor is used as a relative measure of "ozone-forming potential" for the fuel with respect to HC emissions.

Nitrogen oxides (NOx): These chemicals are characterized by the yellowish-brown cloud blanketing our dirtier cities. NOx irritate the lungs, can cause bronchitis and pneumonia, and can lower resistance to respiratory infections. NOx are primary ozone precursors and contribute to acid rain formation, and in some areas are PM10 precursors as well. Vehicles produce approximately 40% of the more than 20 million tons of NOx released annually in the United States.

Carbon monoxide (CO): This gas is toxic in high concentrations, aggravates certain cardiac and respiratory conditions, and may also cause circulatory problems. It has also been implicated in the formation of smog. Vehicles are the dominant source of CO, accounting for two thirds of the 70 million tons released annually in the United States.

Sulphur Oxides (SOx): Besides being a health hazard, these pollutants are the chief cause of acid rain. Over 20 million tons are released in the US each year, but only about 5% is from transportation sources. Since vehicles are such small contributors, SOx measurements are often not made for them.

Ozone (O_3): This is the white haze hanging over many cities: smog. Ozone is formed when precursors (mainly NMOG and NOx) react in the presence of heat and sunlight. These reactions are complex, and the effects of reductions in NMOG and NOx levels vary with the relative concentrations. In fact, under certain circumstances a *decrease* in NOx can actually cause an *increase* in ozone. In general, however, it is desirable to reduce both NMOG and NOx, with stronger emphasis on NMOG in most areas today. The effects of ozone include:
- Billions of dollars in annual health costs
- Nose and eye irritation
- Impairment of respiratory functions
- Chronic lung diseases
- Increased asthma attacks
- Increased bacterial infections
- Premature aging symptoms
- Crop yield reductions (several billion dollars)
- Forest injury and mortality
- Damage to raw materials (such as rubber and dyes)
- Oxidation of structural materials

In 1988, 317 urban and rural areas in the United States earned "non-attainment" classification for ozone because they could not meet federal clean-air standards. More than 100 of our cities may be fairly described as choking on smog. Roughly half of all Americans live in areas that exceed the ozone standard at least once a year.

But isn't there too *little* ozone? What about the Hole In The Sky? Unfortunately, the hole is in the stratosphere, far above land vehicles. Excessive ozone at low altitudes is one serious problem; the destruction of ozone at high altitudes is a different problem altogether. If only we could persuade the unwanted ozone to "take a hike", but we can't. The Ozone Hole is only vaguely related to motor vehicles by the use of CFCs in air conditioners. EVs and other alternative fuels can't really help with this one.

Lead (Pb): Lead accumulates in the body and can affect many systems -- the nervous system in particular. Fetuses, infants and children are most susceptible to low doses. Lead was once of major concern, but aggressive lead-reduction programs have made it a lower priority today. From 1970 to 1990, total lead emissions dropped 97% due principally to the phasing out of leaded gasoline. In 1990, vehicles accounted for less than one third of lead emissions, down from about four fifths in 1981.

Other Toxics

There are several substances emitted in much smaller amounts which are nevertheless of concern because of their higher toxicities. Following are the four most significant with regard to gasoline vehicles, in order of most concern.

Benzene (C_6H_6): Of the four, benzene is emitted in the largest quantity by a wide margin. It is a known carcinogen, and about 90% of benzene emissions are from gasoline vehicles.

1,3-Butadiene (C_4H_6): This is a more potent carcinogen than benzene, but it is emitted in much smaller amounts with about 80% from gasoline vehicles. Benzene and 1,3-Butadiene together account for about 95% of the potential cancer risk from gasoline vehicles.

Formaldehyde (HCHO) and Acetaldehyde (CH_3CHO): These are suspected human carcinogens, and contributors to smog formation. They are less toxic than benzene, and gasoline engines contribute only about 5% of total aldehyde emissions. However, use of the alcohol fuels methanol and ethanol could increase these emissions distressingly. It is expected that alcohol-powered vehicles' emissions will be controlled to limit these toxic emissions, but the risks are not yet clearly defined.

Greenhouse Gases

Carbon Dioxide (CO_2): While carbon dioxide is not an air quality concern, it is the primary greenhouse gas. CO_2 does not have as much heat-trapping ability as the other greenhouse gases, but it is emitted in much larger quantities. For example, in 1988 an estimated 56 *billion* tons of CO_2 were produced in the United States, while the tonnage of other greenhouse gases was in the tens of *millions*. Of this total, automotive fuels contribute nearly one third. The overwhelming majority of CO_2 emissions are from the burning of fossil fuels − those vast pools of carbon that have been locked out of the earth's carbon cycle for millions of years. Releasing these trapped carbon reserves may well upset a delicate global balance.

Methane (CH_4): The smallest of the hydrocarbons, methane is relatively non-reactive and does not contribute appreciably to urban air quality problems. Methane is the primary component of natural gas, used for heating and cooking and increasingly as a vehicle fuel. It is a potent greenhouse gas, trapping heat approximately 25 times as effectively as CO_2. While CO_2 emissions dwarf current methane emissions, there is some concern that methane emissions from vehicles could become a significant greenhouse contributor were natural gas to become a dominant vehicle fuel.

Sources (for this section and Chapter 16)

Bratvold, Delma and David Friedman. (1991). *A Guidebook For Alternatively Fueled Vehicles.* Washington, D.C.: Public Technology Inc.

California Air Resources Board (October 4, 1991). *California Phase 2 Reformulated Gasoline Specifications.* (Staff report, Vols. 1 and 2).

Environmental Protection Agency (November 1991). *National Air Quality and Emissions Trends Report, 1990.* EPA-450/4-91-023, press briefing edition.

Gordon, D. (1991). *Steering A New Course: Transportation, Energy and the Environment.* Cambridge, Mass.: Union of Concerned Scientists.

Theodore Barry & Associates. (1989). *A Comparative Analysis of Electric Vehicles and Other Alternative Clean Fuel Vehicles for Southern California Edison.*

Sinor, J.E. (February 1992). *The Clean Fuels Report.* Niwot, Colo.: J.E. Sinor Consultants, Inc. Vol. 4, No. 1.

Wang, Deluchi, Sperling (September 1990). "Emission Impacts of Electric Vehicles." *Journal of Air and Waste Management,* Vol. 40, No. 9.

Private conversation with Mark Bramfitt, Alternative Fuels Program (January 29, 1992), Pacific Gas and Electric, 111 Stony Point Circle, Santa Rosa, CA 95401, 707-577-7094.

Private conversation with Jerry Martin of CARB, February 6, 1992.

Private conversation with Tim Taylor, Sacramento Metropolitan Air Quality Management District (SMAQMD), January 30, 1992.

Motorcycles can be converted to battery power.

Part I

All About Electric Vehicles

This Baker Electric stands in Kopp Engineering Building, University of South Florida, Tampa, Fla.

Doug Cobb walks past a converted Ford Festiva at the 1991 American Tour de Sol. Note the Solar Car Corp.'s touring Chevy Lumina van in the background. *Photo by NESEA.*

Nissan's Future Electric Vehicle (FEV).

1

What is an EV?

Let's start with a general definition of electric vehicles. EV expert Mike Brown identifies any vehicle that "draws its power from electricity stored in batteries" as an EV. For the purpose of this book, however, we will refer to EVs as those commuter cars, minivans, vans, trucks and other on-road vehicles that are powered by batteries.

*An important distinction should be drawn between **solar-electric** cars and **solar-assisted electric** cars: the first are lightweight race cars that can use the sun's energy to move forward, while the second are cars with solar panels attached to the car's surface (usually the roof) to benefit from "opportunity charging" when parked.*

Mike Brown's Facts about EVs

What is an electric vehicle?
An electric vehicle (EV) is one that draws its power from electricity stored in batteries instead of from the combustion of liquid fuels. EVs include handicapped carts, golf carts, industrial machines (forklifts) and full-sized passenger cars and trucks.

Who should consider owning an EV?
If you have more than one set of wheels, please note why EVs make ideal second cars or commuter vehicles:

Convenience. EVs do not need tune-ups, oil changes, mufflers, fuel pumps, carburetors, etc.

No pollution. No exhaust fumes, no coolant, and no waste oil. Even if you count the pollution created by the electric power plant, an EV is 97 percent cleaner than a conventional automobile.

Efficiency. No energy is wasted when the car is sitting in traffic or while waiting for a traffic signal to change.

Quiet. EVs are almost silent.

Durable. Even the best-kept gasoline-powered car eventually needs a new engine. A standard electric direct-current motor can last for decades, requiring an occasional change of brushes.

A note about the Hybrid EV: when another energy source (usually gasoline or diesel) supplements the batteries and provides additional power to move an EV, the vehicle is called a *hybrid*. In the *serial hybrid*, the additional fuel powers a small generator, which makes electricity to drive the electric motor and recharge the EV's batteries. In the *parallel hybrid*, the additional power moves a separate motor. The additional power unit can extend the range and/or accelerate the EV more quickly.

Some transportation experts (such as Amory Lovins, Rocky Mountain Institute) argue that public policy should focus on the hybrid EV. Consumers are more likely to accept the hybrid since it performs like a conventional car, and most will continue to consume gasoline rather than accept the inconvenience of a pure EV. The no-local-emissions feature of battery power can be used by the hybrid in urban areas and the auxiliary power can provide speed and range, features that most drivers desire in one car. Supporters of the pure EV point out that the most affordable hybrid uses gasoline and has a tail pipe, the principal characteristics that EV pioneers aim to eliminate by switching to battery power. This book will focus on the role that the pure EV can play as the second car in the multi-car household.

2

Why Do We Need EVs?

Limited oil reserves

If consumption remains fairly constant, the current world proven reserves of 670 billion barrels of petroleum will last only 33 years.
Noel de Nevers, University of Utah
Encyclopedia Americana, 1990.

Oil reserves are limited and they're getting smaller every day. The United States has less than five percent of the world's proven petroleum reserves, and imports roughly half of the 17 million barrels consumed daily within its borders. True, a higher price per barrel will stimulate production from domestic wells, but in the end, whether it's 2023 or 2050, eventually petroleum will become too scarce to use as our primary fuel for transportation.

Economic security

In 1989, oil made up 40 percent of the U.S. trade deficit.
Florida Trend magazine, September 1990.

Oil imports accounted for two-fifths of the U.S. trade deficit in 1989, surpassed only by the 45% share held by imported Japanese goods. This growing dependence on foreign oil shows the need for reduced use of petroleum products. Since there are only so many ways to reduce the need for driving (car-pooling, mass transit, bicycling if the weather is pleasant and if the cyclist is in good health), alternative sources of fuels need to be identified. These substitutes for gasoline include methanol, ethanol, natural gas (compressed and liquid forms), and electricity. While this book focuses on battery-powered transportation, all alternatives to gasoline should be evaluated before one makes the switch.

These first two points, *limited supplies* and *economic security*, have focused on the United States, but the conclusion is the same for every nation that chooses to import petroleum: To whom do you owe your allegiance? To an oil-exporting nation or to your country and its economic system?

The next point in support of electric cars applies to the many urban centers around the world where automobile exhausts foul the air.

This car is "off the grid." Florida Solar Energy Center charges this Citicar on the photovoltaic panels in the background.

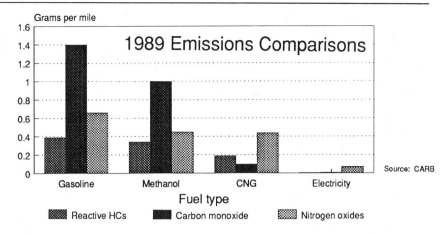

Deteriorating Air Quality

Seventy percent of air pollution is caused by the automobile.
Florida Department of Motor Vehicles

While the percentage of air pollution contributed by cars may vary from region to region, the most important source of most urban smog is generally the conventional gasoline-powered automobile.

In the industrial zones of Los Angeles, the South Coast Air Quality Management District is applying strict regulations to "stationary" sources of pollution (furniture and paint factories, petrochemical industry sites, barbecues, etc.) as well as mobile sources (cars, trucks, and lawn mowers). Although automobiles account for as much as three-quarters of certain pollutants, such as the oxides of nitrogen, the automobile's contribution to total air pollution is closer to half of all other sources in certain areas of Southern California.

One way to address all three concerns (declining petroleum reserves, negative foreign trade, and deteriorating air quality) is to simply drive less. This is not an acceptable solution for most people, so research and development of non-petroleum fuels is advancing rapidly. Alternative fuels like ethanol, methanol, and natural gas each have advantages over conventional gasoline. As the following graph shows, however, electricity may be the cleanest fuel per 100,000 miles. A composite electric power plant, combining the average pollution level of all U.S. utilities, produces much less pollution while generating electricity for battery-powered transportation.

Save The Oceans

*It wasn't **his** driving that caused the Alaskan oil spill. It was **yours**.*
From a poster published by Greenpeace, showing the captain of the *Exxon Valdez*.

In response to the great oil spill of 1989, politicians and the U.S. tourist industry joined with environmentalists to form a coalition to push for restrictions on offshore oil drilling. Despite assurances by advocates of underwater drilling, sophisticated oil-recovery techniques still allow some petroleum to leak out into the ocean. However, the quest for domestic supplies of petroleum will put pressure on Congress to lift the moratorium.

Switching to battery power whenever possible helps to reduce the amount of gasoline transported by tanker and pushes into the future the perceived "need" for offshore oil drilling. Driving a car that does not require changes of motor oil also cuts the potential pollution of groundwater and air. As numerous environmental groups have noted, do-it-yourself car mechanics improperly dispose millions of gallons of used motor oil every year, more than the 11 million gallons of oil spilled into Prince William Sound by the *Exxon Valdez*.

Flexibility

The major advantage of electric vehicles is that they open up a wide range of primary energy options for supplying the transport sector.
D.F. Gosden, Sydney University, Australia.

The beauty of electricity is that it is not in itself a source of energy; it is a medium. Electricity is as clean and cheap as the source that produces it. It is infinitely flexible: virtually every source of energy can be efficiently converted to electricity. A car powered by electricity is a car powered by anything.

With internal combustion engines – even multi-fuel designs – the sources of energy are very limited. Electrics, on the other hand, can immediately take advantage of any and all advances in energy production; they'll just keep getting better and better.

Bob Batson, Electric Vehicles of America, Inc., adds: Electric utilities are regulated to serve the public and provide electricity at a reasonable price. Contrast this with the oil companies, the suppliers of our dominant transportation fuel, who do not operate under the watchful eye of a public service commission. Unlike gasoline, electricity can be generated in many different ways and can be transmitted quickly over long distances. The current infrastructure also allows EVs to be charged in millions of locations, almost any place equipped with an electrical outlet.

They are clean and quiet

Excessive background noise can cause stress-related physical changes such as constriction of blood vessels, a rise in blood pressure, changes in heart rhythm, dilation of the pupils, migraine headaches and ulcers and gastro-intestinal problems... Under urban driving conditions, noise from the exhaust of the internal combustion engine [ICE] predominates; during acceleration, exhaust and other engine-related noises increase dramatically.

In contrast, the EV has only an electric motor and controller, which are typically much quieter than the components they replace in the ICE vehicles.
Dr. C. C. Chan, International Research Centre for
Electric Vehicles, University of Hong Kong

We are so used to gasoline powered cars that we forget how noisy and foul-smelling they really are. Electric cars are clean and almost silent. If you've ever been awakened by a loud car, or had your breakfast spoiled by the fumes of a neighbor's car warming up, you can imagine how much more pleasant life would be if everyone drove electrics.

The next chapter gives a look at what driving in cities was like 90 years ago. If you'd prefer to find out one of five ways to own an electric car right now, skip ahead to Part II, Chapter 19.

3

A Brief History

Electric cars are not new. The first EV was built in 1836 by Thomas Davenport in Scotland, using primitive glass-enclosed batteries. Fifty years later, after the development of the lead-acid cell, garage shop tinkerers were putting reliable EVs on the road. Thomas Edison had a small three-wheeler constructed for his use around 1889. Photos from around 1900 show horse-drawn carriages, carts and wagons everywhere, with the horseless carriages dominated by electric cars and steamers. Gasoline cars were noisy, hard to start, smelly,[1] and not selling well.

There was a time when electric cars were the fastest form of locomotion on earth. France's Camille Jenatzy pushed his *Jamais Contente* ("Never Satisfied") racer to 65 mph in 1899, running a "flying kilometer" in 34 seconds.

The end of the first era of battery-powered transportation came in 1911 when Charles Kettering replaced the hand crank on General Motors' gasoline-powered cars with the electric self-starter. The electric had to this point been primarily an urban vehicle, marketed to the wealthy as an "opera car." The opening of interstate roads such as the Chicago-to-Miami Dixie Highway in 1916 encouraged demand for ranges beyond what electric vehicles could offer. After 1924, no auto maker entered an electric car in the National Auto Show.

Electric cars bounce back whenever a crisis threatens the flow of petroleum. During World War Two, the British government seized 35,000 electric milk lorries (some of which had been running the same delivery routes since 1905), declaring them national assets in the struggle against fascism. Gasoline rationing in the U.S. sparked some interest in EVs, but this quickly died after the war ended.

In 1964, General Motors produced the Electrovair I, a Chevrolet Corvair conversion with silver-zinc batteries and a range of 80 miles. Other manufacturers offered similar prototype conversions of gasoline-powered models, but no production plans were announced.

Some public attention was generated in the mid-1960s when NBC's "Today" television morning news program featured several electric cars, including one built by John Hoke, an employee with the National Parks Service in Washington, D.C. He was encouraged to testify by Senator Muskie in hearings before in a Congressional committee held in 1967 to support an electric vehicle bill.

Federal funds came after the 1973-74 oil embargo. In 1976, Congress passed the Electric and Hybrid Vehicle Research, Development and Demonstration Act, aimed at promoting this non-petroleum form of transportation. The marketplace responded, most visibly with Sebring-Vanguard's Citicar. Nearly 2,200 of these two-person electrics were sold before a negative review of the car in a consumer's magazine, 100 gasoline prices, ended consumer support. U.S. Electric Cars converted a Renault, calling it the Lectric Leopard, and many of these models remain on the road today. When the price of crude oil rose again during the Iran-Iraq war in the early 1980s, Jet Industries (Austin, Texas) used U.S. and Japanese chassis to produce durable EVs that continue to deliver dependable utility today.

---

[1] They *still* are noisy and smelly! Although many internal combustion engines are quieter and run more smoothly than cars built a decade ago, they still depend on imported oil!

Concern for air quality rather than worry about over-dependence on foreign oil became the electric car's most favorable point of support. In 1989, the California Air Resources Board issued a notice of its intent to encourage and require lower-polluting forms of personal transportation. Anticipating this mandate, the City of Los Angeles had already adopted its EV Initiative on May 6, 1988, announcing a competition to support the production of 10,000 electric cars.

Public attention was also directed to alternative cars in March 1989 when the Exxon *Valdez* created the largest single oil spill in the world.[1] Six months later, the California Air Resources Board (CARB) proposed mandates for 2% of total car sales in 1998 to be "zero emissions vehicles."

In the media frenzy that culminated in the 20th anniversary of Earth Day, electric cars appeared again on the front pages of many newspapers. In January 1990, General Motors unveiled a prototype two-seater called the "Impact," aimed at the "performance car" market. The sleek design came from Paul MacCready, who in 1977 won international recognition when his Gossamer Condor claimed the Kremer prize as the first successful human-powered airplane.

In 1990 a new bill to foster the EV industry was introduced by Rep. George Brown of California. It died in committee. The next year, Brown and Senator Jay Rockefeller (West Virginia) again introduced the bill and this time it moved closer to adoption as part of a national energy policy bill (S. 1220, which died on the Senate floor in November 1991).

In April 1991, GM announced it would convert a factory in Lansing, Michigan (the former Buick Riata facility) to produce the Impact, a car that will be "good, clean fun" to drive. Auto industry experts predicted that the first sales would appear in late 1995. Significant government support emerged when New England states and New York agreed to adopt the California air quality standards and sought to form a regional solution to meeting the stiffer Clean Air Amendments of 1990.

The year closed with good news for EV advocates: Rep. Howard Berman's amendment to the Intermodal Surface Transportation Act (H.R. 2950) authorized $12 million in one-to-one matching funds to be shared by at least three EV consortia. The amendment stipulated several provisions to create opportunities for small and medium-sized suppliers to participate in the building of EVs. Passed before the Thanksgiving break, it was the first Federal provision in 15 years to promote the construction of EVs.

What's Happening in Detroit?

In a word: research. The three major auto makers have been focusing on electric vehicles for years. The EV bill that passed Congress in 1976 created a flow of R&D dollars that slowed but never entirely died during the 1980s. The three "OEMs" (original equipment manufacturers, as distinguished from convertors or small-shop contractors) have participated in a number of research and development projects: Ford has developed a motor that is built around the car's axle; GM and Chrysler completed a dual-shaft electric propulsion van under a DOE contract.

The company that has garnered the most attention is without doubt General Motors. Its commitment to develop the Impact has generated significant coverage in the press. (See GM's response in Chapter 5, which explains why you might want to wait for Detroit to produce your electric car.)

---

[1] Note: *The 11 million barrels of crude petroleum dumped in Prince Edward Sound was a fraction of the millions of barrels of crude lost each year in thousands of micro-spills and as a result of irresponsible disposal of used petroleum products. Please take steps to dispose of old motor oil properly.*

The most ambitious joint research effort to date is focused on finding a better battery. The U.S. Advanced Battery Consortium is another investment by the major U.S. car manufacturers in the future. The research will cost more than $260 million by 1995 (half paid for by the Federal government) and seeks to identify the most promising battery technologies for accelerated development efforts.

What's Happening Around North America?

Plans are made in Washington and some important ground-up engineering is no doubt taking place in Motown, Wolfsburg and Osaka, but the real action is in your neighborhood. Electric utilities have been experimenting with EVs since the early 1970s, particularly the G-Van. More than 100 of these four-ton wonders are on the road, purchased by far-sighted utilities like Pacific Gas & Electric, Southern California Edison, Sacramento Municipal Utility District, Detroit Electric, Con Edison (New York) and others.

EVs are also making inroads into corporate and municipal fleets. United Parcel Service has examined the feasibility of electric delivery vans, and one of the most active and consistent use of battery power in mass transit is Denver's rush-hour EVs. Two wireless electric buses quietly cover downtown during the morning, noon and evening rush hours, recharging their batteries between the peak periods of use. Similar buses are also in use in Santa Barbara, undergoing further development by a local company.

With limited space for parking downtown, the "urban town car" is getting smaller and smaller. Before 1920, the Detroit Electric car was first marketed as an "opera car" for women. Today, proposals for micro-vehicles, suitable for one or two commuters and easy to park, are just as likely to run on batteries as on gasoline. The Cushman 3-wheel EVs used for parking enforcement are one example.

How We Got Here

Plentiful, easy-to-extract petroleum is the root of our economy's current addiction to inexpensive fossil fuel. The world as we know it — highways, gasoline stations, plane travel linking continents — began in 1859 when Edward L. Drake drilled for petroleum. The black material was converted to oil for indoor lighting, competing with whale oil. Within fifty years of his first oil strike, the nation's cities were becoming cluttered with horseless carriages and, where intercity roads were paved, the automobile competed with railroads for traffic.

Derived from waste matter and decayed plants, petroleum is composed of a complex mixture of hydrocarbons. Table 1 below shows that roughly 45 percent of the volume of a barrel of crude oil can be made into gasoline. Depending on the grade of the crude and where it was extracted, the fractions will be more or less dominated by the components of gasoline. Demand for specific petroleum products also dictates which fractions will be kept for end products, and which will be "cracked" and formed into other fractions. Certain refineries are limited in their ability to convert one set of fractions to another set. Increasing the amount of gasoline extracted from a barrel of crude reduces the output of other fractions. For example, to get more gasoline for cars from a barrel of crude oil, less aviation gasoline (used for private aircraft), diesel and jet fuel is made.

The refining process is still somewhat of an inexact science. Catalytic cracking, which employs catalysts to break long carbon chains into smaller chains, is sometimes described as "hitting a concrete slab with a sledge hammer": you get all sorts of sizes. Shorter chains of carbon atoms form a molecule that turns to a gas at a lower boiling point than longer carbon chains. So a heavy petroleum fraction can be "cracked" into pieces that boil into lighter fractions like motor gasoline and into heavier fractions like diesel and kerosene-type jet fuel (used by commercial airlines).

Refineries have some flexibility with the percentage of output that they produce: during the spring, they produce relatively more gasoline to prepare for the expected rise in demand for gasoline during the summer travel season; in autumn, many refineries shift to produce relatively more fuel oil for heating. In the long term, however, if electricity and other alternative (non-petroleum) fuels replace the demand for gasoline, major capital expenditures will be needed to change the amount of gasoline derived from crude oil. Currently, about 45 percent of crude oil is cracked and reformed to produce motor fuel for automobiles, with only 9 percent going to kerosene-type jet fuel and 3 percent going to petrochemical feedstocks (used to make plastics). When we drive, we are consuming fuel that could otherwise have flown us to a vacation spot or been used to make a useful plastic product. Those of us who are concerned about the end of the cheap-petroleum era can imagine a world that uses half as much gasoline as today, in which less than a quarter of crude oil is converted to gasoline, with the percentages for other fractions (which have fewer substitutes available) doubling (see Table 3.1).

In the U.S., 6 billion barrels of crude petroleum are refined annually to provide heat and power to factories, businesses, and homes; materials for manufacturing paints, plastics and other petrochemicals; and fuels for transportation. This book offers you information on how to reduce your dependence on petroleum for your transportation needs. Steps you can take to reduce consumption of petroleum include conservation and increased use of renewable sources of energy in the residential, industrial and commercial sectors of the economy. (The next time you visit a hotel, ask if the shower water is heated by solar water heaters.)

You've read a bit about the electric vehicle's past and about the EV pioneers who are today's unsung environmental heroes. The next chapter describes how a state agency and a city council in California jolted the automotive industry into action. We live in exciting times!

The LaserCel 1, powered by a fuel cell, at the Solar Energy Exposition and Rally (SEER), August 1991, at Willits, Calif. *Photo from Solarland Ltd.*

Table 3.1: Fractions in a Barrel of Crude Oil

	Percent (1987)	Gallons	Percent possible
Gasoline	46.6	19.57	23.3
Jet Fuel	10.0	4.20	20.0 *
Liquefied gases (includes propane)	3.4	1.42	3.4
Kerosene	0.6	0.25	0.6
Fuel Oil			
Distillate	20.5	8.61	25.5 *
Residual	6.6	2.77	6.6
Still gas	4.8	2.01	4.8
Coke	3.8	1.59	3.8
Asphalt	3.3	1.40	3.3
Petrochemical feedstocks	2.9	1.22	10.9 *
Lubricants	1.3	0.55	1.6 *
Special naphthas	0.4	0.14	0.4
Waxes	0.1	0.04	0.1
Miscellaneous	0.5	0.21	0.5
Processing gain	-4.8	-2.01	-4.8
	100.0	42.00 gallons in a barrel of crude petroleum	

"Percent possible" assumes that half of the gasoline (for motor vehicles) is not needed (assuming that it has been displaced by electric and other alternative-fuel vehicles) and that fraction (23.3%) is added to other fractions marked with "*".

Still gas is produced in the refinery during the refining and cracking processes.

Jet fuel includes naphtha-type fuel (used principally by the military) and kerosene-type jet fuel (used principally by commercial aircraft).

Gasoline includes both motor vehicle and aviation gasolines. Aviation gasoline is used by small aircraft (single and twin-engine propeller planes).

The processing of petroleum involves breaking certain fractions ("cracking") and forming other fractions. There is a slight gain in volume and this "processing gain" is the difference between the amount of crude oil before refining and the sum of its end-products. *Source: U.S. Energy Information Administration, Petroleum Supply Annual, 1987.*

EVs can bring you perks. *Photo by R. Minner.*

Ed Rannberg with the Badsey EMX electric scooter

4

The CARB and
the Los Angeles Initiative

The Electric Car Rebirth in Los Angeles

Los Angeles, the City of "The Angels," was known as the Valley of Ten Thousand Smokes by the people who lived in the area before Spanish settlers arrived. Millions of new residents moved into the L.A. Basin during the Great Depression. When World War Two ended, increased industrial activity, a lack of air quality standards, and millions of new cars added to the pollution. In the 1950s, the occasional hazy days turned into weeks of unbroken smoke and fog, now called "smog."

The California Legislature formed the California Air Resources Board (CARB) in 1968, giving the new body appropriate powers to deal with the deteriorating air quality. The CARB has a history of using emissions standards to force improvements, rather than just codifying existing technology. This is critical: although the manufacturers are capable of developing new technologies, they are extremely hesitant to act individually because of the costs and risks. By mandating improvements, the CARB spreads the costs and risks over the entire industry -- something the auto makers actually welcome.

On September 27, 1990, the CARB proposed regulations governing stationary and mobile sources of pollution. The plan addressed both major and minor sources of pollutants, from paint and chemical factories to barbecue grills and lawn mowers. Automobiles contribute between 50 and 70 percent of major components of the polluted air above Los Angeles, and the CARB's rules sought to encourage the introduction of alternatively fueled vehicles as part of its general plan to reduce air pollution.

Car makers have been reluctant to invest in mass production of vehicles powered by alternatives to gasoline, since they lack the assurance of a demand for the more-expensive engines needed to use these non-petroleum fuels. The CARB's emissions standards were adopted on September 28, 1990, giving a much-needed push for the automotive industry to retool its assembly lines. Categories established by CARB allow varying amounts of pollutants, from the TLEV (Transitional Low Emissions Vehicle) to the ULEV (Ultra Low Emission Vehicle) to the ZEV (zero emissions vehicle). The introduction of the least-polluting vehicle is mandated for 1998.

The ZEV is of particular interest, since for the foreseeable future "Zero Emissions" means "electric." Electric cars are the only vehicles currently expected to produce no tailpipe emissions. Critics argue that "zero emissions" is a misleading phrase, since electricity must be generated somewhere, and over half of the electricity made in the U.S. comes from coal.

For advocates of petroleum's alternatives, the ZEV is a most helpful concept. Coal emissions can be significantly reduced with expensive "scrubbers" which clean the exhaust air more efficiently than millions of catalytic converters (which cannot be monitored so easily). Renewable sources of energy can supply electricity without emissions *(more on this in the answer to Myth 3 in Chapter 7)*.

EV News carries the latest on EVs: $30/year, 1911 N. Ft. Myer Dr., #703, Arlington, VA 22209

Two Percent of Two Million: It's A Start

The CARB regulations require two percent of all cars sold in California to be ZEVs by 1998, rising to ten percent by 2003. About two million cars are sold each year in California, so each percent increase in new electric car sales will add 20,000 cars that require less (for hybrid-electric) or no (for electric) petroleum products. This might not seem a lot, compared to the 145 million automobiles on the road in 1991, but the following table shows what happens by 2004.

Table 4.1: Potential EV Market in the U.S.

	ZEVs as percent of market	Number of ZEVs in Calif.	Number of ZEVs in Northeast U.S.
1998	2%	40,000	100,000
1999	2%	40,000	100,000
2000	2%	40,000	100,000
2001	5%	100,000	250,000
2002	5%	100,000	250,000
2003	10%	200,000	500,000
By Jan. 1, 2004:		520,000	1,300,000

California represents roughly 14-18% of the U.S. car market, and the Northeast states working to adopt California's vehicle standards account for approximately 35%. By January 1, 2004, more than one percent of the cars registered in the U.S. will be battery-powered. It's a good start.

Kudos to Marvin Braude

Two years before the CARB regulations were confirmed, City Councilman Marvin Braude persuaded the city council of Los Angeles to announce a contest to encourage the development of three types of electric vehicles. The L.A. City Council authorized its utility (the Los Angeles Water and Power District) to spend $3.5 million to assist private companies in designing an electric commuter car. The amount was matched by Southern California Edison. That's like investing fifty cents for every resident in Southern California. In an era of spending cuts and "no new taxes," it is often difficult to muster support for new programs. Councilman Marvin Braude won support for his plan on May 6, 1988, celebrated as Independence From Oil Day by some chapters of the Electric Auto Association.

Considering the public's lack of enthusiasm for clean powered cars (when was the last time you saw 10,000 people picketing your state's capital, demanding cleaner fuel standards?), this governmental support for electric cars is remarkable.

Thank you, CARB and the LA City Council

Electric car advocates can thank the California Air Resources Board (CARB, Public Information Office, P.O.Box 2815, Sacramento, CA 95812, (916) 322-2990) and the Los Angeles City Council (200 N. Hope Street, Los Angeles, CA 90010) for looking ahead and investing in the future. One can argue that both bodies took political risks, since the prices of all cars in the California economy are likely to rise, increasing the cost of living. To sell the more-expensive electric and alternative fuel vehicles, car makers will probably offer rebates and price-cutting incentives. Development costs

5

Why You Should
Wait For Detroit

The title of this book assumes that the Big Three are taking too long to bring electric cars to the showroom floor, so why not just convert an old car to electric? Representatives from Ford Motor Company, Chrysler Corporation and General Motors Corporation supplied the following responses.

General Motors

In March 1991, General Motors announced that its Lansing Craft Centre in Lansing, Mich., would become the first automobile plant in the world to be committed to mass production of electric cars. The first electric car GM will produce in this plant will be based on the Impact prototype that was first shown to the public in January 1990 at the Los Angeles Auto Show. This two-seater is not a conversion of an existing car, but a ground-up vehicle designed to run on electricity while including all the amenities of a production vehicle.

Why wait for Detroit to produce an electric vehicle? Efficiency, performance, safety, style and service are just a few reasons.

Efficiency and Performance: The Impact's obsession for efficiency is reflected in its low energy consumption. Although the range of Impact on a fully charged battery is only 120 miles, it accomplishes this range with slightly more energy than a single gallon of gasoline. A ground-up electric vehicle like Impact has efficiency advantages over a conversion in four areas: vehicle mass, vehicle aerodynamics, rotating drag and accessory loads. In a conversion, specific components of the original production vehicle are removed and replaced with components needed to make the vehicle run on electricity. The modifications to the vehicle to accommodate these components cause the conversion vehicle to be heavier than the ground-up electric vehicle, and thus less efficient. A ground-up vehicle also can be engineered in such a way as to make much more extensive use of lightweight materials, like aluminum, than is usually found in production vehicles.

Ground-up design also creates the opportunity to improve aerodynamics. There are no production vehicles available for conversion today that have a drag coefficient less than 0.26, and most are between 0.30 and 0.40. At higher speeds, the aerodynamic drag increases, resulting in even higher energy consumption. The Impact is so aerodynamically designed, however, that its drag coefficient is only 0.19 -- this not only results in significant energy savings, but also leaves more power available for acceleration at freeway speeds.

All vehicles also have rotating drag, or friction. Because the Impact is designed from the ground up, it is engineered to have less drag than present production in areas such as wheels and brakes, resulting in less energy consumption.

Finally, conversion vehicles use significant amounts of power to manage accessory loads -- air-conditioning, lighting, power brakes, etc. Ground-up hardware designs reduce the energy consumption of these systems. For example, the Impact's electrically driven heat pump provides air-conditioning for the vehicle's interior with only 1 kilowatt of power. Present engine-driven A/C compressors require three to five times as much power.

for cars powered by these non-petroleum fuels will not be recovered for years, and the sales of conventional gasoline-powered cars will have to subsidize the price of ZEVs.

Cynics will laugh at this expression of gratitude (rarely given to public officials today!) and will point out that any city that has not attained the federal air quality standards is required to adopt plans and take action to improve air quality, or face a loss in highway construction money. They will say that we who advocate electric cars and other alternative to gasoline need not feel overly grateful to these officials. After all, the CARB and Los Angeles City Council took their historic stands on behalf of electric cars to meet a federal mandate.

Do not forget, however, that Los Angeles has an extension until 2010 to meet the deadline set in the Clean Air Act Amendments of 1990. Twenty years before Southern California would face losing a single federal dollar, the CARB and L.A. City Council were already taking steps to stimulate the supply of alternative vehicles.

The CARB standards directly affect more than two million new cars every year, and millions more through parallel regulations in other states. While California represents only 14-18 percent of the U.S. market for new vehicles, 51 percent of the total U.S. new car market was considering or had adopted the CARB standards by January 1992, including the 2 percent mandate for ZEVs by 1998. This includes Virginia, the District of Columbia, Maryland, Delaware, Pennsylvania, New York, New Jersey and six New England States (Massachusetts, Rhode Island, Maine, New Hampshire, Connecticut and Vermont). Florida, Texas, Oklahoma, Colorado and Arizona have also strongly supported the introduction of alternative-fuel vehicles with mandated additions to each state's fleets.

Electric car advocates should take a moment to thank the CARB and the LA City Council. Without their leadership, the electric car renaissance would be delayed and would not be spreading as quickly.

The Impact's column of 32 10-volt batteries is located in a tunnel passing through the core of the car, providing an ideal low center of gravity. *Photo provided General Motors.*

Ford engineers Dick Kosik, Jim Bretz and Tony Gambrel with the Ford EV. *Photo provided by Ford Motor Co.*

The result of a more efficiently built electric vehicle is better performance. The heavier conversions will be slower than ground-up engineered vehicles in a flat, 0-to-60-mph run (Impact goes 0-60 in 8 seconds), and the lighter, more energy-efficient cars like Impact can also climb steep hills at a higher speed. It also will accelerate more quickly at highway speeds.

Designing an electric car from the ground-up involves a much greater commitment from General Motors in terms of people, dollars and technology. This commitment has enabled GM to produce a vehicle that consumes two to three times less energy than a typical conversion vehicle, and at the same time provides features that customers expect.

Safety: Safety can also be an important issue when comparing conversions to ground-up electric vehicles. All vehicles produced by automobile manufacturers in the United States must meet federal safety standards. Most manufacturers of conversion vehicles, however, seek exemption from these standards, because it is difficult to modify a complying vehicle without compromising its crashworthiness, and because it is very expensive to certify the vehicle safety performance. Owners of conversion vehicles should consider the care the manufacturer has taken in making the conversion, and the amount of experience, if any, the manufacturer has had in designing vehicles for safety and crashworthiness.

Styling: An obvious advantage of a ground-up electric vehicle is its contemporary style. An efficient electric car must be aerodynamic, and perhaps smaller, to control mass. In Impact's case, the result of ground-up design was a brand new vehicle, like no one has ever seen.

A Real Car from a Real Car Company: GM's electric vehicles will be sold through existing dealerships at a price competitive with cars of comparable value. Advantages to keep in mind when purchasing the GM electric vehicle will be the full warranty that will accompany it, and the ready access you will enjoy to parts and service.

The recent war in the Middle East, the possibility that increasing atmospheric concentrations of "greenhouse gases" may lead to changes in the world's climate and the fact that the entire U.S. economy relies so heavily on energy has forced the public and the government to concern themselves more with the price, availability and use of energy and fossil fuels.

General Motors is continuing its active investigation of alternative fuels as part of its long-term strategy to improve air quality. This includes research and engineering in oxygenate blends, alcohols (methanol and ethanol), compressed natural gas, liquefied petroleum gas and reformulated gasoline, as well as electric vehicles. Consumers can help support this strategy by continuing to drive fuel-efficient GM cars. Since the enactment of the Clean Air Act in 1970, emissions from new passenger cars have been reduced substantially. At the same time drivability, fuel economy, and performance have improved.

The efficiency and safety found in a ground-up engineered electric vehicle, such as the Impact, will help the owner drive away feeling satisfied and secure that he or she has purchased a vehicle designed with the utmost care. This, along with the excitement that comes with the purchase of any new vehicle and the sleek styling and performance that GM electric vehicles provide, definitely make the wait worthwhile.

This concept car by General Motors made quite an impact when it was unveiled in January 1990.

Ford

There are plenty of reasons to wait, says Roberta Nichols, who is leading Ford's program to develop safe, affordable, and comfortable electric vehicles.

The first two reasons why EV advocates *should* wait for Ford to develop a factory-produced electric vehicle are rather obvious: a) production engineered cars are safer than converted cars, and b) production engineered cars result in better overall system energy efficiency and performance.

"That's all very well," you may be thinking, "but why hasn't Ford developed such a car already?" Let me explain it this way: We really try to do what the customer wants and, up until recently, customers haven't been asking for electric cars. We are currently responding to legislation in California that requires two percent of car sales in 1998 to be zero-emissions vehicles, which essentially means electric cars. That government mandate has certainly encouraged us to move our EV research at a faster pace, and it does provide a much-needed incentive.

But we can't go too fast. We need to learn from the past. Remember the diesel-powered passenger car? The first ones came out in 1980 after the second gasoline crisis, and the performance was disappointing. By the time the engines were improved, the price of gasoline had fallen and nobody wanted to buy a diesel car. The customer was not there in 1986 when we produced a beauty: a small 2-liter diesel Escort, with good performance and low emissions. So we had to stop selling it in 1987. It would have moved well in 1981, but it takes five years to get a good car to market, and by then the diesel was too late. By the way, I bet you didn't know that the diesel engine produces *less* carbon dioxide per mile than the best gasoline cars. The diesel engine is a more efficient type of combustion engine than the conventional spark-ignition engine, which makes it a good choice for reducing greenhouse gases or global warming.

Because there's a higher level of awareness about air pollution and our dependence on oil imports today, we hope that the present interest in electric vehicles will remain steady and grow.

How long does it take to develop a new car? The typical car program, starting with a "clean" piece of paper, has taken five years to prepare, although we are working to shorten that time. Starting with an existing car and making a derivative is somewhat less, but with the electric vehicle, much of the technology is quite different. It's a considerable challenge to get the required energy density on board to meet the functional needs of the customer without using up all available space, and without adding lots of weight.

That's why Ford is participating in the United States Advanced Battery Consortium. USABC will leverage the auto industry's resources to try to move advanced battery technology faster.

But the electric motor is much simpler than the internal combustion engine. What's so difficult about converting a car to electric power? An electric motor is essentially a steady-state device, so it requires a very sophisticated control system to provide the flexibility of a typical driving cycle. Also, climate control is a major challenge. EVs in the Northeast will need heat in the winter; EVs in Arizona, Texas, New Mexico, Florida, wherever it gets hot, will need cooling. Heating and cooling are challenges for electric vehicles. If you use resistance heating, you reduce the range of the batteries. If you use a fuel-fired heater, it's no longer a ZEV. Without climate control, the electric car is a substandard vehicle. About 98 percent of our customers buy their cars **with** air conditioning, and a heater is a "given."

There are other challenges to overcome. Our market research shows that people are generally wary about new technology. This is an area where the electric car clubs could collectively help us to raise public awareness of electric cars.

The consumer needs to meet us halfway. Please help us by taking time to educate yourself about the differences between alternative fuel vehicles. Know the advantages and disadvantages of natural gas and methanol. Some choices will be better than others, depending on your driving needs. Whether the car is the second or third car in your household makes a difference. If you use it primarily for commuting, you will need a different car than when you tow a boat to go fishing on weekends, or take the family cross-country on vacation.

Buying an alternatively fueled vehicle is one way to help reduce oil imports, so should we be standing in line to buy your methanol cars? To gain much needed experience, Ford has placed over 1,300 methanol demonstration vehicles in the field, beginning in 1981. But demonstration vehicles are expensive. Next year Ford will have its first pilot production of the flexible fuel vehicle; a 1993 three-liter Taurus that can operate on methanol or gasoline or any random mixture of these fuels. While most of the sales will be to California fleets, private citizens can purchase the cars too. The success of these 1993 vehicles will determine when we move into full-scale production, which we need to do to bring the costs down to levels that are affordable.

Besides, we need to move slowly to deliver the best possible product. The worst thing is to deliver quickly and get a negative reaction. We're happy that there are consumers who are eager to own an electric car or a flexible fuel vehicle (FFV), but building new plants or converting existing ones costs a lot of money. If one starts with that "clean" piece of paper, it requires $1.5-2.0 billion to bring a new vehicle to market.

Unless you have worked in the auto industry, with all of the development work and testing to meet regulatory requirements and safety needs, not to mention delivery of a vehicle that satisfies the expectation of the customers, then you can't possibly imagine the size of the job. It's a mind-boggling task, which most of us don't think about when we step into a car. We just turn the key and go, not realizing that hundreds of thousands of people and years were spent to develop that car. It's that sort of awareness that the public needs to develop. You'll see: before the decade is over, Ford will have an efficient, affordable, safe electric car, designed from the ground up for maximum overall performance, that is fun to drive.

Roberta Nichols joined Ford in 1979 and assumed a leading role in the company's alternative fuel program. She holds a Ph.D. in engineering from University of Southern California. She is responsible for government and public relations for Ford's Electric Vehicle Program Office as well as external affairs of the U.S. Advanced Battery Consortium.

Chrysler
An interview with George Shishkovsky, program manager for Chrysler's EV program:
Are ground-up engineered cars safer than converted cars? Yes and no. I don't think that a generalization that broad can be made. A vehicle engineered from the ground up by a reputable company, such as the Impact from GM, is very likely to be a "safe" vehicle. Vehicles converted by the original manufacturer are also very likely to be just as safe, or safer than, an electric vehicle designed from the ground-up. The original manufacturer has complete access to and understands the original design and development data. The conversion process then has all the benefits of the background information and has the best chance of success. Conversions done by someone other than the original manufacturer do not have access to this design information.

Chrysler is converting its minivan to electric power and we are making sure that the vehicle is just as safe, in every respect, as the original vehicle.

I think that, in purchasing an electric vehicle, the consumer should consider, very seriously, the reliability and track record of the company selling the vehicle.

Obstacle to bringing an EV to market today: The major obstacle to getting EVs on the showroom floor is the batteries. Chrysler has been working with nickel-iron batteries, but there are also nickel-cadmium and, of course, lead-acid batteries. None of these batteries, we feel, will meet the minimum performance and cost requirements for widespread use in EVs. Beyond that, the supply of batteries does not exist for any significant production of EVs.

The United States Advanced Battery Consortium (USABC) was formed by Chrysler, Ford and GM to address this problem. The consortium has set up desired performance specifications for EV batteries and a time table to demonstrate a mass-producible battery.

Why can't we turn out an EV today? We could and have designed electric vehicles. However, a cheap, good-performing supply of batteries is needed to generate a demand for the vehicles. There is no demand for low-performance, high-cost electric vehicles.

Like a car with a 5-gallon tank: Think of the reaction you would have if you were told that your next car could only hold five gallons, and that it would take 6 to 8 hours to refill. That's where we are with electric vehicles today. This will require that the customer change his way of thinking about his vehicle, and that the entire infrastructure (fuel supply) be modified to support EVs.

Things to do now to help the environment: Several things come to mind: first, if you're driving an older car, a "clunker," scrap it and purchase a new car. Those old cars you see on the road produce many times the emissions of a new car. There was, in fact, a program in California sponsored by an oil company that would provide rebates to people who would turn in their old cars and purchases new vehicles.

Second, use a cleaner fuel. The quality of gasoline is just as important in reducing emissions as any of the anti-pollution devices installed on vehicles by automobile manufacturers. A number of oil companies have introduced these reformulated, cleaner gasolines onto the market.

Third, proper maintenance of your vehicle is essential. A number of studies have shown that a vehicle in need of a tune up generates higher emissions. Proper inflation of tires is also important.

When? Chrysler expects to have an electric vehicle ready for the public to purchase in the mid-1990s. Flexible-fuel vehicles, running on methanol, will be available in the 1993 model year, and compressed natural gas vehicles should be available in the 1994 time frame.

Volkswagen

When asked, "When will VW and Swatch begin selling the $6,000 EV?", VW's public relations division sent an informative package, from which the following was extracted:

Volkswagen's corporate statement on the environment begins with Chief Seattle's remarks to President Franklin Pierce in 1855: *What infests the earth also infests the children of the earth. Man did not create the fabric of life, he is merely a thread therein. Whatever you do to the fabric, you do to yourselves.*

Three priorities guide VW's environmental policy: First, conservation before reduction: by limiting the use of natural resources form the outset, the need to reduce their use in the future is minimized. Second, reduction before recycling: by reducing the use of environmentally problematic materials and precious resources, there will be less to reclaim and less to recycle or dispose of later. Finally, recycling before discarding: if every effort is made to reclaim and reuse, what is left or discarded will be minimal. At Volkswagen, every car is built with "green" in mind -- even the red, white and blue ones.

Electric Car: The company offers the CitySTROMer, a battery-powered Jetta. "Strom" in German means "current" as in "electricity" (as well as "stream"), so the name suggests a vehicle that flows through city traffic on electric current. It draws its power from high-energy sodium-sulfur batteries that weigh the same as a traditional lead-acid battery, but can store approximately four times the amount of energy. Range is currently 75 miles with a top speed of 65 miles per hour. Advanced engineering is expected to double the range.

The Golf Diesel Electric Hybrid: For drivers who seek a car without the limited range of the CitySTROMer, VW is planning to offer a hybrid car that adds a diesel engine. Fitted with a specially adapted low boosting turbocharger and an oxidation catalyst, the "lean-burn" diesel engine uses up to 40 percent more air in combustion. This results in reduced particulates and oxides of nitrogen with improved fuel efficiency and up to 25 percent less carbon dioxide emissions than a gasoline engine of the same size. Thanks to the catalyst, half of the polycyclic aromatic hydrocarbons are removed, reducing the characteristic odor associated with diesel exhaust.

During operation, the diesel engine automatically engages during acceleration and at speeds over 31 miles per hour. When the diesel is being used, the electrical generator charges the battery. A small onboard computer immediately determines which is the best power source for the car under a given set of circumstances. The driver can use the drive selector to override the computer and operate the car using electricity or diesel alone.

The Golf Hybrid employs regenerative braking, where the brakes are used to turn the drivetrain into a generator to charge the battery. The car is designed to cut emission by up to 60 percent. With optimum utilization of diesel and electric powertrains, the Golf Hybrid could average more than 100 miles per gallon of diesel fuel.

Nissan

What is Nissan's vision? First and foremost, Nissan's designers and engineers must be responsible and responsive to the performance, styling and comfort needs and wants of our customers. Secondly, the product itself must shoulder a measure of responsibility. This relates to the vehicle's ability to avoid accidents and, in the event of a collision, to protect the occupants from serious harm....

Finally, both Nissan and its products have a responsibility to the environment. As we see it, cars, people and nature depend on each other. We share the same biosphere, the same habitat.

For more than 30 years, Nissan has investigated various electric-based technologies. Though such research is ongoing, one tangible outcome thus far is our Future Electric Vehicle, or FEV, introduced at the Tokyo Motor Show in 1991. The FEV enables us to gain operating experience, to learn more before taking steps toward prodcution. As we've said, we do not intend to manufacture the FEV. Its purpose is developmental.

Perhaps the biggest obstacle to the proliferation of electric vehicles is consumer acceptance. Is today's car owner willing to make significant sacrifices in performance and personal freedom to realize long-term gains in environmental quality? Even if we were to mass-produce the FEV, would it be accepted with open arms by consumers? And are consumers willing to pay for a car that, under today's conditions, is likely to cost more to buy and operate than a gasoline model?

The answer is obvious. But, just as obvious, we cannot allow current public opinion to dissuade us from pursuing such alternatives. We will continue to work hard to develop these technologies, we must also work just as hard at educating the public through a sharing of information and open dialogue. As I've stated, there are some things we can do. And there are things we can do only with the cooperation of others. *From a speech by Kazumasa Katoh, director of Nissan Research and Development, Inc., at the North American International Auto Show, Jan. 7, 1992 in Detroit.*

6

Facts About EVs

Electric cars don't need:
- to consume fuel while stopped at a traffic light
- exhaust pipes
- coolant or anti-freeze
- motor oil
- points or plugs
- carburetors
- oil pumps
- fuel pumps
- water pumps
- air filters
- fuel filters
- oil filters
- fuel injectors
- radiators
- chokes
- head gaskets
- valve grinds
- rings
- engine overhauls
- manifolds
- mufflers
- catalytic converters
- fan belts
- timing belts
- trips to the gas station
- smog certificates (for pure electric)
- distributors
- caps and rotors
- tune ups
- hoses
- pistons
- crankcases
- fuel tanks

Compiled from a list created by Electro Automotive (Felton, Calif.), Joseph LaStella, and from Michael Hackleman's article in the Real Goods mail order catalog, March 1991. Hybrid electric vehicles require exhaust-system inspections if an internal combustion engine is used as an on-board range extender.

Richard Minner in a Solectria Force
(converted Geo Metro).

Here are some additional facts about battery-powered, on-road, street-legal transportation from Mike Brown, who has 27 years of professional automotive experience and has worked with electric vehicles since 1979. He teaches a one-day conversion class for hobbyists through community colleges in the San Francisco Bay area. He also teaches the three-day Pro-Mech Program for professional mechanics.

How much does it cost to operate an EV?

An EV costs less than five cents per mile for electricity and about three cents per mile for maintenance and batteries[1] (which must be replaced approximately every three years). These costs rise significantly, however, if batteries do not receive adequate treatment.

How fast can an EV go?

Many EVs can maintain highway speeds of 55 to 65 mph. The speed record for an EV is over 174 mph (but what's your hurry? Rush hour traffic rarely exceeds 40 mph).

How far can an EV go without recharging?

The average range is around 40 miles,[2] but some EVs can exceed 100 miles on a single charge. For comparison, the average car in the U.S. travels less than 30 miles in a day (9,000 miles annually).

How long does it take to recharge?

Overnight is the ideal time to recharge, since many utilities offer lower electricity rates during off-peak hours. If the EV has an on-board charger, it can be recharged during the day at work as well.

What if I want to take a long trip?

An EV is basically a commuter's car or a household's second car dedicated to local trips, not a travel car. most drivers in the U.S. spend most of their time traveling short distances (less than 20 miles in one direction). Unless you travel a great deal, it is often cheaper to rent a gasoline-powered car for occasional trips than to own and maintain one.

Scott Cornell's converted Ghia.

Note: A typical gasoline car's fuel costs run 6.6 cents per mile at 21 mpg, $1.40 per gallon of gasoline.

[1] The costs cited here come from several of Mike Brown's customers. The cost of operating a gasoline-powered car can often exceed 12 cents per mile for fuel and maintenance. Estimates on the cost of operating an EV vary from expert to expert and car to car, so always request several opinions. See Chapter 11 for a side-by-side comparison of the life-cycle costs prepared by Bob Batson, Electric Vehicles of America.

[2] The 40-mile range may be too pessimistic, since many EVs have a range of over 50 miles.

Essential Facts About EVs

Paul Brasch, editor of *Current EVents* (the newsletter of the national EAA chapter) has compiled a paper to answer many of the questions raised by skeptics who wonder how much of the enthusiasm over EVs is just unexamined optimism. Here are some highlights:

1. Electric vehicles produce no air pollution when used. The pollution released at the average power plant while generating electricity is less than 4% of that produced by a conventional car powered by an internal combustion engine (ICE). *This figure applies to vehicles charged in California. Pollution associated with the generation of electricity varies according to the mix of fossil fuel and sustainable sources of energy used by the utility.*

2. Up to 25% of the energy used to accelerate an EV can be recovered with regenerative braking.

3. More than 1 million EVs could be charged off the power grid in Southern California before any additional generating capacity might be needed, since most would be charged at night when there is excess capacity.

4. Current off-peak capacity in the U.S. could recharge the batteries of 40 million EVs.

5. 95% of all vehicles travel less than 25 miles per day.

6. Los Angeles Department of Water and Power offers EV owners a low off-peak rate of 3.5 cents per kilowatt-hour, discounted from the peak rate of 12.5 cents per kilowatt-hour.

Sources:

1. Quanlu Wang, Mark DeLuchi, and Daniel Sperling, Institute of Transportation Studies, U.C. Davis. "Emission Impacts of Electric Vehicles," Journal of Air Waste Management Association, Vol. 40:1275-1284 (1990). *Note: Paul's figure of 4% refers to California's electricity-generating capacity, and does not apply to the U.S. in general, where plants tend to be "dirtier." However, EVs can be charged with photovoltaic arrays, such as one planned for a parking facility in Boston.*

2. Mark DeLuchi, Quanlu Wang and Daniel Sperling, Institute of Transportation Studies, U.C. Davis. "Electric Vehicles: Performance, Life-Cycle Costs, Emissions and Recharging Requirements," Transportation Research Association, Vol. 23A, No. 3, pp. 255-278 (1989). *Note: Regenerative braking takes place when the electric motor is used to slow down the vehicle. This optional feature can cost up to several thousand dollars extra.*

3. Alternative Transportation News, March 1991, page 11.

4. Electric Vehicle Development Corp (EVDC) Information Network Newsletter, Vol. II, No. 5, quoting U.S. Department of Energy estimates. Other estimates include 38 million by the Lead Industry Association (1982).

5. U.S. DOT, Federal Highway Administration, Personal Travel in the U.S.: 1983-84 Nationwide Personal Transportation Study, Vol. I, II, III 1985-86.

6. Personal communication with Don Siglar, Los Angeles Department of Water and Power, 213-481-5767.

The first Solar Electric Racing Association race in 1991.

Photo by Shari Prange.

7
EV Myths

1. Electric cars won't be practical until 1998.

This myth is based on the justified position that, until government requires industry to conform to a set of standards, there is no incentive for the market to develop the product. So critics of EVs assume that there won't be a useful electric car until the deadline set by the California Air Resources Board approaches (2% of total car sales in California must be zero emission vehicles by 1998).

Reality: What does "practical" mean to you? If you're a public administrator and looking for a quiet vehicle to collect trash, a battery-powered garbage truck is very practical (models are operating today in Japan and Saudi Arabia). If you're a commuter and need a car to take you 100 miles to work at 65 mph, then an affordable electric car is not a reality for you. But if your car just needs to carry groceries and serve as a typical second car in the multi-car household, or if your commute is less than 30 miles one-way, then an electric car will work for you today.

There are approximately 90 million households in the U.S. with 145 million passenger cars and light-duty trucks registered for on-road use (1990 figures). Somewhere around 40 million households have more than one car, and at least half of those homes (20 million) use one car less than 8,000 miles per year. Less than 30 miles per day is well within the range of most electric cars. That's the current target market for electric cars: 38 million (about 25%) of the cars on the road today in the U.S. If you own at least two cars, you probably don't have to wait until 1998 to find a practical electric car.

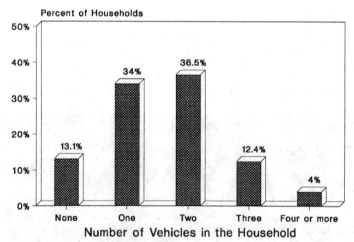

Percent of Households

Number of Vehicles in the Household

Energy Information Administration (1988)
Total Households = 91.6 million

Percent of Households by Number of Vehicles Used for Personal Use (1988). *Source: 1988 Residential Transportation Energy Consumption Survey. Graph appeared in the Household Vehicles Energy Consumption 1988 Report, p. 4, Energy Information Administration, Washington, D.C.*

2. The impact of 100,000 electric cars will be insignificant.

With close to 150 million passenger and light-duty vehicles in North America, converting one tenth of one percent of those cars to electric would appear to have little impact on the level of pollution.

Reality: How do you define "impact"? Sure, alternative-fuel vehicles can hardly hope to dent the U.S. daily demand of 13 million barrels of oil (we imported nearly 6 million barrels every day during 1991). But electric cars act like pebbles thrown on a still pond. One electric car will turn more heads than thousands of other cars passing a busy intersection. This "public-education effect" should not be discounted. Getting 100,000 electric cars on the road (and into schools) before 1998 will prepare the minds of millions of future drivers for commuting in the post-petroleum world.

3. Electric cars don't pollute less: you're just shifting pollution from the car's tailpipe to the utility's smokestack.

People who cling to this myth point to the aging coal plants providing electricity to their region. That brown haze spreading for miles doesn't look any better than the near-colorless gases emitted by many new cars.

Reality: Look at a profile of where we get electricity. Half comes from coal, some from natural gas and nuclear power, less than five percent from fuel oil. So a switch to electric power means a switch away from dependence on petroleum as the prime source of energy for transportation.

Oil- and coal-fired plants work at peak efficiency all the time (converting over 35% of the fuel energy into electricity), whereas automobile engines have an average efficiency of less than 25 percent. In other words, one electric plant uses fuel more efficiently and generates less pollution than thousands of cars.

When one includes the regional polluting from electric power plants, electric cars are 85 to 97 percent less polluting than gasoline cars (depending on the type of emission being measured). The Los Angeles Department of Water and Power distributes a brochure that shows the following profile of pollutants produced while driving a vehicle 100,000 miles (a typical car's life span):

Pounds of gas produced per 100,000 miles

Engine Type	Carbon Monoxide	Reactive Organic Gases	Oxides of Nitrogen (NOx)
Gasoline	2574	262	172
Diesel	216	73	246
Electric	9	5	61

Note: Applies to the Los Angeles area. Pollution levels may be higher or lower in other areas, depending on the fuel used to produce the electricity. Source: L.A. Dept. of Water and Power.

Gasoline contains a number of fractions that do not burn completely and are left in the exhaust gas, whereas coal can be "scrubbed" to remove much of the gases and particles that are not fully burned. It is simply easier to control the emissions of a stationery source than the emissions of thousands of gasoline-powered cars, since the exhaust control system does not have to be made from compact and lightweight materials suited to transporting around with the mobile source.

In the U.S. West, electricity generation is relatively clean. For example, compared to a comparable gasoline-powered car, an EV in California generates only about one percent of the hydrocarbons, three percent of the carbon monoxide and 20 percent of the nitrogen oxides (*Pacific Gas & Electric EV Program brochure*). This is due to the much greater efficiency of a large power plant (30% to 50% efficiency) compared to the relatively small and inefficient conventional car engine (less than 25% efficient).

Even in the eastern part of the U.S., with many more coal-fired plants, the electricity generated to power an EV could create 20 percent less carbon dioxide (according to Professor D.F. Gosden, Sydney University) and significantly lesser amounts of other pollutants than from the combustion of gasoline. *(Mark DeLuchi, University of California at Davis, disagrees, concluding that CO_2 emissions associated with electricity generated by coal plants actually **exceed** CO_2 emissions from the same number of gasoline-powered vehicles. See also Chapter 16.)*

The bottom line is that it is simpler to improve efficiency, reduce emissions and switch to alternate fuels with power plants than with millions of autos.

Future sources of electricity could mean that drivers of electric cars in the 21st Century will pollute even less. Advanced solar thermal electricity generators, neighborhood photovoltaic collecting stations and hydrogen are all renewable and less polluting than the cleanest reformulated gasoline.

4. No more than two percent of the population could ever be persuaded to give up their cars and switch to electric.

This insight is based on the experience of most of us that "talk is cheap." We have seen in a wide variety of circumstances that most people are unwilling to back up their sentiments and beliefs with concrete action.

Reality: Depending on how the question is asked, polls indicate that 80 percent of the U.S. population consider themselves "concerned about the environment," and roughly 15 percent are concerned enough to alter their lifestyle and purchasing patterns to reduce negative impacts on the environment.

How creative are you? Could you persuade half of that 15 percent (or 10 million out of 20 million environmentally concerned car owners) to consider switching to an alternative-fuel vehicle? For the rest, it is only a matter of time. Our job is to bring that time closer.

Shari Prange of Electro Automotive (Felton, Calif.) adds, "Convenience is a persuasive argument. Think of all the time saved **not** taking the car to the shop for service!"

5. All those electric cars will put such an enormous burden on the utility grid, we won't be able to build the hundreds of additional power plants.

It's easy to see where this misconception was born. Electric cars pollute less than gasoline-powered cars, but will we need more power plants because people will not restrict their recharging to night time? They'll want to recharge at any time of day.

Reality: Inexpensive management of the demand for electricity can assist in reducing the need for additional power plants. *(See Things To Do, Chapter 17.)*

EV consultant Victor Wouk addressed this issue more than ten years ago in a letter to the New York Times. He answered a previous Times editorial which expressed concern about electric cars adding to the utility load:

In April 1967, in a paper presented to a conference on batteries for electric vehicles, I showed how, if all automobiles were converted to electricity overnight, the load on the utilities would only double. Since then, calculations done with computer models have confirmed a nominal increase in utility capacity requirements.

However, nobody who is serious about electric vehicles expects them to be introduced at a rate much greater than 100,000 per year, and this would probably not start until the late 1980s, particularly since the Reagan Administration has eliminated all funding for electric car purchases for fiscal 1982.

Even the most optimistic projection for electric cars shows only 20 percent of all automobiles being electric by the year 2020. At that time, the energy required for charging batteries would represent less than 15 percent of the utility energy, and therefore a factor that could be readily absorbed in the normal growth pattern.

Electric cars' batteries would be charged mainly at night, when there is ample excess generating capacity at the public utilities. The utilities would welcome this additional load, which would help to utilize electricity generating capacity more effectively, and help reduce the rate of rise in electricity costs. (The New York Times, April 5, 1981.)

Southern California Edison has sufficient capacity to handle the night-time charging of 600,000 to one million cars, depending on the assumptions used. This works out to be 18% of the current 5.4 million cars registered in the heart of urban Los Angeles (including major sections of Los Angeles, Orange and Ventura counties). One in five cars in downtown L.A. could be a zero-emission vehicle *today* without increasing the electric generating capacity of the L.A. basin.

In Sacramento, where the utility serves one million people (406,126 households and 50,683 industrial and commercial hookups), the current off-peak capacity could support 100,000 electric vehicles, or one EV for every ten people. That works out to be one EV per 4.06 households or one EV per six cars (source: SMUD).

6. Insurance companies either won't insure odd vehicles like electric cars, or they'll price your EV off the road.

The source of this rumor probably points to some negative experience he's had at some point in his life where he was charged a high premium for what the insurance agent considered a "nonstandard car."

Reality: *Marc Rosenberg of the Insurance Information Institute (1101 17th Street, N.W., #408, Washington, D.C. 20036, 202-833-1580) kindly offered this reply to the editors' bold assertion that "electric cars ought to be cheaper to insure, since they generally travel over shorter distances, and have lower operating and maintenance costs." Although Mr. Rosenberg cautions, "Please bear in mind that this reply may not apply to the case of any one specific vehicle," his answer makes the world of insurance premiums a bit easier to understand (**boldface** indicates emphasis added by the editors).*

The cost of private passenger automobile insurance is determined by many factors. The three most significant are: 1) the driver; 2) the vehicle; and 3) location and usage. Any one of the variables can have a substantial impact on insurance premiums, so it is difficult to say what percentage of a policy's cost will be determined by vehicle type.

A driver with a history of moving violations and/or at-fault accidents will be more expensive to insure than a safe driver, regardless of what cars they drive. However, the safety records and repair costs of various model vehicles will make an incremental difference in insurance costs. Likewise, the frequency of accidents, theft and vandalism in a particular community will have an impact on the cost of insuring all cars, but will impact some models more than others.

Insurance ratings of vehicle models are based upon historic data: frequency of accidents, severity of injuries, cost of repairs, frequency of theft, etc. It is difficult to guess what those numbers will look like for models that have not yet been introduced, and there may be off-setting factors. For instance, a car used mostly for commuting and urban driving is far more likely to be involved in traffic accidents, but those accidents tend to be at lower speeds and therefore are relatively less expensive.

Operating expenses are not a factor in determining auto insurance rates. You are not insured for anything that would fall within this category. The same is true of maintenance expenses.

Like any new model car that is introduced, electric vehicles will either be lumped in with existing models or will see a fluctuation in insurance rates for the first few years they are on the market. After that, there will be a body of data from actual experience which will allow insurers to evaluate risk on historic records. **There does not appear to be anything about electric vehicles that would make them more expensive to insure** and the factors you have indicated (low mileage, low speeds, low repairs costs) would be reflected in lower insurance premiums if they are borne out by experience.

7. Electric cars are not energy-efficient because two-thirds of the energy in coal is lost when coal is burned to make electricity.

It's fairly easy to see where this misconception arose. After all, to get electricity, you have to convert a fuel to heat to make steam to turn a turbine to generate electricity, and then there are transmission losses — whereas gasoline is delivered straight to the car, ready to use.

Reality: Suppose someone said to you, "Here are one million Btus of energy, but you must choose how to receive this energy: either as coal or gasoline." Which would allow you to travel farther?

"The gasoline, of course!" you would reply. "I don't have a steam-powered locomotive!" Ah, but you can always convert the coal into electricity. To make this comparison fair (fossil fuel vs. fossil fuel for an EV), we need to subtract the 169,000 Btus needed to convert crude petroleum into gasoline.

How far can I go on one million Btus?

	Gasoline		Coal
	Gasoline		Coal
Start with	1 million Btus	Start with	1 million Btus
Energy in gasoline after delivery to service station	831,000 Btus	Energy left after converting to electricity[1]	320,000 Btus
Btus per gallon of gasoline	125,000 Btus	Kilowatt-hours per 1000 Btus	0.2931 kwhr
Gallons available	6.6 gallons	Electricity available	93.7 kwhr
Car's fuel economy	28 mpg	Energy efficiency[2]	2 mi/kwhr
Miles/million Btus	**184.8 miles**	**Miles/million Btus**	**187.4 miles**
Van's fuel economy	12 mpg	G-Van (1.1 kwhr/mi)	0.9 mi/kwhr
Miles/million Btus	**79.2 miles**	**Miles/million Btus**	**84.3 miles**

[1] This is the amount of energy left after the coal has been converted into electricity at the typical coal-fired utility plant and assumes average transmission losses. Improved technologies and cogeneration can capture significant amounts of this lost energy.
[2] This is a typical "fuel economy" for a converted vehicle. Ken Koch (KTA Services, Orange, Calif.) gets 3 miles per kilowatt-hour in his converted 1972 Mazda. Jim Worden (Solectria, Arlington, Mass.) has plans for "the ultimate commuter car" that will get five miles per kilowatt-hour.

What are the ranges from sustainable sources of energy (instead of fossil fuels)?

Fuel Source	Range in Gasoline Car	Electric
Hydropower	0 miles, charge the car's starter battery	187.4 miles
Sun (8 hours)	0 miles, a warmer car interior	3-10 miles

Assume 320,000 Btus from hydroelectric power. Photovoltaic panels can add 10% to EV's range. According to James Worden (Arlington, Mass.), PV panels in temperate zones can capture enough solar energy in eight hours to drive as much as eight miles.

Researchers at the University of California at Davis have been wrestling with the trade-off between zero tailpipe emissions and energy efficiency. The following energy-loss flow diagrams were developed by Mark DeLuchi and Quanlu Wang and presented at the Transportation Research Board's 70th annual meeting in Washington, D.C., January 13-17, 1990:

Crude oil to gasoline
Crude recovery: 3.1% loss
96.9% retained
|
\|/
Crude transport: 1.1% loss
98.9% retained
|
\|/
Crude refinery: 12.6% loss
87.4% retained
|
\|/
Gasoline transport: 0.8% loss
99.2% retained

Delivered to the service station with 83.1% of the energy that started in the oil well.

Coal to electricity
Coal mining: 1.9% loss
98.1% retained
|
\|/
Coal transport: 1% loss
99% retained
|
\|/
Power plant conversion: 67% loss
33% retained

Delivered to the electrical outlet for charging the EV's batteries, retaining 32.0% of the original energy in the coal.

The "retained" figures are multiplied to give the overall process efficiency.

While gasoline retains more of the original fossil energy than electricity, most of this energy will be dissipated as heat by the inefficient internal combustion engine. The highly efficient electric motor, by contrast, will convert a greater percentage of its "fuel" into traction at the wheels.

Solar George

Note on photovoltaic panels by Larry Alexander: These figures are not accepted by everyone. I think the virtue of panels is proving to be battery-life extension.

Gasoline engine

Exhaust gases: 35% loss
Coolant: 20% loss
Radiation: 20% loss

Engine loss: 75% loss

*25% of the gasoline's energy is
available to perform work on the
crankshaft.*

Alternator, fan: 10% loss
Transmission: 6% loss
Differential: 4% loss
Other axles
 and shafts: 4% loss

Post-engine
 losses: 24% loss

*76% of the energy delivered from the
engine is available for overcoming
friction and for moving the car.*

Retained from engine: 0.25
Retained post-engine: x 0.76

                        0.19

Percent of energy in gasoline that is
available for wheel movement = 19%

Electric motor

Transformer
(charging station): 20% loss
80% retained

Battery charging: 20% loss
80% retained

Motor and controller: 10% loss
90% retained

0.80 x 0.80 x 0.90 = 0.57 retained

*Two-fifths (43%) of the energy in the
electricity is lost between arriving at
the outlet and being delivered through
the motor to the   shaft.*

Transmission: 6% loss
Differential: 4% loss
Other axles
 and shafts: 4% loss

Post-motor
 losses: 14% loss

*86% of the energy delivered by the
electric motor is available for
overcoming friction and for moving the
car.*

Retained from engine: 0.57
Retained post-engine: x 0.86

                        0.49
Percent of electricity's energy
available for wheel movement = 49%

Multiplying the first percentage figure – the percentage of the original energy that was delivered to the gasoline station (83.1%) or to the electric outlet (32%) – **by the second percentage figure** – the amount of energy available for moving the wheels of the gasoline car (19%) or the EV (49%) – **allows us to compare how efficiently a gasoline-powered car and an electric vehicle consume fossil fuels.**

Other Estimates of Efficiency: AD Little has calculated "net energy delivery" (the amount of energy needed to move a small car divided by the energy in the fuel before mining and extraction) for various fuels: gasoline, 11%; methanol from natural gas, 9%; natural gas, 12%; ethanol from corn or biomass, 12%; electricity (from the current U.S. composite), 17%. This comparison assumed for the EV thermal, charger and charging losses at 25% and a vehicle efficiency of 76% compared to 13% vehicle efficiency for a gasoline-powered car. Vehicle efficiency was defined as *road load* (aerodynamic drag and inertial and rolling friction) times *EPA mileage estimates* (10% efficiency in city, 22% in highway, plus air conditioning load).

Fossil energy in ground [1]	100% crude oil	100% coal
Delivery loss [2]	16.9%	68.0%[1]
Energy retained [3] [1] - [2]	83.1% at gasoline station	32.0% at electrical outlet
Percent of delivered fuel converted to wheel movement [4]	19%	49%
Percent of original fuel that is converted into wheel movement [3] x [4]	15.8% of energy in crude oil	15.7% of energy in coal

According to these figures, an EV is no less efficient than the gasoline-powered car in converting fossil fuel into movement. Greater efficiencies could be obtained at the end-use by bypassing the transmission and differential with direct-motor drive, or at the supply end by using a more-efficient method of converting coal to electricity (advanced coal-burning plants). Even if it can be shown that an EV is slightly less efficient than a gasoline-powered car, the fuel-flexibility of battery-powered transportation should give EVs an additional edge in the long-term public debate over how people will be going from point A to point B in the 21st Century.

(Special thanks to Denver Electric Vehicle Council for suggesting this discussion of myths about electric cars. The myth about the "limited range" of EVs is addressed in Chapter 9.)

A Subaru Brat after conversion. Note the space around the motor. *Photo by Ken Bancroft.*

The Ford electric panel van is powered by sodium-sulfur batteries, a technology invented by Ford in 1965. *Photo provided by Ford Motor Co.*

---

[1] Includes coal-to-heat conversion loss and the transmission line loss. This is a conservative estimate, since 40% efficiency (60% conversion loss) is state-of-the-art, and combined cycle plants have attained 60% efficiencies. Many independent power producers who use cogeneration are achieving better than 50% efficiency. In addition to significant efficiency improvements in the generation of electricity, there will be additional improvements in EV components, such as chargers and batteries.

8

Common Questions

Michael Hackleman, editor of **Alternative Transportation News**, *answers the most often-asked questions about battery-powered transportation (from the first issue of ATN). Additional comments from a variety of EV sources have rounded out these replies to give you the most up-to-date information.*

How is an EV better than a conventional car?

Since no fuel is burned during its operation, an electric vehicle needs no exhaust pipe and creates no pollution in the area around the car.

EVs require little maintenance or repair. Parts that move wear out. Engines have hundreds of moving parts. The electric motor has **one** moving part. And this motor does not use gasoline, lubricating oil, antifreeze or coolant. Also, it doesn't need to be tuned, timed or adjusted. There are no points, plugs, carburetors, oil pumps, fuel pumps, oil filters, air cleaner filters, fuel filters, fuel injectors, water pumps, generators, voltage regulators, starter motors, starter solenoids, mufflers, catalytic converters or fan belts. In a gasoline-powered car, these take a bite out of your pocketbook.

You also don't have to wait in lines at gasoline stations or spend five minutes inhaling toxic fumes or add to the air pollution while your EV "idles" in a traffic jam. Nor will you wonder what gasoline will cost tomorrow if there's a crisis halfway around the globe.

Bob Batson of Maynard, Mass. adds: The typical electric motor is designed to operate for 100,000 hours. At 35 miles per hour, an EV could go 3.5 million miles before the motor would have to be replaced. You can't say this for a conventional car's engine.

Why can't I buy an electric car off a showroom floor?

The automotive industry says that electric vehicles are limited in range and performance. They claim that, since the battery pack must be replaced every two to three years, electric vehicles are too expensive to be competitive with gasoline-powered cars. They claim that technological breakthroughs in batteries and motors are required before the electric vehicle will meet performance standards that the driving public has come to expect from automobiles.

Many people and groups do not share these views. Just ask the 20,000 or 30,000 people who use electric vehicles today to travel locally. Most of these people are willing to accept a "substandard" vehicle: no air conditioning, with a top speed of "only" 50 mph.[1] But the major car makers assume that most of the car-buying public is not ready to give up the extras, and that's why it will be years before you can purchase a selection of electric cars from a showroom floor.

What about performance, acceleration and speed?

Driving a car that has been converted to electric propulsion is virtually identical to driving one that has a gasoline-powered engine. The same operator controls are used:

---

[1] Many EVs have top speeds of 70 mph or more, and air conditioning is an option.

accelerator and brake pedals. A good EV will accelerate quickly and reach freeway speeds. The experienced EV owner avoids jackrabbit starts and high speeds, since these activities affect range. High-speed passing and climbing steep hills are also ways to reduce range. Still, if you get stuck in traffic or are stopped at a signal light, enjoy the idea that the electric motor is not running, and not consuming or wasting power! And your immediate environment is not being polluted!

What about range?

At this time, range appears to be the biggest challenge for the owner of an electric vehicle. Standard conversions (gasoline-powered cars that are converted to electric propulsion) will cover on a single charge 70 to 90 miles at low commuting speeds and less than 50 miles at freeway speeds. Lightweight and aerodynamic prototypes double these figures. While this seems a discouraging point, realize that this is well within the *average* daily trip length for most cars.

The daytime range of the electric car is easily doubled by work site recharging. A range of 100 to 120 miles, then, will meet the needs of more than 80 percent of the driving public.

The second car of many households averages less than 8,000 miles per year, or less than 30 miles per day. This activity is well within the range of most electric cars. Some households may find it cheaper to own an electric car and to rent a gasoline-powered car once or twice a month for weekend trips (and avoid the expense of maintaining the car).

John Newell (Belmont, Calif.) adds: Please note that you can go considerably farther with "opportunity charging," by plugging the car at work or at stops along the road. If an EV can cover your driving distance 98 percent of the time and a car rental can be available at your door when needed, why not save money and our environment by using an EV? *For more information on range, see the next chapter.*

Where does the electricity come from?

Utility power is the primary source of electricity for EVs at this time. A battery charger at home will recharge the battery pack in an electric vehicle directly from house current in eight to ten hours. You just plug it into a standard wall socket. High-rate chargers use a plug similar to the one on your clothes dryer (220 volts) and fully charge the vehicle in six to eight hours. Many conversions have the equivalent fuel cost of a gasoline vehicle that gets more than 30 miles per gallon.

Overnight charging is the best way to replenish battery packs. This process can take advantage of cheaper utility rates. Cities like Los Angeles value electric vehicles so much that they will give an owner a special rate, sometimes one-quarter the standard charge per kilowatt-hour. Southern California Edison estimates that it can absorb between 800,000 and one million electric vehicles on the grid before it will begin to need greater power plant capacity. Nationwide, this amounts to tens of millions of vehicles.

A small battery charger can be carried on board the EV, too. Wherever you go, you can plug in to charge. Sympathetic employers may permit on-site recharging, and could be persuaded to offer dedicated parking spaces for EVs. An overnight charge gets you to work as far away as 60 miles, and the recharge performed during work hours gets you home.

Power plants make smog, too. How is this better?

Electric vehicles can be recharged from any source of electricity, including privately-owned wind power and solar-electric power systems. The recent demonstration of utility-scale solar-powered plants indicates that grid power can also use sustainable and non-polluting sources of energy.

Flexibility of fuel source is an important feature of electric cars. If gasoline is limited, car owners wait in lines. If coal for generating electricity is limited or if the system's capacity to produce electricity is surpassed, the utility simply purchases more electricity from another utility. Thus, power plants can be controlled for their polluting and still provide a more versatile source of fuel than gasoline stations.

How can I get an electric vehicle?

A number of car manufacturers have expressed interest in producing electric vehicles for the general public. Some even have very impressive prototypes. However, all of them seem to be waiting for someone else to test the waters. At this rate, the first mass-produced EVs won't appear until sometime around the mid 1990s.

The easiest way to own an EV is to buy or perform a conversion. If you car qualifies as a cost-effective candidate for conversion, you can obtain plans and books that will guide you in this venture. Armed with this information, a good mechanic can do the job in a modest automotive garage. There are also a growing number of entrepreneurs who are buying up vehicles in good condition, converting them and offering them for sale.

While almost any vehicle can be converted, small and lightweight car models that demonstrate good aerodynamics (streamlining) will give you the most performance for the dollar invested. Currently, vehicle-specific plans are available for the VW Beetle, VW Rabbit, Honda Civic, Chevy Chevette, Datsun B210 and Fiat 128. While other vehicles can be converted (and have been), plans help you avoid pitfalls and costly mistakes. The conversion hardware is more readily available off-the-shelf for these cars. *(See Part III, EV Resources, at the rear of this book for detailed information.)*

How much does it cost to convert a car?

There is an old saying, "the more you know, the less you pay." If you just "order" a conversion, you can pay as much as $9,000, and half of that is labor.

Electric propulsion is fairly simple, so don't discount the possibility of doing some or all of this yourself. EV clubs are good places to experience an electric vehicle, to get help in selecting the right system, and to get the scoop on hardware and people experienced in doing conversions.

The motor, controller, and battery pack for a modest conversion will cost about $5,000 (1991). Package deals, (conversion kits) might be cheaper, but don't count on it. Control accessories and other conversion pieces can add another $1,000. Labor varies considerably.

Is there a way to extend the range of an electric vehicle?

Adding more batteries increases range, but it also results in a heavier vehicle. An alternative is to use an extra power source. An EV that uses two or more power sources (one of which is a battery) is referred to as a "hybrid" EV. The power produced by the extra energy source will vary considerably with the type and design, but it is designed to augment the power from the battery pack, adding to overall range, performance and other operational characteristics.

The most common hybrid EV is one that uses a genset, or engine-driven generator. Imagine a lawn mower engine connected to your car's alternator or generator through a V-belt. This would be a low-power unit, but when added to an EV, it becomes an on-board charging system. The engine itself can be fueled with gasoline, propane, alcohol, hydrogen or diesel, depending on the type and your own preference of fuel.

In the genset, the engine is relieved of the task of producing propulsion (as in standard cars) and is assigned the task of producing electric power. The electricity produced by the genset goes toward the motor for direct propulsion or to battery storage. When the auxiliary charging unit (ACU) or range extender is operating, the power it produces is never wasted. It's used or stored. Compare that to an internal combustion engine (ICE) car stuck in a traffic jam or waiting for a signal light to change. The ACU can also be operated at its most efficient and least-polluting speed; your current car's ICE rarely remains at its most efficient speed (45 mph), since ever-changing driving conditions require the driver to vary from this least-polluting condition.

This type of hybrid is called a "series" hybrid, because the flow of electricity is into the motor. A "parallel" hybrid avoids the electric motor and is connected to the drive shaft. It converts the liquid fuel into mechanical motion and directly turns the transmission and the wheels (it cannot be used to charge the batteries, since it is not a generator).

Hybrid EVs address two fears held by the driving public: low performance and getting stuck somewhere with a dead battery pack. City driving favors use of the battery pack; freeway driving favors ACU operation.

Use of an ACU increases overall system complexity and initial costs. It may increase overall vehicle weight, too.

What about solar-powered cars?

A solar-powered car is an electric vehicle with a large solar panel on it. The solar panel is made up of photovoltaic cells that convert the sun's energy into electricity to help run the motor or store the energy in the car's battery. It's another type of hybrid vehicle.

Putting solar modules on an electric vehicle doesn't make the car a solar-powered vehicle. To achieve any real benefit, hundreds of cells are required at great expense and the vehicle must be very lightweight. This makes the vehicle fragile, bulky and prone to theft. A better plan is to put the solar cells on the roof of the owner's home (or on a garage roof at work) and to charge the vehicle from them. Grid power exchange, alternating battery packs (charging one set of batteries at home while a second set is powering the car), and pack-to-pack charging are all possibilities.

Solar cars demonstrate the simplicity of alternative transportation and represent a form of independence from imported oil. Solar car races attract public attention and stimulate people to question their assumptions about how cars can be powered.

What about air conditioning and heat?

In the first edition of *Why Wait For Detroit?*, Jim Tervort of Sebring Auto-Cycle described his three-wheeled auto-cycle's cooling system: "The Zzipper comes equipped with a 2/30 air conditioner: crack open the two doors and travel at thirty miles an hour, and you'll have all the ventilation you need. If you tend to get stuck in traffic, you can always install a 12-volt oscillating fan."

However, standard air conditioning technology can be used in an EV, although doing so will affect the vehicle's top speed and range. A/C units suitable for EVs are not widely available as of this writing, but several of the "manufactured conversions" have an A/C option, and EV parts suppliers are beginning to offer them.

For heat you have two primary options: electrical or kerosene. A small kerosene heater is fairly simple to install and it produces virtually no emissions. However, with such a heater your vehicle will not be a true Zero Emission Vehicle (ZEV); this is important where special incentives are provided for ZEVs, such as the California tax credit. Electrical heat is simpler and available from several suppliers, but like A/C it will affect your top speed and range.

For converted EVs, Kevin McDonald (New Concepts Engineering) suggests installing an electric coolant heater and retaining the car's heater core. By heating a small quantity of engine coolant, the heat will convect naturally toward the car's heater core. The heated coolant will retain a higher temperature longer than heated air will, while using less battery power.

How much do heating and air conditioning reduce your speed and range? It varies with your driving pattern and the vehicle design, but figure a 5-miles-per-hour speed reduction and a 5-to-25-percent range reduction. Bear in mind that this is for continuous operation. A typical range loss would be less than 15 percent. It's all a matter of trade-offs. If you can get by with a slightly reduced range, you can travel in comfort.

What about electromagnetic radiation?

This question was raised by the editors' spouses, who refuse to believe that EVs are harmless in this regard until we can give concrete evidence.

If there is a concern, the motor and the cables can be shielded to prevent the electromagnetic radiation from entering the passenger area. Shielding will result in a slight increase in weight (less than twenty pounds).

Lew Gulick, editor of EV News, adds: "There have been test measurements showing that you're worse off sitting in front of a computer." Look for more on this subject in the EV periodicals.

Shari Prange reports that *Home Power* editor Richard Perez has tested a converted VW Rabbit and concluded, "This is a healthy vehicle. You'd get more EMF sitting in front of a computer monitor."

EMF test	Millivolts	Milligauss
Ambient	1.60	0.11
Front Seat Maximum	63.20	4.21
Minimum	0.80	0.05
Average	6.20	0.41
Back Seat Maximum	199.20	13.28
Minimum	0.00	0.00
Average	7.10	0.47

The VW Rabbit in the photo received the first EV conversion kit approved by CARB to receive the $1,000 tax credit. *Photo by Shari Prange.*

9

What About Range?

What happens when the batteries go dead?

When you first heard about electric cars, you probably wondered whether the limited range of the average affordable EV (usually around 30 or 40 miles[1] for a car costing under $10,000) would affect the car's usefulness. Perhaps you thought, "That's not practical for me. I might drive too far and get stranded!"

We could explain how the EV owner can avoid worrying about running out of electric power. (Just keep track of the miles covered since the last charge.) But all you need to know is this:

OVER HALF OF ALL AUTO TRIPS ARE UNDER 7 MILES

The average trip by car in the city is 8 miles
30 percent of all trips by car are between 7 and 20 miles
56 percent of all trips are less than 7 miles
A car with a range of 40 miles can handle 85 percent of all passenger journeys within cities.
Source: Audi AG, Germany

Average number of vehicles per household: 1.8
Average miles per day per vehicle: 26.48
Average Trip length: 9.8 miles
Average commute by car: 8.5 miles
Source: Statistical Abstract of the U.S. (1988).

Most electric cars can cover between 30 and 40 miles on a charge, or up to 85 percent of the average vehicle's trips. EV pioneers regularly exceed 100 miles in competitions. *(In 1991 Gary Jackson, a physicist and a member of the EVA of Southern California, drove his converted VW Rabbit 188 miles on a single charge. The average speed of the vehicle over a closed course, including one stop per mile, was 20.13 miles per hour.)* However, most consumers have been taught by repeated exposure to persuasive and seductive advertising to demand a car that will handle all of their perceived needs: a car that will fly over gulches, climb steep rocky hills overlooking the Grand Canyon, and zoom past cars stuck in snow banks.

If you regularly drive beyond the range of the average electric car (more than 40 miles), you might consider purchasing a "hybrid" vehicle. This is an electric car with a "range extender." The extender can be a second motor or a small electric generator, which can be powered by gasoline or an alternative fuel (methanol, ethanol, etc.).

Another option: alter your travel needs. This is often possible for the two-car family. The primary car can be used for longer trips, and the second (electric) car can cover the local, errand-running trips under 20 miles in length. *One-car families should*

---

[1] While maximum range on a converted electric car can often exceed 50 miles, battery life can be extended by limiting travel to less than 60 to 70 percent of the car's maximum range.

consider the economics of renting a second car if they rarely travel farther than 50 miles in a day.

Third, install an on-board charger. Wherever you stop, there's usually someone who will let you plug in for a short time. At work, at a friend's home, or at a convenience store, you'll be ready. Just make sure to bring a long extension cord. With the 15-amp limit of most wall outlets, an hour of charging uses less than 15 cents of electricity.

Eventually, electric vehicles could be the majority of cars in many cities. They will be the preferred mode of transportation in urban areas that need "zero emission vehicles" to comply with air quality standards.

Vehicle Trips By Purpose and Percent

Purposes	Percent of trips (1990)	Average vehicle trip length (miles)	Percent of miles traveled
Work	26.1%	10.9	32.8%
Other Personal Business	24.1%	7.2	20.1%
Shopping	20.2%	5.1	11.9%
Other Social and Recreational	11.2%	10.1	13.0%
Visit Friends and Relatives	8.8%	11.3	11.4%
School and Church	5.3%	7.4	4.5%
Totals	95.7%	---	93.7%
Other purposes	4.3%	---	6.3%

Each of the remaining categories, lumped together as "Other Purposes," accounted for less than 2% of the vehicle trips. Work related business 1.8% of trips (average trip length of 14.0 miles, 2.8% of miles traveled); Doctor/dentist 1.1% (10.5, 1.3%); Vacation 0.1% (80.0, 0.8%); Pleasure driving 0.3% (20.9, 0.6%); Other 1% (10.7, 0.8%). **Note:** *the category of Vacation in 1983 had the following results: 0.2% (113, 2.1%). A "trip" is defined as any one-way travel from one address to another. When travel is to more than one destination, a separate trip exists each time the following criteria are satisfied: the travel time between two destinations exceeds five minutes and or the purpose for travel to one destination is different from the purpose for travel to another. The one exception is travel within a shopping center or mall. It is to be considered travel to one destination, regardless of the number of stores visited. If there was more than one reason for the trip, the primary reason was collected. If there are two or more reasons and they each involved different destinations, then each reason is classified as a separate trip. Source: The 1990 Nationwide Personal Transportation Study, U.S. Department of Transportation.*

Dr. Michael Symons, 3 Wrench Place Kenthurst, NSW 2156, Australia (02) 654-1571, Suzuki 800cc converted to 72 volts with a Curtis 72 volt controller and one 12-volt battery for accessories. Range 80 km (50 miles) in stop-and-go driving conditions.

10

How Safe Is An EV?

When they first see a Citicar (a small electric car built in 1974-75), many people say, "I would never drive a glorified golf cart on the highway!" The image of a small vehicle the size of a golf-cart is not what most people see in their minds when they think of driving a car. However, electric cars can be larger than golf carts and still deliver adequate service.

Ken Koch, an experienced EV converter, notes that if it weren't for the word *ELECTRIC* on the side of his car, most people wouldn't notice the 1972 Mazda passing them at 65 mph. He commutes 28 miles one way to work and reports that his car is the same size as many fuel-efficient cars on the road.

Critics point out that smaller cars are less visible and have less material and bulk to cushion the driver and passengers. While many electric cars are smaller than the larger cars on the highway, so are many sub-compact gasoline-powered cars. Smaller cars can be parked more easily and their profile is less wide. John Newell, former head of the Electric Auto Association, points out, "The width of a compact car is approximately 5 feet while a luxury car is six feet, six inches. Which is the larger target? Cannot we say that a compact is 30 percent less likely to have an accident?" (Crash statistics prove this argument to be false, but it is an attractive way of looking at the issue!) A smaller chassis means less weight to move around, an important factor in keeping the number of batteries to a minimum. This is why most conversions tend to be smaller cars.

How safe is an EV? As safe as many conventional cars that many people reading this book use every day. All vehicles can be made safer if they are designed like Indianapolis 500 race cars: drivers often walk away from complete wrecks, thanks to thoughtful engineering.

A discussion with an engineer at the
National Highway Traffic Safety Administration

"If a gasoline-powered car is converted to be electric, how does this affect the ability of the car to withstand a crash?"

Engineer: Crash tests are done by the manufacturer to check the vehicle's ability to protect passengers and driver. The Federal government also has a crash test program, which we apply to any car sold to the public as a new car.

To start, the vehicle is given a weight rating. The federal standards don't speak to how the car is powered or driven. It's a standard based on vehicle weight. The classes are passenger vehicles, multi-purpose vehicle (MPV) and heavy truck, over 10,000 pounds GVWR [gross vehicle weight rating].

The crash testing is one aspect to look at, but you also have to consider other factors, such as defogging. Electric vehicles generally don't have a high temperature source to draw on to clear up fogged windows.

When a car is converted to electric, chances are that the weight will increase and it will be distributed differently than the car maker intended. You carry all those extra batteries. There's suddenly this big dead weight that wasn't there when the car was designed. Even if it's spread over the car in pieces, these batteries might not be secured very well, so they can be jarred loose in a crash.

Without some well-thought-out structural changes to the car's suspension, I would say that the additional weight is not a good thing for the car's capacity to withstand a crash and protect its occupants.

"What about a half-ton pick up truck? If the truck is rated to carry 1000 pounds, and 500 pounds of batteries are added, wouldn't that be all right? It's as if the truck is carrying around a load of 500 pounds wherever it goes. What's wrong with this?"
Engineer: It's not clear to me that a permanent addition to the truck within the rated weight limits is bad, but I've never seen tests. The tests we did on electric cars in the 1970s showed rollovers and the acid of the battery leaked all over. I would say that this is not likely to be a clean conversion, since it's not like you're putting in a ethanol engine when it used to be a gasoline engine.

Editors' conclusion: some converted EVs are probably not a great idea ... unless you aren't traveling at highway speeds. With proper engineering, a converted car can be made safe. The most efficient cars are the cars engineered from the ground up, like Solectria's Flash and the Clean Air Transport LA 301 (the car that won the Los Angeles competition). These "purpose-built" vehicles have lighter and safer structures because the metal is designed to serve a specific purpose, such as supporting batteries.

Response by John Newell, long-time EAA member and EV owner
Put your finger into your battery acid. The specific gravity is low enough to avoid serious acid burns. The engineer from NHTSA failed to compare gasoline burns and acid burns. My battery-powered Ford Escort conforms to all Federal Motor Vehicle Safety Standards. As for a dependable source of heat to defrost the windshield, just plug in an electric hair dryer (adapted for 12 volts).

Response by Mike Hackleman, editor of *Alternative Transportation News*
1. Batteries must be securely clamped down to prevent movement in a roll-over.
2. Most conversions put batteries in the trunk and under the hood, so passengers are less likely to be affected even in a high-speed collision.
3. Batteries should be distributed to maintain the original front-to-rear weight ratio, not just to fill available space.
4. A conversion that adds up to 1,000 pounds of additional weight to a car is "safer" than the same make of car using a gasoline engine: a) properly maintained batteries won't explode, but gasoline can catch fire; b) in a crash, the energy of the collision is transferred in an inverse proportion to the weight of the vehicles (the heavier vehicle wins).

Response by Mike Brown, Electro-Automotive
With proper attention to detail, safety should not be a problem. Battery weight should be well-distributed and kept low. Batteries should be secured in place, held down snugly, and enclosed in a box with a securely latched lid. All efforts should be made to take advantage of the original crash protection that was designed into the car.

Response by Bob Batson, Electric Vehicles of America
The light-weight pickup truck is inherently safer than the conversion of passenger vehicles. That is why we at Electric Vehicles of America specialize in electric trucks. Our current test truck is an electric Dodge Ram 50 pickup truck. This type of vehicle is ideal from a safety viewpoint because:
1. Although its curb weight is 2,500 pounds, about the same as a Ford Escort, it is designed for a Gross Vehicle Weight (GVW) of 4,200 pounds. This means that its frame, brakes, transmission, and other components are designed for this weight. This is significantly greater than the GVW of most EV conversions.
2. The pickup allows you to keep all of the batteries out of the passenger compartment and from the engine compartment, if you so desire. Keeping the

batteries out of the passenger compartment is better for the passengers. Keeping them out of the engine compartment allows you to have easier access to the motor, controller, vacuum pump, and other components. This is called "maintainability."

3. Our pick up has been converted to a tilt-bed. This allows the batteries to be located under the bed. The advantage from a safety standpoint is that the center of gravity is lowered and the vehicle is better from a crash-protection viewpoint.

4. Finally, the pickup truck allows greater safety by separating redundant safety components. For example, we use a contactor and a fuse at each end of the battery pack: one contactor and fuse at the negative terminal of the first battery and a contactor and fuse at the positive terminal of the last battery. The pickup allows separation between these components in case an accident does happen.

Bob Batson also offers these observations about "design philosophy."

EVs not only come in all shapes and sizes, but they also come with different **design philosophies**. Ten years ago, EVs had basic differences in the voltage of the battery pack and the type of control system. Control systems were voltage switching, resistance control or SCR control. Today, most all control systems are MOSFET or pulse-width modulated.

However, there are still subtle differences in system design that require closer examination. These include:

The arrangement of the components not only within the vehicle, but their arrangement to each other should be considered. Some people separate the battery pack from the motor and control system. This allows the battery pack to be totally isolated from the other components until the power system is energized. If the components are modularized with multiple components in a single module, you must ask yourself if this is the way you would design it, or would you prefer to separate these components?

Redundancy of safety components. Some EVs have only a single fuse and contactor. What is the impact if that contactor fails in the closed position? I recommend at least two fuses, one on the positive side of the battery set, and the other on the negative side.

The wiring arrangement. Are power cables run side by side? Are they protected from chafing and wear? Is their size adequate for the designed current? What will be the impact on the electrical system if you have an accident?

(For more details on how to build a safer EV and on what to look for when purchasing an EV, see Chapter 23.)

The general manager of the Sacramento Municipal Utility District (SMUD) drives a battery-powered pickup truck.
Photo by R. Minner.

11

How Much Does It Cost To Drive An EV?

This is one of the most widely argued points in electric car circles. Some people claim that EVs are cheaper than conventional cars only when you don't include the replacement cost of batteries, while others insist that the true daily expense of driving, in cents per mile, is one third less than the cost of driving a gasoline-powered vehicle.

A Converted Pickup Truck Makes Cents

Bob Batson (Electric Vehicles of America, Inc.) analyzed the electric G-Van's ownership costs and found that a vehicle with fewer batteries has a more-favorable balance sheet over its life-cycle. He assumed that a pickup truck with 60,000 to 70,000 miles has lost its internal combustion engine and that the truck has another 40,000 miles available under battery power. Where the G-Van needs 216 volts (36 6-volt batteries), a pickup can give adequate service with 96 volts (16 6-volt batteries). To keep the pickup truck's cost estimate conservative, Bob pro-rated the G-van's costs in the 96/216 ratio (16 batteries vs. 36 batteries or 4/9). He has found that his costs have actually been lower.

Comparison Chart Showing Cost Per Mile

All costs in cents per mile	Converted Pickup Truck	G-Van	Gasoline powered Van
Cost of vehicle	27.0	84.4	22.5
Battery cost	7.6	14.0	---
Fuel cost	2.0	5.6	13.0
Vehicle maintenance	4.2	4.6	10.0
Total	40.8	108.6	45.5

Bob Batson's tilt-bed pickup truck. The batteries are located in front of and between the rear axle to provide a low center of gravity and to keep the batteries away from passengers.
Photo by Electric Vehicles of America, Inc.

Assumptions	Converted Pickup Truck	G-Van	Gasoline-powered Van
Purchase price Salvage value	$12,000 10%	$60,000 10%	$18,000 20%
Battery cost Number of batteries	$1,520 16 batteries $95/battery	$4,700 36 batteries $130/battery	not applicable
Years and miles per battery pack	2.5 years 20,000 miles	4 years 32,000 miles	not applicable
Fuel costs and fuel efficiency	5 cents per kilo-watt-hour 0.4 kwhr/mile	5 cents per kilo-watt-hour 1.1 kwhr/mile	$1.30 per gallon of gasoline 10 mpg
Hours of labor and cost of parts per 1,000 miles	0.3 hours $30 for parts	0.4 hours $30 for parts	1.0 hour $60 for parts
Life of vehicle	40,000 miles 4 years	64,000 miles 8 years	64,000 miles 8 years

Charts compiled by Bob Batson, Electric Vehicles of America, Inc., using G-Van comparison figures published by the Electric Power Research Institute (EPRI).

Converted Pickup Truck: Purchase price assumes $2,000 value at time of conversion plus the $10,000 conversion. Salvage value is assumed to be 10% or $1,200, since the electric motor will be in good condition.

Salvage value of all batteries is assumed to be 5% of purchase price.

G-Van: EPRI estimates that the purchase price of a G-Van, in quantities of 10,000 vehicles, will be around $14,000. However, this table uses the 1991 price of $60,000, the amount quoted by Conceptor Industries at a conference held in Washington, D.C. in November 1991. Salvage value is pegged at $6,000 or 10% rather than the 20% assumed by EPRI.

Gasoline-powered van: Salvage value of 20% or $3,600 is based on EPRI comparison.

Note: actual battery purchase cost for Bob's 96-volt truck is about $1,000, but a higher figure is given to keep the results conservative. Averaged over 40,000 miles, this estimate assumes that he'll spend $3,040 on batteries, buying two sets of batteries, replacing the first set at 20,000 miles. His actual life-cycle battery cost could be in the range of 3.2-to-4-cents per mile, since simple precautions (proper battery maintenance and not driving beyond the vehicle's range) will allow him to replace the batteries at 25,000-to-30,000 miles. He will need only 1.33-to-1.6 sets of batteries ($2,030-to-$2,440 total).

Per-mile costs of a people-mover: Bob Batson's cost comparisons for a low-mileage demonstration vehicle offer utilities a low-cost way to put electric vehicles in front of the public, while using a vehicle already owned by the utility. However, the principal market for the EV will not be for a converted pickup, but rather for what the father of the Citicar, Bob Beaumont, calls a "people-mover." EV advocates at a major utility in California describe this people-mover as the 50-50 EV: a lightweight two-passenger car that travels 50 miles at a steady 50 mph.

What does it cost to drive a people mover? Bob Beaumont points out that a lightweight car like the Citicar (1100 pounds) had a 48-volt system capable of delivering about 10 kilowatt-hours. At 10 cents per kilowatt-hour, the fuel cost was $1 per charge and the Citicar could easily get 30 miles per charge at 3.3 cents per mile. The 1500-pound, two-passenger

Renaissance people-mover (built from the ground up) has 72 volts, holding 15 kilowatt-hours, costs $1.50 per charge and goes at least 40 miles at about 4 cents (3.75¢) per mile.

Replacement cost for the 6-volt deep-cycle batteries is about $65, so the 12 batteries cost $780 or about $800. The lead acid battery is good for 300 to 500 charging cycles. Taking the low end, 300 cycles of 40 miles per day is 12,000 miles; dividing $800 for batteries by 12,000 miles gives two-thirds of a cent per mile for the battery cost. Add the 3.75 cents per mile for electricity and you get a fuel cost of slightly less than 4.5 cents per mile.

Let's compare the cost of purchasing a light compact car for local travel, such as a Geo Metro (the typical 1992 model costs around $7,000). Maintaining an EV costs virtually nothing, and for the first 24,000 miles the maintenance on the new Metro (besides oil changes and tune ups) is covered by warranty. The savings derived from owning an EV, says Beaumont, come after 24,000 miles when you start having to replace fuel pumps and any of the 10,000 parts in the conventional car. The Renaissance people-mover costs $500 more than the Metro ($7,500), but has fewer than 1,000 parts.

Let's assume that traffic jams bring the Geo Metro's efficiency down to around 40 miles per gallon in the city (50 mpg/highway, 45 mpg/city). That's 3.5 cents per mile for gasoline costing $1.40 per gallon, so the fuel costs for a purpose-built electric people-mover is about a penny higher than the fuel costs for the most efficient compact car running on the industrial world's cheapest gasoline.

Like most EV advocates, Beaumont observes, "How do you account for the human factors? How do you put a price on clean air? On quiet operation? On owner satisfaction, on not having to take the car to the garage for regular maintenance?" He adds that if the purpose-built lightweight people-movers like the Renaissance can be charged for 5 cents per kilowatt-hour, then the total fuel cost drops below 3 cents per mile, less than the fuel burned by the Geo Metro in the city. Researchers like DeLuchi, Wang and Sperling have concluded that "mass-produced EVs will have lower life-cycle costs than comparable conventional gasoline vehicles. By the turn of the century, *electric passenger vehicles could be viable as second cars* in multi-car households and in other limited markets." If the consumer is willing to make a few trade-offs, such as slow acceleration in a converted EV, a top speed of 35 mph in the Mini-el, or a smaller passenger compartment in the Renaissance, then the turn of the century is here today.

Here is an example of the costs of "real world" use of electric vehicles.

Model: 1975 Electric 4-door Honda wagon, converted in 1981 by Bill Williams

Energy consumption: 0.43 kilowatt-hours per mile. *Operating cost:* 3.1 cents per mile (at 7.5 cents per kilowatt-hour). *Conversion cost:* $3,845 (labor not included). *Cost of vehicle before conversion:* $5,000. *Curb weight:* 1964 lbs. as gasoline-powered, 2990 as electric. *Motor:* 20 horsepower Prestolite. *Batteries:* 18 6-volt batteries, each 65 lbs. *Cost for a set:* $1,080. *Total Battery Weight:* 1170 lbs.

Top Speed: 70 mph. *Cruising speed:* 50 mph. *Acceleration:* 0 to 30 mph in 11 seconds. *Range (in town):* 65 miles (to 80% discharge). *Usage:* commuting to work and errands, average of 35 miles per day. *Distance covered:* 54,000 miles. For more information on this conversion, send a self-addressed, stamped envelope to Williams Enterprises, P.O. Box 1548, Cupertino, Calif. 95015.

Comparing Bill Williams' Honda with a Gasoline Car

Power source:	Electric	Gasoline
Vehicle Cost	9.3	18.5
Conversion Cost	11.1	--
Batteries	4.3	--
Maintenance	3.1	5.0
Fuel cost	3.1	8.0
Cents per mile	30.9	31.5

All costs are in 1991 dollars. Gasoline figures come from AAA. Cost of the gasoline vehicle is assumed to be $10,000.

Data on the converted electric Honda

Miles travelled: 54,000. *Cost of Vehicle before conversion:* $5,000. *Actual cost of conversion:* $3,845 (1975 dollars). *Conversion cost assumed for calculation:* $6,000 (1991

dollars) – current conversions are closer to $9,000, if you include labor, which works out to be 16 cents per mile over 54,000 miles. *Note: The calculation from the American Automobile Association assumes the cost of the average new car. To adjust the calculation for a used car, divide the purchase price by 54,000 miles to get vehicle cost per mile. 35 miles per day x 360 days:* 12,600 miles per year. *Years to cover 54,000 miles:* 4.28 years. Assume two years as the life of the battery set. *Consumption of battery over 54,000 miles:* 2.14 sets of batteries needed. *Cost of one set of batteries:* 18 x $60 = $1,080. 2.14 sets of batteries x $1,080 = $2,312 ... Divide by 54,000: 4.28 cents/mile. (A trained "battery wizard" can extend the life of the battery at least six months.)

Scott Cornell did a side-by-side comparison of his gasoline-powered 1980 Volkswagen Rabbit and his battery-powered 1975 Volkswagen Rabbit. He included fuel and maintenance costs, and extrapolated actual figures (gathered over two years) for a projected ten-year, 100,000-mile life span. His figures came to 17 cents per mile for the gasoline car, 14 cents per mile for the electric. He purchased the car for $2,500 and he estimated his cost of conversion to be around $3,500.

Cost for Operation of Vehicle for 100,000 miles	Gasoline	Electric Car
Batteries ($45 each)[1]	135	3500
Brakes (at 50,000 miles)	200	200
Fuel (35 mpg, $1.10/gal; 3 mi/kwhr, $0.10/kwhr)	3143	3333
Purchase price ($3,500 EV conversion cost)	7100	6000
Maintenance[2]	1077	150
Resale value	- 1500	- 1500
Tires (at 50,000 miles)	200	200
Insurance (gasoline, $720/year; EV, $120/year)	7200	1800
Total	$17,555	$13,683
Cost per mile (cents)	17.6	13.7

[1] Gasoline, one battery every 3 years or every 33,000 miles; EV, 15 batteries every two years or every 20,000 miles (75 batteries). You can find this price if you shop around.

[2] Costs do not include labor, since Scott does his own car maintenance. Gasoline: Oil change (every 3,000 miles @ $9) $297; radiator flush (every two years @ $8), $40; smog check (every 2 years @ $45) $225; tune up (every 20,000 miles @ $50) $250; valve adjustment (every 40,000 miles @ $80) $160); alternator (rebuild once at 70,000 miles) $30; belts and hoses (at 50,000 miles) $75. EV: Brush replacement (at 50,000 miles) $30; distilled water (1 gallon/500 miles @ $0.60) $120. Based on a telephone conversation with Scott Cornell.

[3] Scott's actual total cost for the used 1975 VW Rabbit and EV parts was $2,500, but the higher figure is used to make it a more realistic comparison. The $7,100 figure was the price paid by Scott when he purchased it new. Based on Scott's actual costs, he spent 17.6 cents/mile on the gasoline car and 10.2 cents/mile on his EV.

Why is the insurance cost so low? Scott says that his insurance agent classified the EV as a recreational vehicle, since it has low mileage. It is also his second car, so he receives a lower cost of coverage. "My All-State Insurance agent considers the EV to be a lower-risk vehicle, since I don't use it to commute daily. I bicycle to the train, so the EV is exposed to less risk."

The resale cost of the gasoline car is an actual figure. Scott expects to get more than $1,500 for the motor and components if he sells the EV. The purchase price of the EV is lower than the gasoline car (which was purchased new) to highlight what EV owners have learned: a 15-year-old car with an electric motor is more reliable than most younger gasoline-powered cars, since there's less that can go wrong with the drive system.

Other estimates: The consulting firm of Booz, Allen & Hamilton (Bethesda, Md.) compared the life-cycle costs of alternative fuel vehicles in 1988 and concluded that a 2-passenger EV would cost 22.85 cents per mile to own in 1995 (6 cents/kwh), compared to gasoline at 19.58 cents ($1/gallon), CNG at 28.09 cents (81 cents/gallon) and methanol at 24.37 cents (72 cents/gallon). Life-cycle costs included initial cost, operatin cost, maintence, ancillary cost (insurance, title, registration, etc.; assumed to be 5% of purchase price) and salvage value (20% of purchase price without the battery and engine). The EV was assumed to use sodium-sulfur batteries.

In 1989, William Hamilton (the prolific author of the most comprehensive studies addressing virtually all impacts of widespread EV ownership) calculated per-mile costs for a household EV at 15.5 cents compared to 14.9 for a conventional car with an internal combustion engine (ICE). He projected that an electric van would cost 21 cents per mile versus 21.6 cents per mile for an ICE van. *(Source: Technical Background Report, prepared for EG&G Idaho, Inc. and the U.S. Department of Energy.)*

12

What Happens To
All Those Batteries?

Lead has been extracted from the earth for millennia. This "primary lead" is roasted out of ore and was the principal way that industry obtained the metal until about 30 years ago. The lead-recycling business began in the 1950s when entrepreneurs discovered that recycling lead from batteries was simpler and avoided many costs associated with the roasting of primary lead.

In 1969, one of these entrepreneurs, Wiley Sanders, Jr., started a recycling company with a truck, a smelter and a battery cracker in Troy, Alabama. From this small beginning grew a company that today generates an annual revenue in excess of $120 million by processing 132,000 tons of lead each year. The following describes a visit to this facility.

The process

Eighty percent of the lead processed by Sanders enters the factory in used batteries. The balance comes in scrap metals that must meet a mandated quality control. Radioactive lead shielding in x-ray machines is not accepted and the company maintains a quality control program to evaluate incoming shipments.

Virtually every part of a battery is made ready for reuse. After the battery's casing is cracked, the plastic container is washed and crushed, and turned into polypropylene pellets, which are conveyed to a large storage tank.

The electrolyte is not recycled at the Sanders plant. The salts and remaining sulfuric acid are mixed with lime to balance the pH, and the mixture is then treated and leaves the plant as treated discharge water. All discharges must meet standards issued by the Alabama Department of Environmental Management (ADEM) and the Federal EPA.

The lead in the batteries is in two forms: elemental lead and lead oxide. Both are mixed with lime, cast iron, and coke (a form of coal that provides electrons to reduce lead oxide to lead). Airborne dust containing lead is captured in a baghouse, which is a large building that acts like a filter. The small particles of lead and dust fall to the bottom of the baghouse and are conveyed to an agglomeration furnace. Here they are compacted into a block and the material is returned to the furnace for reprocessing.

The air leaving the baghouse is often cleaner that the air entering the furnace, since the filter captures virtually all airborne dust particles. The system catches 95 percent of the airborne emissions, and the state monitors the content of the exhaust air for lead and sulfur dioxide.

A 35-pound battery contains 18 pounds of lead, 12 pounds of sulfuric acid, and about two pounds of plastic that is recycled. About half of the remaining two pounds is consumed in the blast furnace as heat, leaving about one pound of non-recyclable materials. Each battery creates approximately 8 ounces of hazardous waste, which must be transported for off-site burial at a cost of over $100 per ton. Each year the plant handles at least 12 million batteries, so roughly 6 million pounds of hazardous waste is transported off-site for disposal as compared to 420 million pounds of recycled products. This represents a 98.58 percent reduction of the solid waste stream, since the lead smelter reduces the amount of buriable waste from 35 pounds in the lead-acid battery to a half-pound.

Emission levels

The principal concern about how the Sanders operation affects the surrounding ground water is focused on what the company's environmental manager calls "the sins of the past." Sanders has closed several of its on-site landfills because they were found to be a potential source of groundwater contamination. Since November 1988, all water that enters the facility, including rain water, has been captured, treated and released under a permit, which is regularly monitored. According to records kept by the ADEM, the amount of lead in the exiting water has never exceeded the permitted daily average concentration of 0.119 pounds per day. In fact, the average for 1990 was 0.0445 pounds per day, or 16.23 pounds per year. Thus, the annual water run-off is less than the amount of lead in one battery, yet Sanders handles 12 million batteries every year.

The principal concern with lead in the closed landfill is whether the heavy metals will eventually migrate into nearby potable water sources. To monitor the flow of metals from the landfills, 61 wells have been placed at strategic points around the plant. Several of the wells were drilled below the clay layer and into the aquifer that runs near the plant. According to several engineering studies, the clay barrier is sufficiently thick and dense to capture the hazardous elements. A small amount of lead-contaminated water that does escape from the closed landfill is captured in special wells that return the water to the plant's on-site water treatment plant. It is estimated that by the year 2000 virtually all of the heavy metals contained in the on-site landfills will have migrated out and been captured by the recycling wells or been captured in stable compounds within the landfill.

The interior of a lead smelting plant.

A Sanders Lead lab technician analyzes a sample.

An Average 36-pound Battery Produces:
18 lbs. recoverable lead
9 lbs. sulfuric acid
3 lbs. polypropylene casing
3 lbs. sulfates and oxides
3 lbs. polyvinyl chloride separators

Courtesy of the Lead Industry Association.

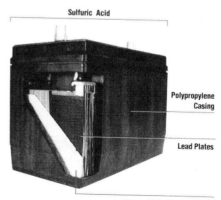

Anyone who claims that sending even one pound of lead into the groundwater is too much should consider the consequences of shutting down a plant like Sanders. While other smelters might eventually recycle the batteries, if even one battery (that would have been recycled at Sanders) is thrown into an unlined dump, the potential amount of lead leaking into the groundwater will be more than when Sanders is operating.

Lead from 7,000 batteries

Under a permit with the Alabama Department of Environmental Management (ADEM), Sanders can emit three pounds of lead per hour from stack #5 and 2.82 pounds per hour from stack #1. The total actually emitted during a recent test (June 1990) was 0.12 pounds per hour (stack #1) and 0.29 pounds per hour (stack #5), less than one-tenth of the maximum level allowed.

A second method of monitoring lead emissions into the air is to set up filters at locations around the plant at various distances. The federal standard in 1990 for ambient air was 1.5 micrograms of lead per cubic meter of air, or 1.5 millionths of a gram. Since installing a number of air-cleaning devices (principally the bag house), the facility has rarely exceeded that standard.

According to Nate Hartman, an official in the Air Division of ADEM, "The trend for the last quarters of 1990 is positive. While we can't say with a certainty of one that we've solved the problem of air emissions, it's very encouraging. This is principally because the company has people like their environmental affairs manager. When we detect a problem, he's there to meet with us and to deal with the problem. He knows both sides, industry and regulatory agencies, so he doesn't waste time making up excuses. He gives it to us straight. This affords us the ability to work with Sanders to design a solution."

How much pollution would be associated with the recycling of lead-acid batteries from 30 million electric vehicles? The annual consumption of batteries would probably not exceed 180 million batteries, or the capacity of 15 plants like Sanders. Since Sanders recycles 12 million batteries annually while releasing into the environment the amount of lead found in 447 batteries, the pollution associated with recycling 180 million batteries would be equivalent to dumping fewer than 7,000 batteries each year (6,705). One hopes that we are prepared to accept this amount of lead in the atmosphere (at least until a more benign battery is developed for the commercial market) in exchange for reducing our dependency on oil imports – and reducing other air pollutants by millions of tons.

(Special thanks to the manager of Sanders Lead Co., Troy, Ala. for assisting with the preparation of this article.)

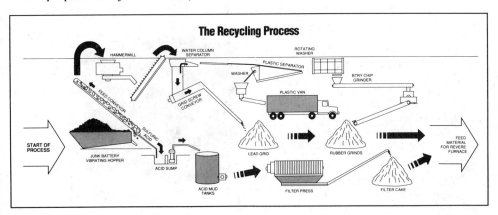

The Recycling Process

How many batteries a year?

The Sanders facility in Troy, Ala. operates 24 hours a day, 365 days a year. Sanders handles 300 tons (600,000 pounds) of batteries per day. That's 33,000 batteries per day, 12 million batteries per year. (This assumes that all of the lead that is processed at Sanders comes from batteries. Generally, 20 percent of the lead comes from other sources.) The plant processes 300 tons of lead each day and 109,500 tons of lead each year.

Annual lead pollution associated with recycling 12 million batteries: **16 pounds** of lead per year into the groundwater, plus 0.4 pounds per hour x 24 hours x 365 days = **8,040 pounds** of lead per year into the air, giving a total of **8,056 pounds of lead released annually** (18 pounds of lead in a battery). This is the amount of lead in 447 batteries. Thus, when 12 million batteries are recycled, less than **1 in 24,000 pounds** is lost to the environment.

If just ten percent of the batteries currently handled by Sanders were dumped improperly, the environment would have to absorb the lead in 1.2 million batteries or 21.6 million pounds of lead.

Write to Washington

A threat to the nation's recycling capacity for handling lead is eating away our country's ability to guarantee that lead in batteries will not be misplaced. Entrepreneurs in the Far East, principally Taiwan and the People's Republic of China, are not forced to work under the same environmental restrictions as smelters in the U.S., so they can afford to offer more for a used battery. The abuses have been well-documented: Bill Moyers' program on public television (which aired October 2, 1990) focused on the improper dumping of waste batteries in unprotected pits in several Pacific Rim lead "processing" sites. While firms like Sanders can afford to pay only $1.50 per battery, Taiwanese "recyclers" can offer more than $2 per battery because their disposal costs are much lower (thanks to virtually no environmental regulation).

The result is that, since August 1990, U.S. lead smelters have lost about one-third of their usual customers. These companies depend on a high volume of batteries to pay for their overhead costs. To keep the secondary lead market affordable, the pollution abatement costs are also spread over a large volume of batteries. If plants are handling only 60 or 70 percent of their usual volume of used batteries, they will eventually shut down, since they cannot raise their prices to cover their costs. In other words, the U.S.'s capacity to safely handle used lead-acid batteries is threatened by unscrupulous waste handlers overseas.

Various proposals exist on how to remedy this situation, including a ban on exports and imports of lead-acid batteries. This temporary restriction of free trade would be on the basis of concern for the environment, say its advocates, and would be lifted as soon as other countries pass and enforce laws as stringent as the standards in the U.S.

To level the playing field, U.S. Rep. Esteban Torres of California introduced a bill that establishes incentives for recycling lead-acid batteries. It is in the interest of every EV owner, both present and future, to contact your member of Congress to urge them to support this and similar legislation until they are made law.

Key facts on battery recycling

Americans replace over 70 million batteries each year.

Up to 23 million of these batteries are improperly discarded, either in incinerators, landfills or along the side of the road.

These 23 million batteries contain over 400 million pounds of lead (that's 200,000 tons!) and this lead can enter our air, soil and water.

If 30 million cars were switched to electric power, another 180 million batteries could need recycling *each year*.

Lead is our industrial society's most recycled material: approximately 90 percent of lead that is thrown away is smelted for re-use.

Until the lead-acid battery is replaced by a cleaner technology, we need incentives to encourage recycling of lead batteries. Congress is considering a bill called The Lead Battery Recycling Incentives Act of 1991.

The bill was filed in 1991 in the House of Representatives as H.R. 870 – sponsored by Rep. Torres (Calif.).

The bill was filed in the Senate in 1991 as S. 398 – sponsored by the late Senator John Heinz (R-Penn.) and Sen. Tim Wirth (D-Colorado).

The bill proposes a system of battery recycling and lead reclamation that is economically and technically efficient as well as environmentally sound. For more information on the bill, contact Rep. Esteban Torres, 1740 Longworth Building, Washington, DC 20515; (202) 225-5256. *(This plea appeared in a number of EV newsletters in 1991. Contact the Torres office for updates.)*

What happens to used motor oil?

*"Why should I be worried about lead?
My car uses **unleaded** gasoline!"*

Your car's used engine oil could be adding lead to the air

When you change your car's oil filter and oil every 3,000 miles, where does the waste oil go?

In 1990, 1.4 billion gallons of motor oil were replaced, and 784 million gallons (56%) was burned for fuel. 500 million gallons were dumped in storm sewers and landfills.

In 1990, 1.45 million pounds of lead went into the atmosphere in the U.S., and 588,000 pounds came from the burning of used oil. *The incineration of used motor oil is the single largest source of airborne lead.*

Over 40 percent of the lead entering the atmosphere each year comes from the burning of used motor oil *(figures in millions of pounds)*. Source: Environmental Protection Agency; Hazardous Waste Treatment Council. Seen in **USA Today**, November 13, 1991, p. 10A.

Sources of airborne lead   588,000,000 pounds – burning used oil

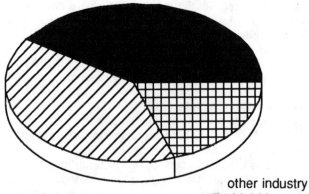

574,231,000 pounds – metals industry

other industry
287,800,000 pounds

How "green" is the EV?

Many EV advocates have focused almost exclusively on the environmental benefits of electric-powered transportation: no reactive organic gases, low oxides of nitrogen (which are precursors of low-atmosphere ozone), and no carbon monoxide, except for what is created at the power plant.

Even the possibility that power plants also contribute to global warming doesn't stimulate many EV advocates to think about the downside of widespread battery-powered transportation. They will cite studies that conclude that, if the electricity produced comes from coal or other fossil fuels, carbon dioxide will be produced in roughly the same amount as when a conventional car burns gasoline. According to *Worldwatch Magazine* (November 1990), based on the current mix of electric power plants in the U.S., greenhouse gases would be reduced by 9 percent if EVs replaced conventional cars. Of course, electricity made from renewable energy sources (such as hydropower or direct solar energy) does not contribute to the greenhouse effect, a fact overlooked by critics who call the EV the "elsewhere emissions vehicle."

Further support is found in a paper titled "Electric Vehicles and the Greenhouse Effect," produced by a pro-electric car Australian researcher and read at the December 1990 meeting of the Tenth Symposium on Electric Vehicles in Hong Kong. The author, Professor D.F. Gosden, concludes that, when generated by a coal-fired plant, the electricity consumed by an EV produces an average of 20 percent **less** carbon dioxide than conventional petroleum-powered vehicles. Gosden points out that the amount of CO_2 can be reduced by using renewable fuels and by improvements in EV charging technology. He also notes that a major advantage of electric vehicles is the flexible choice of power source, since a wide range of fuels not normally available for transportation (wood, hydroelectric power, coal, nuclear) can be used to produce electricity.

480 million batteries

EV advocates point to the second car in the non-rural household as the most logical vehicle to convert to electric. Most families with a second car drive it less than 25 miles per day, well within the range of most converted EVs. In 1991, there were approximately 140 million cars and trucks in the U.S. and 90 million households. Let's assume that 30 million of the cars in multi-car households were converted to electric power: what would happen to the 480 million deep-cycle batteries that would be replaced every two years (assuming 16 batteries per car)?

The switch to electric could dramatically increase the mishandling of dead lead-acid batteries, and could inflict an additional burden on our nation's limited hazardous waste dumps. But you can make the switch without feeling guilty, because people in the lead smelting business are working to recycle lead responsibly. As this article has demonstrated, the quantities of lead being dispersed are not insignificant, but this should not deter you from investing in an EV. Mass production of the nickel-metal-hydride battery (or a similar benign technology) will be in place by the time you need to replace your first set of lead-acid batteries.

A 6-volt battery being inspected.

13

What's Your Source of Electricity?

Nuclear? Coal? Solar? Hydro? Name any two sources of energy for making electricity, and someone will argue that one is better than the other. The very nature of energy politics focuses on costs and benefits and forces one to choose between one form of fuel over another.

Instead of choosing sides, let's step back and note that there are three things we can do to help our descendants as well as ourselves:

(1) reduce the need to import oil

(2) clean up the air in cities

(3) increase our use of sustainable sources of energy and decrease our dependence on non-renewable fuels.

(However you define "sustainable," the spirit behind this goal is the "seventh generation" philosophy articulated on the acknowledgement page in the front of this book.)

A New Coalition: The ETC

United by our common interest in reducing petroleum imports, diverse interests can work together to build a viable alternative to the gasoline-dominated economy. Let's begin by recognizing that there is strength in diversity. Some petroleum substitutes will work in cities, others in rural areas. Some fuels may work in tropical and subtropical areas, but are not appropriate for areas that have harsh winters. While propane might not be a viable alternative to gasoline in Florida or Arizona, many farm vehicles run affordably on propane in the Midwest.

Starting with a "different is stronger" attitude, it is healthy to see different regions relying on divergent forms of fuels for energy use. Renewable energy advocates, clean coal supporters and the nuclear lobby need to unite to fight the planet's gasoline addiction. Rather than try to accomplish all three goals at once, let's work on #1: reducing imports of petroleum. After oil consumption has been cut in half, then let's argue about what deserves to be the next national priority.

Until then, let's work together to get the imported-oil monkey off our backs. We can do further refinements down the road and argue over which is the best way to produce electricity, and whether methanol or compressed natural gas should be the alternative fuel of choice. We can argue later whether it's wise to rely on a substitute fuel like propane (derived from petroleum) or on a true alternative fuel like ethanol (when derived from a sustainable biomass resource). Let's first agree and work together to switch away from gasoline.

After all, it is too easy to characterize the advocates of a particular source of energy as repugnant just because we happen to believe that the energy source is undesirable. Sincere people believe that clean coal, solar power or nuclear fission is best for our country or planet to use to produce needed electricity.

Fortunately, there's a second reason for sincere people who have differing viewpoints to work together. In addition to reducing oil imports (to help boost our economic and energy security), we need to clean the air. The Clean Air Act Amendments of 1990 require cities, counties and states to develop ways to reduce air pollution, or suffer cuts in Federal transportation grants. Today, support for electric vehicles rests most significantly on the need to improve the air quality of our urban and suburban areas.

Whatever you believe our current options are for generating electricity, you will find someone who agrees with you in the Electric Transportation Coalition. This lobbying and advocacy group based in Washington, D.C. brings together the most diverse interests for discussion and support of electric vehicle legislation. The ETC has assisted Rep. George Brown with the preparation of his EV bill and the ETC staff is up-to-date on the latest efforts to promote sustainable alternatives. Why not write to ETC and find out how you can help? You can start by writing to your member of Congress about bills that will prepare us for a world filled with a variety of alternative fuels. *Electric Transportation Coalition, 1050 Thomas Jefferson Street, Sixth Floor, Washington, D.C. 20007, 202-298-1935. The Coalition's quarterly newsletter is distributed to members (organizations that pay annual dues costing thousands of dollars) and to interested members of the public. Enclose a contribution to defray the cost of postage and mention that you are interested in supporting EV legislation.*

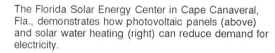

The Florida Solar Energy Center in Cape Canaveral, Fla., demonstrates how photovoltaic panels (above) and solar water heating (right) can reduce demand for electricity.

Other Alternative Fuel Coalitions and Sources of Information

Natural Gas Vehicle Coalition (703-527-3022) and American Gas Association (703-841-8499), 1515 Wilson Blvd., Arlington, VA 22209; American Methanol Institute, 815 Connecticut Ave., N.W., #800, Washington, D.C. 20006, 202-467-5050; California Energy Commission, 1516 Ninth Street, Sacramento, CA 95814; for an informative booklet about natural gas vehicles, send $2 to SFEAA, 101 SE 15th Avenue, #5, Ft. Lauderdale, FL 33301.

Cliff Hayden (far left, representing the Americas), Dr. C.C. Chan (far right, representing Asia), and C. Dierkens (2nd from the right, representing Europe). Thanks to the cooperation of these "three wise men," the Electric Vehicle Symposium will be hosted in Europe (1992), the Americas (1994) and Asia (1996). *Photo from EVS-10 provided by Dr. Chan.*

14

Aren't We Trying to Use *Less* Electricity?

We are told by numerous renewable energy advocates and utility consumer groups that it is cheaper to reduce demand through energy efficiency and conservation than to build any sort of plant (nuclear, coal, whatever). So why are some environmentalists telling us it's all right to drive electric cars, which will only *increase* electricity use?

Ken Koch, a long-time member of the Electric Vehicle Association of Southern California (EVAOSC) and a supplier of electric car parts (KTA Services), explains the concept of peak versus off-peak charging.

Charging At Night
By Ken Koch, KTA Services (Orange, Calif.)

Critics of battery-powered transportation argue that placing thousands of electric vehicles on the power grid would require the utility companies to build newer and larger facilities. Consumers would have to pick up the tab in the form of increased utility rates. Fortunately, most electric cars are charged during the "off-peak" hours, when there is surplus capacity (usually between 10 p.m. and 6 a.m.). In the Southern California area, the mix of power generated by the Los Angeles Department of Water and Power and Southern California Edison totals about 12,000 megawatts, half of which is generally idle during off-peak hours.

Here's a conservative estimate: assume that one-third or 4 megawatts of capacity is available between 11 p.m. and 5 a.m. The system can generate 24 million kilowatt-hours over these six off-peak hours. If an average electric car drives 30 miles per day and requires 20 kilowatt-hours to recharge, a total of 1,200,000 electric cars can be supported without additional investment in plant capacity or in reducing off-peak consumption in other areas.

Even if half of the vehicles are utility trucks, which consume twice as much power as cars, we're still looking at 400,000 trucks and 400,000 cars. Adding 10,000 electric vehicles to the grid as proposed in the Marvin Braude EV initiative (adopted by the City of Los Angeles) will use less than one percent of the region's off-peak electrical capacity.

Shari Prange of Electro-Automotive (Felton, Calif.) adds,

A power plant cannot be turned off quickly when people turn off the lights and go to bed. Electric cars that charge at night can help level the demand. This allows power plants to operate more efficiently and many utilities offer a cheaper "off-peak" rate to encourage greater use between midnight and 5 a.m.

Photo by Shari Prange

Here's A Controversial Idea:
Let's Help Our Utilities Make A Profit

By Bob Batson, Electric Vehicles of America (Maynard, Mass.)

Unfortunately, it appears that the electric utility industry is in a "Catch-22" situation. They are currently being forced by numerous environmental groups and government agencies (called Public Service Commissions in many states) into selling less of their product (electricity). The intent behind "demand-side management" and "nega-watt" thinking is to reduce the amount of carbon dioxide that is produced.

However, let's examine what happens when a business sells less of its product: the overhead costs must be spread over a smaller number of sales, so pressure builds to force up the cost per kilowatt-hour sold. Reduced demand for electricity means you need fewer power plants, so fixed costs should eventually decline. Until those unneeded plants are shut down, however, the utility's overhead is covered by lower revenues.

Most utilities have a mix of generating capacity: nuclear, coal, oil, natural gas-fired, gas turbines and a range of renewable sources (geothermal, solar, wind, biomass, and hydropower). The nuclear and coal units provide the base capacity: they are typically kept running continuously, since they are more costly to start and stop and work most efficiently when they operate without interruption. Oil and gas-fired plants are usually used as "cycling units": they operate during the day when the industrial need for electricity is greatest and they either significantly reduce their production or shut down entirely in the evening. If they shut down every night, the life of the equipment is shortened and maintenance costs increase. Gas turbines and hydroelectric power plants are used for the peaking load during the day when air conditioning demand is highest (in the summer) or in the early morning in areas that depend on electric heaters during the winter. Gas turbines have the highest operating cost and hydropower is limited by the capacity and location of dams.

During the past ten years, 'round-the-clock manufacturing has decreased in the U.S., so there has been minimal increase in demand for electric power at night. So more and more base-load generating plants (primarily coal) have been required to operate at a low load (which is inefficient) or shut down every night (which increases maintenance costs).

For example, a 400-megawatt coal-burning plant might be cut back to 80 megawatts just to keep heat in the plant's system. This is inefficient, since it takes 12,000 BTUs to generate a kilowatt-hour under this low-load operation, whereas the plant at its most efficient rating can make a kilowatt-hour with only 10,000 BTUs.

Electricity is readily available during off-peak hours, which depend on the customer demand, but generally is between 10 p.m. to 5 a.m. This periodic excess capacity is one reason why utilities support the introduction of electric vehicles. There are numerous benefits to both the utility and all paying customers when additional uses can be found for off-peak electricity:

- The cost of electricity stabilizes or decreases because more of the product is sold using existing generating plants.
- Emissions are minimized because it is easier to clean up a few smoke stacks than a million automobile tailpipes.
- Smog (urban air pollution) is substantially decreased because emissions that are released are typically outside urban areas and are released through tall stacks, not at the ground level.
- The units that are now shut down or cycled each day will be operated closer to the maximum efficiency. Less cycling means less maintenance; improved efficiency means less fuel burned.

The "Catch-22" situation centers on the clashing of two good ideas: energy conservation and shifting to off-peak loads (for more efficient operation). The electric utility is not allowed to encourage electricity use, even in off-peak hours. This is a rule developed to encourage conservation and demand-side management. However, our real objective should be to maximize efficiency.

So how do we turn the tide? The answer is education and economics. Education of the public, government groups, environmental organizations and businesses. We need to make them aware of the penalties we are paying for not using the idle generating capacity and we need to highlight the benefits of expanded use of electric vehicles. By providing economic incentives to encourage EVs, the off-peak use can increase, adding revenues to the utility that can be used to delay the next rate increase. These incentives include:

- reduced electricity rates for EV users (usually monitored with a separate meter and timed for off-peak charging)
- tax incentives for EV owners

It is up to us as individuals and as organized groups to promote the use of EVs and improved off-peak use of electricity. Some environmentalists refuse to support EVs because EVs plug into the grid, tapping electricity from high-sulfur coal-burning plants (a major contributor to acid rain). However, widespread acceptance of battery-powered transportation will encourage the installation of photovoltaic garages, like the one in Basel, Switzerland, operated by Fridez. The commuter leaves the car at the train station and during the day, instead of adding to the peak demand for electricity, the EV gets charged by highly efficient PV arrays. So let's work together with utilities to put to work proven ideas to use our electric grid more efficiently.

For more information about alternative sources of energy, contact the Rocky Mountain Institute (1739 Snowmass Creek Road, Snowmass, CO 81654) and the Campus Center for Appropriate Technology, California State University (Humboldt), (Buck House #97, Arcata, CA 95521, 707-826-3551).

EVs help manage demand: This graph depicts the drop in demand for electricity between 11 p.m. and 6 a.m. The grey area represents the capacity in the utility's system that could be used to charge EVs. Some utilites operate close to their off-peak maximum capacity and would have to turn on additional power plants to charge EVs or reduce current off-peak demand for electricity (by persuading customers to invest in more energy-efficient appliances). Other utilities work under rules that penalize excessive operation of oil-fired units, which might be the only power plants available for charging EVs at night. Another drawback: the off-peak period is usually the time set aside for routine maintenance of power plants. (source: Steve Sim, Florida Power & Light).

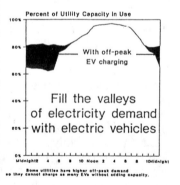

Percent of Utility Capacity in Use

With off-peak EV charging

Fill the valleys of electricity demand with electric vehicles

Some utilities have higher off-peak demand so they cannot charge as many EVs without adding capacity.

Charging stations at SMUD's headquarters. *Photo by Richard Minner.*

15

Future Developments

*Warning: This chapter contains material that might encourage you to wait for the **Super Battery** and dissuade you from converting a vehicle to battery power today. Discussion of future batteries should not be used to justify waiting to convert a car! A purchase of an electric car today tells both the auto and battery industries that there is one more person in the market who is ready for the post-petroleum era. If you have a severe case of Super-Battery Lust, you can always change your batteries when the next generation of electricity storage emerges.*

Current research funded by the U.S. Government focuses on the single factor that limits range of all electric vehicles: the battery. The U.S. Department of Energy has joined an effort initiated by Chrysler, Ford, General Motors, major utilities and battery manufacturers to invest $260 million between 1991 and 1995 in the pursuit of the "super battery."

What will the Advanced Battery Consortium (USABC) invest in? The goals for the consortium include finding a battery that will double current best technology while making it cost competitive with lead-acid batteries. This chapter describes some of the leading candidates, as well as three emerging technologies that USABC has overlooked. Later in the chapter we'll take a look at developments in Europe.

Mature alternatives to the lead-acid battery

Nickel-iron: Thomas Edison developed and sold the first nickel-iron batteries, which have an alkaline (not acid) electrolyte. They hold more energy per pound than lead-acid batteries, offsetting their higher initial cost. A potential drawback: while the U.S. has 12 percent of the world's nickel-bearing ore, less than three-tenths of one percent of these resources can be mined economically with current technology at current market prices. Although the U.S. would not be self-sufficient in the near term, Canada controls 15 percent of the world's resources and 16 percent of the ore that can be mined affordably. EV consultant William Hamilton has calculated that current production facilities, secure resources for nickel and planned expansion could satisfy demand created by an increase of one million EVs per year (*Technical Background Report*, prepared for EG&G Idaho and U.S. Department of Energy, 1989). While charging, the nickel-iron battery generates slightly more hydrogen than its lead-acid cousin does, but watering and gas-management systems compensate for this tendency.

John D'Angelo (UtilityFree™) adds: I don't know why the general consensus of the nickel-iron is negative. I suspect the reason is *most* people have never extensive hands-on experience with them. I have found that nickel-iron batteries used in an EV will outperform any lead-acid battery, especially in colder conditions.

Nickel-cadmium: While nickel-cadmium batteries can be as much as four times more expensive than lead-acid, they have excellent performance. The cycle life can exceed 3,000 cycles and the battery can hold almost twice the energy of a lead-acid. Cadmium's availability and difficulties associated with its disposal (cadmium is very toxic) are two potential drawbacks. *(John D'Angelo reports that there's a cadmium recovery facility in North Carolina.)*

Technologies under development

Zinc-bromide: The low cost of its materials makes this battery attractive. However, for a variety of reasons, it is not likely to see commercialization.

Nickel-zinc: Another alkaline battery, it is thought to be better suited to shallow discharging cycles (typical of short suburban EV driving) rather than deep discharging. While it delivers more power than lead-acid batteries, it is not likely to be commercialized.

Zinc-chloride: A complex system is needed to take advantage of this high-energy battery. During recharging, chlorine is generated, so a sophisticated capturing method must be used. A bulky battery, it is better suited to storing off-peak electricity for peak use.

Sealed Bi-polar Lead Acid (SBLA): This lead-acid battery is called "bi-polar" because it is not made into 6-volt or 12-volt modules. If you need a battery system of 120 volts, you get one long battery with two poles (positive and negative). This reduces the internal resistance between individual batteries, since the SBLA acts like one large battery. Developed by the Jet Propulsion Laboratory as part of the Star Wars (Strategic Defense Initiative) research effort of the mid-1980s, the SBLA is being refined for use in electric vehicles by Arias Research Associates. One cell has been discharged and charged through 3000 cycles and is still going strong. This is equivalent to a ten-year life span, assuming a charge six times per week.

Unlike the conventional deep-cycle lead-acid battery, the plates of the SBLA do not take part in the charge-discharge cycle, so they do not have to be smelted after becoming sulfated. The "recycling" is more a matter of dissassembly, where thin silicon wafers are repacked with lead dioxide paste. "This completely removes the Mephisto scene that we are familiar with at lead smelting plants," notes Paul Schutt, whose company is coordinating an electric vehicle manufacturing consortium in Southern California.

High-temperature batteries

Lithium-iron sulfide: Developed in the early 1970s, its electrolyte is a salt (lithium chloride) which must remain above 400°C (752°F). Widespread use may be limited by the supply of lithium.

Sodium-sulfur: Another high temperature battery, the sodium-sulfur battery has received much support in the U.S. Its materials are in abundant supply, and it's being produced in small quantities as part of its development. This battery must be kept at 350°C (660°F) and it will probably be available in the mid-1990s. Its ability to store large quantities of energy makes it a favorite of many battery analysts.

In both of these systems, the superheated contents are much better insulated than the standard car battery and the molten salts are separated in small cells for added protection.

Lithium-polymer: Based on thin-film technology, the lithium-polymer battery is expected to cost about 20 percent more than a conventional lead-acid battery while delivering twice the energy and a 50,000-mile life span. With an anticipated operating temperature range between 65°C and 120°C (150°F and 250°F), it has the potential for fast-recharging (some analysts predict less than 90 minutes). Scaled-up models will probably have a long shelf life and be able to withstand external temperatures up to 180°C (355°F). Drawbacks include a thermal control problem (which may indicate higher internal resistance when discharged at a fast rate) and an intolerance to over-charging. This battery has yet to be built, but looks promising for the late-1990s.

Aluminum-air: This is not a conventional rechargeable battery. Instead, aluminum plates are added every couple hundred miles to replace the aluminum "consumed" in the chemical reaction. The aluminum reacts with atmospheric oxygen in the sodium hydroxide electrolyte solution to form sodium aluminate. This then deposits as aluminum trihydroxide, which must be removed. The basic components may one day be made small enough to fit in a standard passenger car. Most analysts agree that aluminum-air will be restricted to a larger vehicle (van or bus).

Nickel-hydrogen: Under development by a number of researchers, including Johnson Controls in Milwaukee, the nickel-hydrogen is quite expensive ("but so were photovoltaic cells ten years ago," John D'Angelo reminds us), so innovative financing may be needed. It could be developed as a 30-year battery, purchased with a mortgage and moved from car to car as the EVs are retired. Advantages include long life and safe operation. Currently used in spacecrafts and deep-water vehicles.

Future battery options are the principal focus of the USABC effort, but other means of propelling a car exist:

Fuel Cells: Sometimes called a "reverse battery," a fuel cell unites hydrogen and oxygen to form water while producing electricity. The main drawbacks are the fuel cell's expense and size. Current projects focus on a fuel-cell bus, ready for testing in the mid-1990s. *For information on fuel cells and other alternative fuels, send $4 for Electrifying Times, Solarland Ltd., 63600 Deschutes Road, Bend, OR 97701.*

Cliff Hayden, former director of GTE's fleet of 200 EVs and numerous other alternative-fuel vehicles, shared these observations at the NESEA Solar/Electric Vehicle Symposium in Boxborough, Mass., in October 1991:

Sometime before 2000, we will see widespread acceptance of hybrid EVs. Where an EV makes good sense from an environmental standpoint, there is every reason to believe you will see small on-board generators to provide extended range.

In the longer term, I believe most of the future vehicles in the 21st Century will be electric, passenger cars particularly, but they will be hybrids. They will use a fuel cell which is non-polluting and zero-emissions. It will take on fuel, either compressed natural gas or methanol or any fuel that can be converted into electricity. You'll pull into a fueling station and you'll have the extended range. I think it's coming, but I don't know exactly what form the fuel cell will be.

Inductive Power: Some visionaries see cars being pulled by magnetic fields coming from electric wires buried in major roadways. The force is "induced" in the passenger car, allowing the car's batteries to rest while the electric motor moves the car. The idea is winning some support in California but has little chance of making a significant or widespread impact. Another proposal: inductive charging, where the batteries are charged by the magnet in the roadway (the car can be moving or at rest, depending on the system envisioned).

Three additional promising technologies also exist: nickel-metal-hydride, iron-redox, and a new form of the lead-acid battery developed by B.A.T. in Utah.

Nickel-Metal Hydride: Ovonic Battery Company of Troy Michigan calls it a "green battery": no cadmium, no lead. The metal hydride is made form a patented alloy of vanadium, titanium, zirconium, chromium and nickel (V-Ti-Zr-Cr-Ni). Nickel-metal hydride (Ni-MH) batteries have been developed for use in laptop computers, cellular telephones, videocameras and medical instruments. Ovonic has licensed the manufacturing of its battery to a number of companies and a battery for EVs is expected to be available commercially in the near future.

Still, there's one sure way to direct dollars toward the development of a nickel-metal-hydride battery: through your economic vote. Ovonics has issued manufacturing agreements with Gates Energy Corporation and Harding Energy Corporation (see the "Batteries" section in **EV Resources** for the addresses). A portion of every dollar spent on a nickel-metal-hydride AA battery goes to pay a royalty to Ovonics. Part of that royalty will be invested in further research. So, join the adventure! Invest in a benign battery today!

Iron-redox: Little information is available on this technology, only the word of Bob Beaumont, who claims that the battery is worth examining, even if just to find out whether it is a dead end. Anyone interested in pursuing a low-cost investigation is urged to contact Ralph Zito, 2563-A Eric Lane, Burlington, NC 27215.

B.A.T.'s Patented Electrolyte: *The third technology that USABC is likely to overlook is under development at Battery Automated Technology. The following is extracted from a paper prepared by Joseph LaStella, B.A.T., 2471 South 2570 West, West Valley City, UT 84119.*

The Ultra Force battery is the result of research to develop a deep-cycle battery adequate to power electric cars using a new patented electrolyte which retards sulfation of battery plates and has a much lower impedance (reduced resistance to the flow of electricity).

Lower impedance allows recharging to take place   quickly. Power output is sustained at higher rates, extending operational time between fully charged and fully discharged batteries. Lower impedance also reduces the stress on battery operation, increasing the number of cycles from as few as 400 to as many as 1,500 cycles. This is especially evident in cold weather operations. Finally, heat build-up is reduced, reducing water consumption and lowering maintenance costs.

The Ultra Force electrolyte virtually eliminates the corrosion around terminals, the most common battery-service chore. Corrosion-free terminals mean full voltage and lower resistance to delivering electric current, giving more efficient battery operation.

The Ultra Force batteries do not begin to produce significant amounts of hydrogen gas until they are overcharged to almost 17 volts. This is a substantial safety margin over the 14.2-volt level for regular lead-acid batteries. This translates into more leeway for accidental over-charging and allows a higher charging rate.

Looking Into The Crystal Ball at Hydrogen

*To provide yet another look to the future, Joe Stevenson edits a fascinating bi-monthly publication called **Solar Mind**. This article appeared in the September-October 1990 issue and gives a much-needed alternative perspective.*

The true cost of oil: The recurring justification for non-investment in renewable transportation sources and electric cars is the catch phrase "cost effective," as in "hydrogen as a fuel isn't cost-effective yet." What this means is that until the cost of gasoline grows to equal the cost of hydrogen production, let's forget about it. It is odd that the cost of gasoline is the only measure for our choice of energy. When will we begin to see that the true cost of oil use is not limited to the pump price? If we consider our health and environmental costs along with the military and other governmental costs, I believe we will find that gasoline is at least ten times as expensive as hydrogen. Even at today's gas prices, hydrogen can be produced for a little more than thirty cents per gallon more than gasoline. And hydrogen doesn't pollute or create more carbon dioxide. It doesn't burn up engines and carburetors and other engine components. It is clear there are other ways to get around on this planet if we want to explore them. The first step to be taken is to find the clarity within ourselves that we are ready to change. The next step is to see that if we demand vehicles that are clean and quiet, there will be a supply.

Electric cars have existed since the turn of the century and offer the most immediate option. Sad to say, there are only ten thousand or so in the entire USA. The technology now exists (batteries, motors) to build an electric car that could travel 500 to 1,000 miles on a single overnight charge, and also at freeway speeds. Because there has been no demand for such materials, their current cost is high. Also on the horizon are solar-powered and -charged vehicles which represent the most exciting promise. Just think of a highway full of cars propelled by wind, sun and hydrogen, all renewable and clean.

Hydrogen is the purest of all combustible fuels. It can be prepared from water at a cost similar to gasoline and can be made in decentralized locations (your home). When burned, it gives up only water vapor. In electrolysis (separation of water), the by-products are oxygen and freshwater. The fear of explosion associated with hydrogen has been relieved with the discovery of what are known as hydrides. These compounds attract and bond with hydrogen at normal temperatures, releasing the gas at higher exhaust temperatures. Under rigorous testing, all fires created in and around tanks containing hydrides could not spread and eventually self-extinguished.

For more "future thinking," subscribe to Solar Mind, 759 South State Street, #81, Ukiah, CA 95482.

The Ultimate Electric Vehicle

James Worden, a senior research engineer and founder of Solectria Car Corp. (Arlington, Mass.), made these remarks at the NESEA Solar/EV Symposium, October 27, 1991. His car, the Flash, can stretch more than five miles out of one kilowatt-hour.

The Flash is a three-wheeled commuter car, all-composite, with no continuous metal frame in the car. Its three-wheel design might appear unstable, but it's practical. In a full skid it won't tip over because of its low center of gravity.

Three wheels is a block in some people's minds, but we're talking about the ultimate commuting car here. Education has to be part of the ultimate car. The car has to be lightweight and efficient enough to go 30 miles after charging its batteries in the sun for eight hours.

The dream of my existence is building a practical, safe and fun vehicle, a car that you can drive through your entire average commute without plugging into the utility grid. The photovoltaic panels built into the Flash can convert enough solar energy and store it as electricity to take you 30 miles after a full day of charging. How many people fit with that? How many people drive less than 30 miles a day? I think we can safely say that the majority of us do.

Two trends will direct the future development of EVs: the evolution of motor vehicle safety standards (developed by the National Highway Traffic Safety Administration) and the integration of EVs into the European mass-transit system.

A New Category of Cars
By John Hoke

Let's face it: the best vehicle for zipping around a city or for doing errands in a suburb is not a gasoline-powered automobile. What we need most is not just an affordable electric vehicle, but an electric **runabout.**

You might call it a mini-car or a town car. I call it a runabout, because that's what you do with it: run about your neighborhood doing errands, run about downtown, ducking into narrow parking spaces. Such vehicles operate in Europe and Japan, often with a clearly posted speed limit. Some aren't allowed to go faster than 40 mph (60 kph), so they carry a sign, a 60 with a red line through it, to indicate the vehicle's speed limit.

In the U.S. we have communities where people can ride golf carts on residential streets. They can cross heavily traveled streets but are not allowed to operate the carts upon them. Well, this "runabout" would be a bit hardier than a golf cart, but not by much. It doesn't have to go fast, so there's no need for it to withstand rigorous crash tests.

I envision downtown traffic will adopt the law of the boat operator: **Power gives way to sail.** The larger automobile, capable of highway speeds, will give way to the "underpowered" runabout. Currently, there's far more innovation on the water than on the American road. After all, what's the sense of taking a motor capable of 150 horespower to go eight blocks down to the grocery store? That's like taking a battleship to the grocery store when a rowboat will do just fine.

As for safety standards, the 30-mph crash test hardly applies to such a vehicle. This new class of car will be operating at half the speed of conventional cars, so a 15-mph crash test seems more logical.

I doubt if I've taken my car over 60 mph more than 5 times since I bought it three years ago. I wander around Bethesda, never exceeding 40 mph unless I'm on Canal or River Roads, which I could avoid if my vehicle was strictly for runabout duty.

Let's put some enjoyment back into downtown driving. After 13 years of driving a battery-powered runabout, I know firsthand how fun it is. *Between 1975 and 1988, John Hoke accumulated over 78,000 logged miles in a Sebring-Vanguard Citicar. This article first appeared in* **Electric Vehicle News**, *March 1992.*

European Initiatives Shape Future EVs
By J.W. (Bill) Yerkes

The environmental movement's motto, "Think globally, act locally, " has found expression in the emerging electric vehicle market in Europe. Differences in geography and political makeup are shaping the EV's evolution.

Switzerland: The home of the original Tour de Sol is committed to preserving its "Disneyland" appearance. Tourists are encouraged to come ride the train system, see the beautiful views, travel over the clean rivers.

Environmental catastrophes, such as the Chernobyl accident, have shaped the Swiss interest in cleaner technologies. The 1985 chemical spill by a Swiss chemical company, which killed fish and plant-life and contaminated drinking water for millions of Germans, French and Dutch, was embarrassing for a country known for pristine views and mountainscapes. Concern for the environment now has encouraged greater cooperation between the cantons (Switzerland's political units, like states in the U.S.), who have limited the Central national government to running the army, trains and postal system. In a national referendum, voters recently agreed to stop future development of nuclear power plants and to phase out current nuclear capacity by expanding photovoltaic and natural gas-fired electric plants.

Thanks to extensive exploitation of rivers for hydroelectric projects and a centuries-old tradition of self-sufficiency, the Swiss have led the world in seeking ways to reduce dependence on imported oil. It's now possible to drive a small Swiss built electric car to a train station, park the car, and take the train to your destination, renting an EV for local driving. While you are at work or away on the trip, the car's batteries are charged by the electric grid or by photovoltaic arrays.

Groups of citizens have organized events to educate the public about electric vehicles. Switzerland has held national "Solarmobile" electric car shows in Basil Switzerland and this year in Bern for the last three years. The show, held in early March or late February is exclusively for electric vehicles (in Switzerland, called Solarmobiles because they can be recharged by solar generated electricity). The annual Tour de Sol takes place in a different city each year. The educational benefits of the competition are already reaping new consumers who are willing to purchase "under-achieving" vehicles as a part of a national effort to make the transportation system clean, environmentally friendly and reliable. These activities in Switzerland for the last seven years have generated a unique to Europe mini-industry of small electric car builders. These cars, built in Denmark, France, Italy, Germany and

Switzerland all find a market in the Swiss vision of independent transportation and self sufficiency.

Germany: The forces shaping the EV industry in Germany differ sharply with the "short distance commuter" EVe that is evolving in Switzerland. While the central government in Germany has more authority than the central government in Switzerland it is voting for unlimited speed and powerful cars on the Autobahn. It is the municipalities that are leading the EV effort by gradually closing off more of the access to the cities to the internal combustion engine (ICE). Dusseldorf started the trend with weekend closing of the downtown area to automobiles. Munich, Freiburg and many other cities have now closed the centers of their cities to the automobile. The zones of exclusion are being enlarged each year and other cities are finding a renaissance by banning thousands of noisy cars and trucks with gasoline and diesel engines. Munich has a plan to gradually expand the "no ICE zone" to cover most of its central business district. Since most households in Germany have only one car the EV mostly likely to succeed in Germany will need to leave the city and move onto the Autobahn to the next city. The compromise being worked on by germany's automakers is a hybrid car with battery for the city center and super clean auto or diesel engine for the highway.

Geography in Switzerland makes it easier to justify the EV's limited range, since a railroad station is not far from any corner of the country. Narrow valleys in Switzerland tend to trap emissions, even from the less-polluting hybrid car, leading eight towns to ban all gasoline and diesel engines. In Germany, however, the extensive autobahn system and the movement to close downtown areas make the hybrid EVe more attractive. Germany's open terrain requires a vehicle that can cover longer distances than the typical pure EV, and the hybrid can operate on battery power when the traveller enters a no-emission zone.

Volkswagen is the leader in developing a parallel hybrid EVe, which has a separate drive system for the ICE motor. VW's "CityStromer" can run on a super "EcoDiesel" which gets 75 mpg on the highway and switches to pure electric in the city. In normal driving the computer starts the car with the electric drive and the diesel takes over when reaching 30 mph limiting its pollution at idle and low speed. The combination of the two systems with the computer is similar to the LA301 being developed by Clean Air Transport (CAT) for the Los Angeles initiative. Volkswagen has also used this same system in the new CHICO concept car shown for the first time at the Frankfurt Auto show in late 1991. The CHICO is a small two plus two city car of minimum size. It uses two cylinders of the POLO 4 cylinder engine (POLO is smaller but similar to the GOLF but not imported into the U.S.). By using pieces of high volume production engine and drive systems VW is positioning itself the make reliable EV's at with low cost high volume components.

Both the CHICO and GOLF CityStromer use an advanced, sealed Nickel Cadmium battery developed by DAUG (Deutsche Automotive Union Gesellschaft) and licensed for high volume production to Hoeppeke a battery production company. This battery gives twice the performance of the best lead acid battery systems and performs well in cold climates which lead acid does not. DAUG is a joint venture of VW and Mercedes Benz started in the 1970's after the oil embargo. The new battery uses nickel plated polymer fibers instead of solid nickel placque to reduce cost. Clever developments by DAUG on the very old Nickel Cadmium system have allowed the battery to be welded shut and sealed completely within a stainless steel case. The battery will last for the life of the vehicle and can be recycled into a new battery and have another life at that point. The Cadmium cannot be dumped into the environment because of the completely sealed design of the battery. Batteries like this are now being used in jet aircraft and in space because they are completely sealed and maintenance free. As demonstrated by the Japanese the Nickel Cadmium battery can also be recharged in very short times compared to any other system. Volkswagen is probably the world's leader in practical EV solutions that could be used in Los Angeles. They are now working with SWATCH to produce a low cost, popular EV prototype and the results should be interesting.

BMW has also introduced prototype electric cars for Germany (don't forget the BMW Isetta BMW motorcycles) with high profile show-cars at Frankfurt which were all electric. Mercedes has taken the usual high cost approach with its hydrogen storage program and is hanging back to see what will happen. Mercedes along with SWATCH was a sponsor of the Swiss Biel solar race car which won the World Solar Challenge across Australia in 1991.

France: In contrast to the local Cantons in Switzerland and the Cities in Germany the French have a more central socialist government which is directing the EV efforts. The French program is backing SAFT, one of the world's largest battery manufacturers to develop advanced Nickel batteries. Originally the SAFT program was fixed on Nickel Iron, but these batteries proved to not be as reliable, so the program switched in 1989 to Nickel Cadmium which can be recharged fast and has a higher in-out storage efficiency. SAFT has these EV batteries available now and they provide 55 watt hours per kilogram, very high power levels and excellent winter performance. The two major French car groups, Peugeot (Citroen is now a part of Peugeot) and Renault have both built several series of small passenger cars and small vans using the SAFT batteries. You can even buy an electric version of the old 2CV small delivery van with an electric motor. I suspect that would sell in Los Angeles where being "cute" is important. EVs in France will use nuclear power which now provides more than 85% of the electrical energy for the country. Don't forget that France too has an excellent modern train system including the TGV (Train Gran Vitesse) which has gone over 300 miles per hour (faster than the German Maglev). All of this transportation system is powered by France's nuclear reactors. Electric cars could make Paris a much nicer city.

Italy: FIAT's electric car effort is impressive. An electric version of the FIAT PANDA has been in production for 5 years now, and the "NEW 500" or Cinquecento that FIAT is starting to produce in poland is designed from the ground up for either electric or gasoline drive. Unfortunately for us the electric Peugeot and FIATS will not be available to the U.S. because our 30 mph crash tests has been valued over ease of parking and energy efficiency. One hopes that vehicles dedicated to urban use will be allowed to meet a lower crash standard since most urban accidents involve much slower speeds.

In short, local forces, in Europe, are determining how the EV is evolving, much the way the automobile has: smaller, easier-to-park vehicles for urban cities, fast cars for the autobahn, and minivans and larger vehicles for the U.S., market. EV advocates will learn much by monitoring how Europe is leading the world in identifying niche markets for this new transportation technology. *Bill Yerkes, Founder of ARCO Solar is presently prototype development manager at a large Aerospace company's high tech center. He has travelled to Europe and monitors the development of batteries, aerodynamics and other high technology spin-offs in the transportation field.*

Sources used in this chapter: Fetcenko, M.A. et al. "Ovonic Metal Hydride Battery Technology," IBA Conference, Seattle, Washington (1990); Walsh, W.J. and J.B. Rajan, "Advanced Batteries for Electric Vehicles." Argonne National Laboratory, Argonne, Ill. (1985).

Dr. C.C. Chan is developing a switched reluctance motor. *Photo by J. Kayman.*

16

Comparing The Alternatives

Substitute Fuels vs. Sustainable Fuels

By Richard Minner

The primary goals to be achieved by moving beyond today's gasoline are improved air quality[1] and reduced reliance on finite fuel resources, particularly those from unstable foreign suppliers. The four major players in the gasoline-alternatives game are reformulated gasoline (RFG), methanol (M85), natural gas (CNG), and electricity (EVs). Each provides a different trade-off between potential benefits and ease of adoption; each provides a good cost/benefit ratio. The EV is the long-term favorite, because it provides the greatest benefits and because it will continue to improve while the others become more expensive.

Furthermore, the EV is often the only practical alternative for individuals who want to contribute today: reformulated gasoline offers relatively small benefits and will not be available until 1995 or 1996; methanol and natural gas require sizable capital outlays to establish distribution channels and refueling stations, hence they are targeted almost exclusively to fleet use and will remain so for several more years. Before comparing the alternatives further, let's look at some details.

Reformulated Gasoline – RFG: Gasoline is complicated stuff and one can make it many different ways. Until recently, refining has focused on cost and power; by shifting our priorities we can reduce emissions considerably. Phase 1 reformulated gasoline became mandatory on January 1, 1992. This first-phase reformulation focuses on simple improvements with relatively small benefits. Then beginning in November of 1992, "oxy-fuels" will be required in carbon monoxide (CO) non-attainment areas during the winter months. The oxy-fuels are made by adding oxygenates such as alcohols or ethers to gasoline. This increases the oxygen content to yield lower CO emissions. However, the oxy-fuels do little else and can actually increase other emissions, especially in warmer weather. Hence they are restricted to wintertime, which fortunately is when CO levels are the highest.

Phase 2 reformulated gasoline is of primary interest here. It is slated to come on line in 1996 and promises significant reductions in overall emissions. Although the emissions reductions per vehicle are not as great as for the other alternatives, reformulated gasoline will improve the emissions of all existing vehicles – something no other alternative can do. On the other hand, it will only improve the emissions of those vehicles produced before it becomes available. Why? Because when reformulated gasoline is the standard, automobile manufactures will use it in meeting the new-vehicle emissions requirements which they would have to meet regardless. Nevertheless, for the remainder of this century, use of reformulated gasoline is likely to produce greater emissions benefits than all other alternatives combined. This includes a significant reduction in toxic emissions, primarily benzene and 1,3-butadiene.

Reformulated gasoline will buy much-needed time in the air-quality department, but it retains all the other problems associated with gasoline: finite resource, dependence

---

[1] See the primer "Know Your Air" at the front of this book.

on foreign supply, risk of oil and gasoline spills and contamination. Indeed, it is an important step, but it will not take us far enough by itself.

Methanol – M85: Methanol (methyl alcohol) can be made from a variety of sources, including coal and biomass; it therefore has the potential to be renewable and/or to reduce our fuel imports. Unfortunately, by far the cheapest methanol is produced overseas from inexpensive natural gas; even with the current low demand, the United States is a net methanol importer. Methanol is only slightly more expensive than gasoline, but the price could rise sharply if future demand triggers capital outlays for new production facilities. A gallon of methanol has only about half the energy of a gallon of gasoline, so range is reduced unless the tank is enlarged. Methanol is highly corrosive and requires that many parts of the car be made of special materials. Vehicle conversions are not recommended because of the need for strict quality control. Standard storage tanks and pumps cannot be used for methanol: corrosion-resistant versions must be installed at service stations. Methanol is more toxic than gasoline and must be handled carefully. Groundwater contamination from a spill is a special concern because methanol is completely soluble in water and cannot be easily extracted. Other safety risks are comparable to those of gasoline. Overall toxic emissions are somewhat less than for RFG, because though methanol vehicles emit much more formaldehyde and acetaldehyde, they emit much less of the more potent toxics benzene and 1,3-butadiene.

Nearly all methanol vehicles are Flexible Fuel Vehicles (FFVs), designed to run on a wide range of mixtures of methanol and gasoline. The typical maximum and optimal blend is 85% methanol with 15% gasoline, known as M85. This fuel flexibility overcomes a major barrier to adoption: fuel distribution and availability. With an FFV, one can always use gasoline where methanol is not yet available. The downside is that drivers may be inclined to use gasoline to increase range or reduce fuel costs, thereby foregoing methanol's benefits. Fortunately, with fleet use this is not a significant concern, and modest government incentives could further encourage use of methanol over gasoline.

Natural Gas – CNG: This is the same gas (primarily methane) used for heating and cooking in many homes. For vehicles, the primary form is Compressed Natural Gas (CNG), in which the gas is pressurized to around 3000 pounds per square inch. In 1988 there were approximately 30,000 CNG vehicles operating in the United States, and about 700,000 worldwide. Natural gas can also be stored as Liquefied Natural Gas (LNG) at much lower pressures but at extremely low temperatures. LNG presents handling difficulties and is not widely used in vehicles. CNG/gasoline dual-fuel vehicles are possible, but they require separate fuel tanks and systems (unlike the methanol FFV). Conversions are also relatively simple, but the primary focus for natural gas vehicles is on ground-up dedicated-CNG vehicles, which have the greatest emissions benefits.

The bulk of natural gas comes from underground reserves, which are inherently finite. Fortunately, for now, the United States has a good supply, and when our relatively stable neighbors Canada and Mexico are included the supply is ample. Natural gas can also be made renewably from biomass, but the acreage required to make a significant contribution may be prohibitive.

Natural gas is widely available and distributed, but installing compressors for refueling is expensive: approximately $3000 for a home slow-fill installation, and from $90,000 to $400,000 for a fast-fill service station (5-vehicle and 75-vehicle capacity respectively). Fast-fill refueling is more expensive, but it allows a refill in 5 to 10 minutes. Slow-fill stations are relatively cheap but refueling takes 4 to 8 hours. Perhaps the largest problem with CNG is the capital required for converting service stations. Because of this, the primary focus for CNG will remain fleet use for several more years.

As with methanol, CNG has only about half the energy of an equivalent volume of gasoline, so range is reduced unless the tank is enlarged. Moreover, the fuel tank is considerably heavier than a gasoline tank of similar capacity. On the plus side, a ground-up CNG vehicle will have slightly more power than a gasoline vehicle with the same size engine.

Although the public generally perceives gaseous fuels as more dangerous, CNG has proven to be quite safe in use. The tanks are well made and have survived remarkable durability tests in extensive worldwide applications without leakage or rupture. Natural gas dissipates readily and presents less risk of fire than gasoline, though there is a potentially serious risk in enclosed areas. CNG is nontoxic, noncarcinogenic, noncorrosive, cannot contaminate water or land through "spills", and overall is considered less hazardous than gasoline. CNG also produces essentially no toxic emissions.

In comparing the alternatives, one must bear in mind that there are numerous complicating factors, including (but not limited to): many different types of vehicle; regional differences in fuel availability and emissions benefits; air quality is seasonal emissions vary with tuning and performance; vehicle characteristics change with age; vehicles receive varying degrees of maintenance; fuel costs vary with the level of investment; and vehicle production costs vary with production volume.

A detailed analysis would easily fill a book twice this size. The material here is intended to give you a good idea of the tradeoffs, but it really only scratches the surface. That said, see Figure 16.1 for a representative comparison of passenger-car emissions for each alternative fuel. EVs are the clear winner here, especially in California with the relatively clean electrical generation mix. Figure 16.2 compares estimated per-mile costs. Batteries are the largest recurring cost for EVs. Bear in mind, however, that this cost will fall as battery life and production volume increase, while the costs for the other fuels will certainly continue to rise. The EV's primary limitation remains range and refueling time. But remember – once again – that the EV's limited range is still sufficient for most driving needs. Finally, Table 16.1 presents an admittedly subjective "Report Card" covering a wide range of factors. Although not precise, it gives a good overview of the strong and weak points for each alternative. For more details, contact the Sacramento EAA (see Part III, EV Resources; enclose a self-addressed, stamped envelope with your inquiry).

There are several other alternatives that bear mention, although they are not major players at this time.

Liquefied Petroleum Gas – LPG: This oil-derived fuel powers some 350,000 trucks, farm vehicles, school buses, and other fleet vehicles in the United States, and several million vehicles worldwide, but it is still used primarily for space heating and as a chemical feedstock. LPG vehicles have had a somewhat lower life-cycle cost than gasoline or diesel vehicles, so they have been attractive for fleet operations where supplies are adequate. The emissions benefits of LPG are significant, but less than those of CNG, and LPG does nothing to ease dependence on unstable foreign sources. In short, LPG compares unfavorably to CNG and will likely remain only a niche fuel.

Ethanol (ethyl alcohol): Made by fermenting various plant materials, this is the same alcohol found in alcoholic beverages. By far the largest experiment with ethanol has been in Brazil, where over a million vehicles run on ethanol produced by a highly subsidized domestic sugar industry. The experiment has been largely unsuccessful and is being reconsidered. The primary problems are the high costs and the troublesome increase in formaldehyde emissions. Overall emissions from ethanol are only slightly less than from gasoline.

In the United States, ethanol as a fuel is limited almost exclusively to gasohol, made affordable through subsidies of about 6 cents per gallon. This may seem small, but gasohol is only 10% ethanol, so the subsidy for the ethanol itself works out to about

90 cents per gallon of gasoline-equivalent. (A similar subsidy for EVs would mean free electricity!)

In 1988, 95% of the ethanol produced in the United States came from corn, using 5% of the domestic corn crop. Making ethanol from corn is expensive and provides little to no reduction in greenhouse-gas emissions. However, in the future it may be cost-effective to produce ethanol from woody lignocellulose and herbaceous crops (such as trees, shrubs, and grasses) and from waste biomass, so ethanol has the potential to be a renewable fuel with zero net greenhouse-gas emissions. *EV entrepreneur Jim Tervort (Sebring, Fla.) adds: Let's give the farmer a break and promote E-85. It will also assist our grain surplus problem and give at least 25-percent better mileage per gallon than M-85.*

Hythane: This is a newly emerging variation on CNG (methane). Natural gas is mixed with 5 to 7 percent hydrogen, with the potential to yield significant emissions benefits over pure methane. At present, the costs and relative safety are not well defined, but hythane could substantially improve the outlook for CNG.

Hydrogen: Although it can be burned relatively cleanly in an internal combustion engine, hydrogen is put to much better use in fuel cells to power EVs. Fuel cells[1] are much more efficient and have effectively no emissions. Hydrogen can be produced from water by electrolysis, thus it is possible to convert any source of electricity -- in particular the clean and renewable ones -- into hydrogen fuel. The hydrogen fuel cell could therefore one day act as a type of battery. The advantages are that hydrogen has a very high energy density so that rapid refueling is possible. For now hydrogen remains too expensive to produce and presents storage difficulties. When stored in pure form (gas or liquid) it is extremely volatile and can be explosive. It can be stored safely in metal hydrides, but the resulting weight increase reduces much of its advantage. A newly developing storage method using highly porous carbon granules is a promising compromise, but much work remains. Although many feel it will not be widely used as a vehicle fuel for more than twenty years, hydrogen is definitely one to watch.

Food: That's right, food for eating. Food to power the body that walks or rides a bike. No discussion of alternative fuels would be complete without at least mentioning human power -- the most overlooked, but the simplest of all the alternatives. The energy efficiencies are not the greatest, the range is limited and it takes a while to refuel, but human power has the lowest emissions by far, does not depend on foreign sources, is clearly the quietest, and with proper infrastructure (such as protected bike routes) it is the safest. It is the only alternative that can actually improve your health -- as long as the smog isn't too heavy.

Perhaps the most important thing to do when comparing the alternatives is to note the sources of your information. Vehicle fuels are a multi-billion dollar market and strong biases abound. Moreover, the issues are extremely complex and it is possible to support practically any position using the variety of data available. We have made every effort to compare the alternatives in an evenhanded manner, and our bias is clear: we are impatient for cleaner air and reduced dependence on foreign oil.

In conclusion let us note that, although EVs do not get straight "A"s, they are far above average in many respects and getting better every year. Moreover, we are unlikely to see significant improvements in the production or supply of any combustible fuel: they will just continue to increase in cost. Even hydrogen will be put to best use in fuel-cells to power EVs. Although EVs are not yet all cars to all people, when we consider electricity itself as a fuel it is a clear winner because it is so flexible. By choosing electricity we are, in a sense, not forced to choose at all.

---

[1] See Chapter 15 for more on fuel cells.

Table 16.1: Alternative Fuels Report Card

Characteristic of fuel	Gaso-line	RFG	M85	CNG	EV	X
Overall emissions	D-	D+	C	B	**A**	10
Toxic emissions[d]	D	C	B-	**A**	**A**	7
Emissions variability[e]	D	D	D-	B-	**A**	7
Global warming	D	D	D	C-	B-	8
Other environmental risks	C-	C-	C-	B	**A**	8
Helps with existing vehicles	F	**A**	F	F	F	7
Domestic supply	D-	D-	D+	**A**[a]	**A**	10
Finite resource[b]	F	F	C	C	**A**	9
Life-cycle costs, today	B	B-	B-	**A-**	B+	6
Life-cycle costs, future	D	D	C	C+	**A**	7
Fuel price stability	F	F	C-	B+	**A+**	8
Refueling and range	**A**	**A**	B	B-	D	6
Cargo area/payload capacity	**A**	**A**	B+	B	C[f]	6
Fuel distribution & availability	**A**	B+	B-	C+	**A+**	9
Vehicle performance	**A**	**A**	**A**	**A**	B[f]	6
Cold starting	B-	B	C+	**A-**	**A+**	4
Fuel toxicity	C	C	D	**A**	**A**	2
Fuel corrosiveness	B-	B-	D-	**A**	**A**	2
Noxious fumes	C	C	C+	B	**A+**	5
Noise	C	C	C	B-	**A+**	1
Overall safety of the fuel	B-	B-	B-	B	**A-**	7
Future outlook, to 2000	C	B	B+	**A-**	B+	8
Future outlook, beyond 2000	F	D	C	B	**A**	8
Grade Point Average	C-	C	C	B	B+	151[c]

[a] Canada and Mexico are included. [b] Assumes methanol is made from finite sources, not biomass (a sustainable source of energy). X = the weighted rating (1 to 10) that indicates the importance of the characteristic. [c] This is the total of the weighted factors. [d] Includes benzene, 1,3-butadiene, formaldehyde and acetaldehyde. [e] This is a reflection of how the emissions vary with vehicle use, age and maintenance. [f] This grade would be lower for applications that require quick refueling and long distance driving. The weighting factors in the extreme right column of this table do not reflect any specific vehicle. The weighting for characteristics like range and cargo capacity would be lower for a commuter vehicle and would be higher if the fuel was needed to power a large vehicle for a family.

Relative Emissions
Comparisons With Gasoline

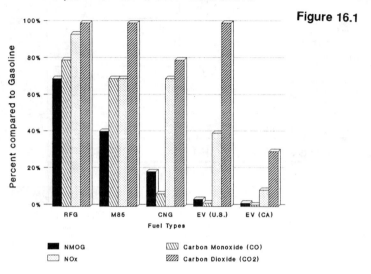

Figure 16.1

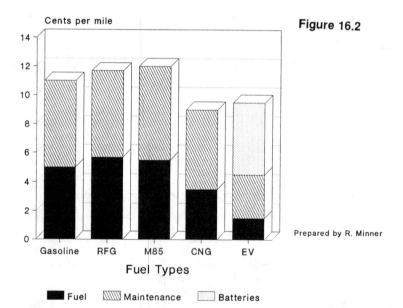

Figure 16.2

Prepared by R. Minner

Notes: emissions per passenger-mile are more important. Ride sharing, car pooling and mass transit can reduce emissions far more than any of these alternative fuels. Of course, ride sharing in a lower-emissions vehicle is all the better still. Methanol: low value of CO_2 emissions compared to gasoline is for when made from natural gas (97%); high when from coal (198%). Electricity: low figures are for the California mix of electrical generation; high are for the U.S. average mix. Cost of electricity: assumes off-peak discount, which is becoming widespread.

See the remarks by Ken Williams, transportation manager for Peoples Gas Systems, on page 131.

17

Things to Do

What can one person do? What does it matter? With over 150 million cars on the road, what difference does one electric car make?

"Nobody made a greater mistake than he who did nothing because he could only do a little." Edmund Burke, 1750-1814 (*quoted in 50 Simple Things You Can Do to Save The Earth, Earthworks Group, Berkeley, Calif. 1989, another book you might want to read for ideas on "what one person can do."*)

"Everyone has their own coefficient of wanting to matter. I tend, as I get older, to want to matter a lot. I want the fact that I existed to matter." *Harry Chapin (the song writer and performer who died in a car accident in 1981)*

Use whatever motivates you to make a difference. If all else fails, try patriotism: history buffs will recall that two people rode to alert the Minutemen in April 1775. The lyrics from this 1960s ballad, "The Ride of Paul Revere," can inspire us to move away from dependence on petroleum.

The Ride of Paul Revere
In '75 upon an April night,
The air was chilly and the moon shone bright.
He floated past the man 'o war,
Landed on the Charleston shore,
Where the finest steed was ready for
The ride of Paul Revere

Ride, ride, though the night be cold,
Ride, ride, till the truth be told,
Ride, ride like that man of old.
Ride like Paul Revere!

I wonder if 200 years ahead
If we will ride or if we'll stay in bed?
If faith and freedom within us die
And then we hear the midnight cry
And the hoofbeats cross the moonlit sky,
Will we ride with Paul Revere?

(Permission to reprint requested from Pace Communications, Los Angeles)

This book is just one more "midnight cry." You hear dozens of them every year on the radio, see hundreds of headlines and TV news reports that remind you of our dependence on imported oil. While this book is written from a North American perspective, the same urgency exists in other countries where dependence on imported petroleum products undercuts national budgets and the financial capacity to invest in needed improvements in many countries. If he were alive today, Paul Revere would be riding the streets to warn us about the pollutants that we inflict on each other daily.

Here are a few suggestions, grouped into three categories: **Learn, Persuade, Do** — how individuals can make a difference and reduce our economy's dependence on imported oil while improving the well-being of the planet and its passengers. In short, here's how to become an environmental and balance-of-trade patriot.

Learn:

1. Join an electric car group

See the list under "EV Organizations" in **EV Resources**. Or start your own chapter of the Electric Auto Association (EAA). Contact EAA headquarters at 415-591-6698 or 1-800-537-2882.

2. Attend annual electric car events

The Electric Car Calendar

April: • Solar Electric Racing Association (SERA), Phoenix, Arizona
• SunDay Rally, Florida Solar Energy Center, Cape Canaveral 407-783-0300
• Texas Land Commission, Annual Alternative Vehicle Fuels Market Fair and Symposium, Austin, Texas, 1-800-6-FUEL-99.

May: • American Tour de Sol (Albany, N.Y. to Massachusetts) Northeast Sustainable Energy Association (NESEA)
• Lightwheels, New York, N.Y. 212-431-0600
• Auto-Free New York/Transportation Alternatives, 212-941-4600
• Canadien Coupe Solaire, Montréal, Canada
3575 Blvd. St. Laurent, Montréal, P.Q. H2X 2T7 514-982-0492

Aug: • Clean Air Revival, San Francisco
Electrathon racing and demonstration of electric vehicles
(regional trials around the U.S. Call 415-495-0494 for updates)
• Solar Energy Expo and Rally (SEER), 239 South Main St. 707-459-1256
Willits, Calif. 95490: *The Solar Energy Capital of the World*

Sept: • EAA's annual rally in San Francisco Bay Area

Oct: • NESEA's Fall conference, Boston, Mass.
• EVAOSC's annual rally in the Los Angeles area
• Laguna Seca Solar Electric Auto Race, Box 3232, Monterey, CA 93942
408-375-1685

3. Subscribe to an EV magazine.

For the latest information (new companies, new car models), invest in a good periodical. See the listing in *EV Resources* at the end of the book.

4. Buy books on EVs

Bob Beaumont's Book: The controversial entrepreneur who gave 2,200 people the joy of battery-powered commuting is back with the full, no-holds-barred story about the Citicar. Some have called it "the car that set the EV industry back ten years"; others admire Beaumont's team for its tenacity and for offering the public an alternative to gasoline. Get the behind-the-scenes details:

how one man built the first major electric car company since the 1920s
how his company became the fifth largest manufacturer of automobiles in the U.S.
how a workable electric car is built from the ground up
how a single article in a consumer magazine contributed to the company's demise
how hundreds of Citicar owners outlasted the critics and are still driving their cars today with excellent safety records

Proceeds from the book will help fund pre-production costs of a new electric car called the Renaissance. For information, write to: Bob Beaumont, Columbia Auto Sales, 9720 Owen Brown Road, Columbia, MD 21045, or call 301-799-3550, 301-799-5724 (fax). Beaumont continues to develop EVs: his key group of colleagues is in place and awaiting funding, ready to begin production of an appropriately sized EV.

Michael Hackleman's series: *Better Use of Utility Supplied Electricity; Electric Vehicles: Design and Build Your Own; Transportation Sources and References; EV*

Engineering Guidebook; and At Home With Alternative Energy. Mike has also compiled a video series called **Hand Made Vehicles**. Available from Earthmind, P.O. Box 743, Mariposa, CA 95338, or call 310-396-1527.

For an unusual, do-it-yourself, off-road three-wheeled EV construction project, inquire about *Solar Wind,* by K. W. Krutz, 2387 West Oakland, Hemet, CA 92545 ($10 postpaid). This one will turn heads!

Coming in December 1993: *The EV Encyclopedia: A Guide to Electric Vehicles* with extensive articles on fascinating topics. Results from the survey conducted by SFEAA, a full analysis of John Hoke's 71,000 logged miles, photos and anecdotes about other long-distance record holders, detailed descriptions of all sorts of EV trivia.

5. Learn about alternatives to gasoline and diesel

In a world without plentiful petroleum, liquid fuels can be extracted from wood wastes. Researchers at the National Renewable Energy Laboratory in Golden, Colorado are using a high-solids (35%) anaerobic digester to produce natural gas from garbage. Driving cars powered by renewable fuel sources will help your country to move away from dependence on imported oil.

For a book on ethanol (a reliable fuel that EV-hybrid designers and users might consider), write to Bill Kovarik, Communications Dept., Radford University, Radford, Va. 24142.

For information about methanol, contact the California Energy Commission, Publications Office, 1516 Ninth Street, MS-13, Sacramento, CA 94244-2950. They are conducting tests with more than 2,000 flexible-fuel vehicles; over 100 service stations in California are equipped to dispense methanol. > > > see page 67 < < <

6. Learn about Demand Management

Some utilities in the U.S. have taken an aggressive approach to promoting conservation and electric load-shifting. Most providers of electricity face two peaks in demand, following the routine of everyday life. In the morning, people turn on the toaster, take a shower, turn on a heater, and increase their demand for electricity. That level increases as businesses open for the day and air conditioning and motors turn on. In the evening, the oven turns on, the refrigerator is repeatedly opened and closed (increasing the need for cooling) and various appliances are put in use.

The peak in the morning occurs between 7 and 9 a.m. and remains level until the second peak arrives. Air conditioning loads in the summer force the afternoon peak load to take place between 2 and 5 p.m. Winter heating shifts the afternoon peak to between 5 and 8 p.m. (as the day cools off, the demand for heating a cool house creates the peak).

In Denver and other innovative utility service areas, utilities offer a smart box to keep a household's electric demand below a specified maximum. As the household or commercial establishment demands more electricity, the "smart box" monitors the total kilowatts being used at any moment. When the demand for power approaches a pre-determined maximum, the smart box shuts off major appliances or pieces of equipment in the work place, rotating the shut-off period according to a program worked out in advance.

This "rotating internal black out" allows the homeowner and commercial establishment to keep demand for electricity below a certain maximum level. Public Service Company, the utility in Denver, charges for kilowatt-hours at a lower rate if you agree to keep your power demand (KW) within a low maximum level. The monthly bill displays your maximum demand (averaged over 15-minute intervals).

This explanation of demand management is given here to stress the following point: **It's possible to charge your electric car any time during the day and still pay a lower rate for the electricity consumed.** If you charge your car at your place of work (which is equipped with this load-stripping device), you can still qualify for a lower cost per kilowatt-hour.

Persuade:
7. Help shape public opinion
Surveys indicate a reluctance in the general population to adopt a new type of car or to pay the hidden costs of petroleum dependency. Any change that involves some restriction on our mobility is looked on negatively, despite the obvious benefits to the environment and future generations. An opinion poll conducted by Cambridge Energy Research Associates (CERA) and Opinion Dynamics Corporation in January 1990 found that **64 percent of Americans oppose an extra tax of 50 cents per gallon on gasoline.** That's generally regarded as the minimum price increase needed to make a significant impact on gasoline consumption.

In other countries that import petroleum, drivers pay at least $2.50 per gallon, or at least one dollar more than the U.S. driver. Yet nearly two-thirds of the U.S. population is telling their representatives in Congress, "Don't raise our gasoline taxes." Eighty percent of the people polled identified themselves as environmentalists, but they are also saying, "We don't care about the environment enough to raise our gasoline price to half of what drivers in Japan pay."

Sixty-four percent of the 1,250 people in the CERA survey also said they would accept a refinery in their community if it reduced dependence on foreign oil. This is not an opinion poll, this is an addiction talking through these people! You can see the difficult work that faces the EV advocate who hopes to turn public opinion toward a more sustainable future. Here's how you can help turn the tide:

a) Display a bumper sticker: My Next Car Will Be Electric, The Future Is Electric, My Other Car Is Electric, as well as:

This Car Is Solar Powered

A solar advocate's job pays for the gasoline

(suggested by Dick Piekarski, member of the American Solar Energy Society)

Electric Cars Today, No Smog Tomorrow

(available through Solar Electric, Santa Rosa, Calif.)

I Am Polluting The Atmosphere

(it certainly takes a sense of humor to display this one)

Don't Drive Yourself To Extinction *(Lightwheels, 212-431-0600)*

Where to obtain these bumper stickers: see **EV Resources**.

b) Write letters to the editor. It has been estimated that fewer than three people in 100 regularly write letters to publications. To increase your chance for publishing, relate your opinion to a story that has appeared in the newspaper.

c) Participate in public opinion polls on electric cars For instance, call General Motors' line: 1-800-25-ELECTRIC. If you'd like to participate in a number of surveys, write to the Florida Electric Auto Association and we'll send you several (P.O. Box 156, Titusville, FL 32781).

The Texas General Land Commission has an alternative fuel number, which offers information primarily on natural gas, propane and battery-powered vehicles. The annual alternative fuels fair and symposium, hosted by the Land Commission, takes place in April: 1-800-6-FUEL-99. Ford's toll-free number is 1-800-ALT-FUEL.

d) Tell the big auto makers you want an EV now! Why not write to the Big Three and ask when you can purchase an electric or flexible-fuel vehicle? *General Motors,* Public Relations, Attn: Toni Simonetti, 30200 Mound Road, Box 9010, Warren MI 48090-9010 Tel. 313-986-5717. *Chrysler,* Customer Relations, 12000 Chrysler Drive, Highland Park, MI 48288 Tel. 313-956-5346. *Ford Motor Corp.,* Customer Relations, The American Road, Dearborn MI 48121 Tel. 313-322-3000

e) Tell everyone about EVs and the coming post-petroleum era! Buy or copy a video, get a stack of EV brochures (the Florida Electric Auto Association sells 100 for $10) and spread the word. Photocopy newspaper and magazine articles and share them with friends. Share your enthusiasm for the exciting time, the challenges and choices that we face in the next thirty to fifty years as we seek to depend less on imported oil.

If you aren't excited about being alive today, when you have an opportunity to be an environmental patriot, then send a stamped, self-addressed envelope to the Florida EAA, Attention: "It's Exciting!", Box 156, Titusville, FL 32781. Include an extra stamp to cover photocopying costs.

8. Ask your local institutions to purchase EVs

a) Write to your Member of Congress. Suggest that an electric car or other alternative-fuel car be purchased for local district business. Ask your legislators about EV legislation and their positions on these issues.

b) Urge your local utility, city council and public safety officials to consider purchasing an electric car for local trips. Ask your utility's demand-side management team about using electric vehicles to boost off-peak demand. Bob Batson (Electric Vehicles of America) estimates that pay-back on investment in a community-wide program to encourage conversion to electric vehicles should be fairly rapid. "The personnel and power plant are available at night. The only variable cost is the fuel to produce the electricity. This is why many utilities offer an off-peak rate that is discounted by 70% from the peak rate. Most utilities shut down during the off-peak time, and it's in the utility's interest to encourage more people to consume electricity to help operate the electric plants more efficiently."

c) Ask your local car dealer when you can place an order for a non-gasoline car. If enough people request battery- or methanol-powered vehicles, production of these drive systems will be encouraged. Besides, dealers have been told by upper management that the cars are coming, and it would be nice for the public to show a little interest, even enthusiasm, for the efforts made to offer alternatives to petroleum-powered vehicles.

d) Encourage fleets in your area to convert existing vehicles to electric and other alternative fuels. For sources of information, see page 67.

Do:

9. Help build the EV Support System

Let's imagine that you are riding around in your first EV. You've followed the directions given in other chapters (you've become an expert at reading a hydrometer), but you notice that it's time for a mechanic to check your brakes. You've also watched the batteries grow weaker over time -- you have been keeping the battery surfaces clean, washing them once a week, but you suspect there's a short or a drain somewhere in the system.

What do you do? Look up "Automobile, Electric -- Dealers" or "Vehicles, Electric -- Repair" in the telephone directory? Believe it or not, by 1993, newspapers in certain areas of North America will carry such listings in their classified ad sections. Why? Because several innovative colleges will have trained dozens of EV mechanics by then and they'll be advertising their services.

Not everyone who prints up five hundred business cards reading "EV Repairs and Maintenance" is certified to be offering that service. You should look for someone who has attended a hands-on EV mechanics course of training or who has earned a certificate from a college or vocational-technology (vo-tech) school.

EV News carries the latest on EVs: $30/year, 1911 N. Ft. Myer Drive, #703, Arlington, VA 22209

a) Earn an EV Repair and Maintenance Degree
The following schools offer courses in EV Mechanics:

Pasadena City College
Pasadena, Calif.

Jordan Energy Institute
155 Seven Mile Road
Comstock Park, MI 49321
616-784-7595

Humboldt College
Campus Center for Appropriate
Technology, California State
University, Buck House #97
Arcata, CA 95521, 707-826-3551

York Technical College
452 South Anderson Road
Rock Hill, SC 29730
Dr. Ed Duffy 803-327-8000
With 17 EVs assigned to its maintenance facilities, York is the leading
center for EV training in North America. Its Electric Vehicle Program is
integrated in York's Transportation
and Engineering Technology programs, and students learn hands-on
how to maintain an EV fleet. York is
a U.S. Department of Energy site
operator and has a cooperative relationship with Duke Power, an innovative utility. York has developed an EV
training program which can be repli-
cated through partnerships with other
technical colleges. York seeks to
work with industry to fill the need for
providing continuing education of
automotive mechanics.

Mike Brown is training mechanics
through his **Pro-Mech** Program:
Electro-Automotive
P.O. Box 1113
Felton, CA 95018
408-429-1989
This is an electric car conversion
training program for professional mechanics. The aim is to establish an
international network of trained EV
technicians who already have a professional automotive background, a
tooled shop facility and an ongoing
business. These technicians will
receive hands-on training, wholesale
parts supply, sales referrals and technical support from Mike Brown. Courses offered in Santa Cruz, Calif., or
on-site by arrangement.

Through a university in New Mexico,
Jack Hedger is training an adult education class how to build a battery
charger and how to convert a gasoline-powered car to electric:
Dr. Jack Hedger
P.O. Drawer 1077
Deming, NM 88031
505-546-0288
Designer of a solar-powered battery
charger; holds a patent on a solar
tracking apparatus.
*Also available: manufacturers of
electric vehicles, such as Conceptor
Industries (converters of the G-Van),
often arrange training sessions for
their customers. Request details from
individual companies.*

To California Assemblyman Sam Farr
In Appreciation Of His Efforts
To Encourage Clean Electric Vehicles

0000001   1,000

STOCK CERTIFICATE

ONE THOUSAND SHARES OF STOCK IN

THE FUTURE

NEGOTIABLE IN CLEAN AIR

ELECTRO AUTOMOTIVE
INFORMATION SERVICES LP
POST OFFICE BOX 1113
FELTON, CA 95018-1113
(408) 429-1989

Conversion Kits,
Components, Books,
Videos, & Training

In December 1991, California
Assemblyman Sam Farr received this
"stock certificate" from Electro
Automotive of Felton, Calif., "in
appreciation of his efforts to encourage
clean electric vehicles." You, too, can
invest in The Future by converting a car
to battery power (for $7,000 in parts
and $3,000 in labor).

Alternative Fuels Universities

The engineering departments of the universities listed below have entered vehicles in at least one alternative fuel vehicle competition (solar, natural gas, methanol):

Alabama
Arizona State
Auburn
British Columbia
Cal Poly (San Luis Obispo)
Cal Poly (Pomona)
Cal State (Los Angeles)
Cal State (Northridge)
Clarkson University
Concordia
Colorado State
Crowder College
Dartmouth
Drexel
Ecole Poly
F.I.T.
GMI Institute
I.I.T.
Iowa State
M.I.T.
Mankato State University

University of Maryland
Michigan State
Western Michigan
University of Michigan
Michigan Tech
N.Y.I.T.
Nebraska
Northwestern
Ohio
Oklahoma
Old Dominion
Ottawa
Penn State
University of Pennsylvania
University of Puerto Rico
R.I.T.
Rose-Hulman Institute of Technology
San Jose
Stanford

Stark Technical College
Tennessee
Texas (Arlington)
Texas (Austin)
University of North Texas
Texas Tech
Toronto
Villanova
University of Virginia
Virginia Tech
Western Washington University
Washington U.
University of Waterloo
West Virginia
Wichita State
Worchester Poly

If you are interested in studying a fuel of the future, these universities have professors who have demonstrated their commitment to a post-petroleum world.

If you know someone who is looking for a career, why not write to several of these universities and ask for course catalogs?

b) Organize an electrathon event. Another source of EV experts will grow out of the work of Steve Van Ronk and his Clean Air Revival network. He's coordinating EV-building projects in over 20 schools in the Bay Area. His particular interest is the Electrathon, a three-wheeled vehicle that has been given its own class by the Sports Car Club of America (SCCA). The materials cost less than $1,500, making it an affordable project for most schools.

Clark Beasley introduced electrathon racing to North America. For more information, write to: 23725 Oakheath Place, Harbor City, CA 90170, 213-539-9223.

Exposing high school students to a challenging project like building an EV is hardly a new idea. R.H. Patterson of Pembroke, Ontario taught his students (ages 15 to 17 years) to build nearly a dozen EVs during his 27 years as an instructor of electrical technology.

In the San Francisco Bay area, Steve Van Ronk is breaking new ground by coordinating the EV programs in local schools and by sponsoring electrathon rallies. Centering the students' attention on a competition with an affordable vehicle is new, and his efforts should bear fruit rapidly. Anyone interested in starting their own electrathon club should contact Steve (415-495-0494).

c) Sponsor a student at the Sebring Auto-Cycle Institute. A third way to develop a pool of EV experts will involve learning the craft "the old-fashioned way": through apprenticeships (often referred to as "internships"). Sebring Auto-Cycle, located an hour south of Disney World offers internships to "people who are committed to social change, who want to donate their time and learn a skill under an unpaid apprenticeship," says company president Jim Tervort. "It would be a big help to small companies, not just Sebring Auto-Cycle, to have students invest in the future and help put affordable EVs on the road."

10. Buy or build an electric car

There's a need for people who want to be EV owners. They are the pioneers, the front line in the battle to reduce dependence on imported oil, today's Minutemen. The spirit of Paul Revere is running through the streets of our cities, past gasoline pumps and across the headlines of the business section, shouting, "Use gasoline efficiently! Switch to alternative fuels!"

Regarding California's goal of requiring two percent of auto sales in 1998 to be zero-emissions vehicles: Editor Richard Minner suggests, "Wouldn't it be remarkable if nobody had to count? This might be dreaming, but what if the electric car market is flooded with so many orders for conversions that it becomes *obvious* that the CARB goal is moot? What if the goal is exceeded just by public demand, not by the force of regulation?" Let's work to make this dream come true.

11. Rent an electric car

Surprise a rental car company today: say, "I want to help reduce air pollution. What kind of electric car do you rent?" Who knows? If enough people inquire, maybe some of the car rental firms in "non-attainment" areas will start offering EVs for rent. (Urban areas that exceed the federal standards for air pollution are called "non-attainment areas," since they do not attain the mandated air quality standards.)

12. Time-share an electric car

A new concept in car ownership: one person holds the title, but the monthly car loan, insurance premium and electric bill are paid on the basis of miles driven, plus a charge for hours away from the charging station (even if only a few miles were driven, a minimum hourly or daily charge will encourage drivers to use the EV for its primary mission: short trips at speeds below 45 mph). This is a way for a one-car household to obtain a tenth or a quarter of an EV and share the fixed cost of vehicle ownership with others.

A Japanese company has developed a system based on a plastic card: a magnetic strip identifies the user, who is billed for miles driven and electricity consumed. The program involves 150 subscribers, five vehicles and seven charging stations. Interested readers can inquire about the success of the venture by writing to the Japan Electric Vehicle Association, 2-5-5 Toranomon, Minato-ku, Tokyo, Japan.

13. Improve the local infrastructure

Persuade your local government to offer incentives to electric and alternative-fuel cars. George Gless and Ron Putnam of Denver Electric Vehicle Council offer these suggestions for working closely with your local utility.

a) Convert sick vehicles. When the engine in a vehicle in the fleet of your local government or local utility needs to be replaced, persuade the fleet manager to consider conversion to electric or alternative fuels. You need to make the conversion as easy as possible, so assemble a list of suppliers of EV parts and brochures from electric car organizations like EPRI and the Electric Transportation Coalition. *(Look for a special chapter in the "big book,"* **The EV Encyclopedia***: Tips for Fleet Managers.)*

b) Arrange better insurance rates for EVs. Electric cars generally travel shorter distances, so turn this into a positive feature. Insurance represents a major fixed cost of owning a car (no matter how far you drive, two miles or 15,000 miles each year, the fixed cost still has to be paid, whereas a variable cost increases with use). The cost of insurance ought to reflect the amount of risk that the driver and vehicle will encounter. If you drive less than 20 miles per day at speeds under 45 mph (a typical suburban driving environment), you are exposing the insurance company to much less risk than the person who commutes at highway speeds over 60 or 100 miles a day.

Most insurance companies charge a lower premium if the customer drives a shorter distance. This tip advocates an even lower premium for cars that have a lower top speed. If your electric car can't go faster than 45 or 55 mph, the insurance company is assured that you will not be in a 75-mph crash with a tree.

c) Obtain local incentives to encourage EV use. Cities can choose to become safe havens for electric cars. Colorado offers a $200 rebate on the purchase of items related to owning an electric car: no state sales tax on batteries, tires, wires, parts, and no license fee.

Other incentives can make electric car use less of a hassle. By improving the city's infrastructure and making it more friendly to EVs, a city can encourage more people to invest in electric cars.

Wherever there's a streetlight next to a parking space, a coin-operated electric outlet can be installed.

Allow only electric and alternative-fuel vehicles to park in special "green spaces" next to the blue handicapped parking zones.

Encourage your local utility to offer a lower rate per kilowatt-hour for outlets dedicated to charging electric car batteries.

Encourage restaurants, car-wash and gasoline service stations, offices and shopping malls to install coin-operated electric outlets.

Here's a list of other incentives, obtained from an electric car advocate in Southern California:

Federal incentives

Subsidies to support the manufacture and sale of EVs in non-attainment areas (where the air quality falls below the federal minimum clean air standards).

Expanded federal fleet purchases of electric cars.

State incentives

State income tax credits (up to $1,000 per vehicle purchased in California).

Reduce registration tax and license fees for electric cars.

No state sales tax on electric cars.

Local incentives

Special consideration for EVs in all major building and zoning approvals.

Lower electricity rates for meters dedicated to charging electric car batteries.

Permit stationary sources of pollution to be offset by replacing mobile sources of pollution with EVs.

Ban internal combustion engines from urban areas (Milan, Italy is experimenting with ICE-free weekends).

Let's work to get our federal, state and local governments to offer these and other incentives. *California residents, take note!* The California tax code grants a tax credit of 55 *percent of the costs (including installation charges) of a device designed and installed to convert a motor vehicle, which is intended to be used on the public roads ... to a low-emission motor vehicle. The credit allowed shall not exceed $1,000 per automobile or $3,500 for a commercial vehicle.* California Senate Bill 2600, adopted in September 1990. (Author, Senator Vuich; co-author, Senator Leonard). For more information, see Chapter 19.

14. Get to the kids

If you own an electric or flexible-fuel vehicle, or you know someone who owns a car powered with a non-conventional fuel, arrange time to show the vehicle by visiting a school at least once a month. Teachers are looking for opportunities to make math and science more interesting, and you will be helping to show future drivers that there is hope, there are alternatives to importing oil. Dare to be a role model for the post-petroleum era. Explain how cars don't have to go from 0 to 60 mph in less than 8 seconds to be practical. Show kids how to save 10, 20, even 50 percent on their family's transportation fuel bill (if batteries are cared for properly), and how practical an electric car can be as the second car in a multi-car household.

Schools are often defined as "the future sitting inside four walls." Want to make a difference? Persuade your employer to let you work an extra half-hour on four days, then take 2 hours off to volunteer in a local school. Two hours a week can change the world (of future car buyers). Let's share our message of "use less oil" to build an eco-army of environmental patriots.

Bruce Severance has produced a video called *The Race to Save Our Earth*, available from Speed of Light, Solar Energy Education, Box 485, Altadena, CA 91001. Solar racer kits allow kids to experience the power of photovoltaics first-hand.

Students find EVs fascinating. This van was converted by teenagers in Canada.

15. Save gasoline.

a) **Drive slower!** The U.S. Department of Energy has sponsored a campaign called "Do Your Part, Drive Smart." One poster suggests, "if you slowed down to read this, you saved gasoline." This is related to a study performed in 1984 on 16 car models. The study determined that virtually every car is most efficient within the range of 35 to 45 mph. If you want to get the most miles out of every gallon of gasoline that we are importing, then leave a little earlier and drive 45 mph. Instead of racing across country or to Disney World at 65 or 75 mph, cut back to 55 or 50 mph and you'll still "save gasoline and the planet."

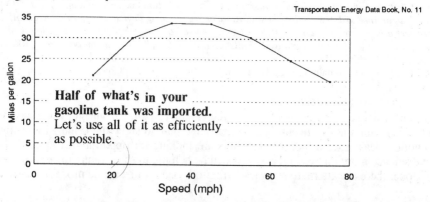

Transportation Energy Data Book, No. 11

Half of what's in your gasoline tank was imported. Let's use all of it as efficiently as possible.

Ask yourself: is it worth reducing the world's petroleum reserves by an additional gallon just to save ten minutes? If you are driving an ambulance or racing to work when your alarm clock broke, sure, it's worth the extra gallon or two. But let's look for opportunities to save gasoline. As the quote in italics on the acknowledgements page (at the front of this book) points out, the seventh generation will thank you! And slower driving speeds should prove safer for you, too.

b) Read a book on how to reduce gasoline consumption. Robert Sikorsky's book is an excellent resource for ideas on how to reduce pollution while making every gallon stretch farther. Look for **Car Tips For Clean Air: How to Drive and Maintain Your Car to Cut Pollution and Save Money.** Sikorsky also wrote **How to Get More Miles per Gallon.** Both are "required reading" for anyone who wants a simple, 1-2-3 guide to being a "greener" auto owner. It's even printed on recycled paper. Perigee Book, Putnam Publishing, New York (1991), 111 pages. As Sikorsky observes, "You hold the keys to clean air."

c) Pay for parking at work. The Association for Commuter Transportation (ACT) points to these facts:

- Nine out of 10 U.S. commuters who drive to work park free.
- When employers charge a market rate for parking, one out of five employees joins a car pool or takes mass transit.

Employer-subsidized parking increases traffic congestion and works against tax dollars invested in subsidies for mass transit. Why not persuade your boss to charge for parking? The collected fees could be used to subsidize van pools and car pools. For more information: ACT, Suite 200, 808 17th Street, N.W., Washington, D.C. 20006, 202-223-9669. If you're interested in other fuel-saving ideas, write for the guidelines presented in *Transportation Control Measures*, a document available from U.S. Environmental Protection Agency, Motor Vehicle Emissions Laboratory, 2565 Plymouth Road, Ann Arbor, MI 48105.

d) Ride a less energy-intensive form of transportation. Ride a bicycle instead of driving a car. Take a bus instead of a car. For trips less than 500 miles, take a train instead of an airplane.

16. Encourage battery recycling.

In 1991, several members of the U.S. Congress filed bills dealing with the improper disposal of lead-acid batteries. If you're concerned about the issue, write to Rep. Esteban Torres, 1740 Longworth, U.S. House of Representatives, Washington, D.C., 20515 or call for an update at 202-225-5256.

17. Turn off the air conditioner.

Well, we got your attention. Most of us are not as committed as environmental patriot Jim Treacy. He's the EV owner who told millions of TV viewers, "Frankly, if it's a choice between going to war with Iraq and not having air conditioning, I think a lot of people would choose to not have air conditioning" (ABC's *PrimeTime Live*, September 6, 1990).

If you use an air conditioner, take some advice from a clean-air expert. Michael Lorion of AirMax makes a living by removing thick mats of fungus from the sides of air conditioning ducts in buildings. Save energy by cleaning the evaporator coils in your car's air conditioning system. Keeping the coils clean of mold and fungus will also improve the smell of the air passing into the car. For more information, call 305-665-3238 or write to AirMax, 5875 S.W. 69 Street, South Miami, FL 33143.

18. Retire an older car.

Thirty-seven million cars (30 percent of the cars on the road in 1990) lack catalytic converters, since they were made before 1981 (*New York Times,* October 24, 1991, p. A20). Half of the carbon monoxide emissions comes from just under 10 percent of the cars (*Wall Street Journal,* Feb. 6, 1990, p. A6). Keeping these older cars properly tuned helps to reduce emissions, but the kindest act for future generations (and your neighbors) is to retire your pre-1981 automobile. A smaller, newer car also uses gasoline more efficiently. Of course, you could convert it to electric...

19. Save electricity.

Install a solar water heater, an energy-efficient "upside down" refrigerator (with the motor on top) or a geothermal heat pump. For more information, contact the American Council for an Energy-Efficient Economy, 1001 Connecticut Avenue, N.W., Suite 801, Washington, D.C. 20036 (202-429-8873). For the latest on heat pumps, write to the International Ground Source Heat Pump Association, 101 Industrial Building, Oklahoma State University, Stillwater, OK 74078-0532 (800-626-4747, 405-744-5175), or the Earth Energy Association (202-223-1606).

By reducing your demand for electricity, you can save electricity for someone else to use in their EV — so that no new greenhouse gases are generated even if a coal-burning plant is used to make the electricity.

20. Become an EV Book Contributor!

Have you seen an electric vehicle in your town? If you send us a description and the story behind the vehicle, we'll include it in future editions of the big book, *The EV Encyclopedia,* and you'll be acknowledged as a contributor. Send information about who owns the vehicle, plus a contact address and phone number. Black-and-white photos are preferred, but color prints with adequate contrasting colors can often provide acceptable results.

Positive and negative lead plates are stacked on a US Battery assembly line in Evans, Ga.

Part II

Own An Electric Vehicle Today

Concept drawing of the LA 301, Clean Air North America's first hybrid electric car.

Bruce Meland in a solar-powered three-wheeler. *Photo courtesy of Solarland*

18

Why You *Shouldn't* Wait For Detroit

*"What do you mean, **why wait for Detroit?!** Why would anyone even try to compete?" is probably on the minds of some readers. Who in their right mind would want to go head-to-head with the three sets of Big Three in Michigan, Germany and Japan? A small firm in Central Florida says, "There's a niche for us, too!" and has been rising like a phoenix from the remains of the company that in 1974-75 produced 2,200 battery-powered Citicars.*

Jim Tervort, President
Sebring Auto-Cycle
Sebring, Florida

Why design, build and offer an electric vehicle (EV) for sales at this time? This question has many strong answers. There is a growing number of environmentally responsible individuals, organizations and corporations who will demand pollution-free transportation. The impetus for this alternative is coming from metropolitan areas with the greatest pollution problems.

10,000 EVs in L.A.: The South Coast Air Quality Management District (SCAQMD) is mandating the replacement of 10,000 gasoline-burning cars in the Los Angeles area with electric vehicles in the near future. Other regions will be using SCAQMD's experiment to guide their pollution abatement programs. We can anticipate a solid, demand-driven need for non-polluting electric vehicles.

To assure a successful introduction, I have designed a low-cost conversion for a Dodge Colt to take you shopping, commuting, and running around on short errands. Eight 12-volt lead-acid batteries provide energy to a time-proven and reliable DC electric motor. The ZEV Colt accelerates to 52 mph while giving a range of 45 to 50 miles in city driving, depending on driving conditions.

A combination of state-of-the-art and proven technologies have been used to convert the Colt to battery power. All of the electronics and running gear have been tested in the field for many years. Dedicated personnel and experience qualifies Sebring Auto-Cycle, Inc. to offer the public a non-polluting alternative to the fossil-fueled automobile. We have been involved in the design, testing and manufacturing of more than 4,000 electric vehicles since 1973. That's why you don't have to wait for Detroit or anybody else to get into an EV.

Editor Richard Minner gives another three reasons for looking for an EV now:
Q: If the big auto makers will be selling EVs in just a few years, why not wait till then?
A: 1. There's no telling just how long "a few years" will actually be. Given the California law, it should be before 1998, but no one is promising how much sooner.

2. The faster we deploy electric cars, the faster people will learn about them and the faster demand will rise. Let's get those EVs on the road – the sooner the better.

3. Cost. Even when EVs start rolling off the big assembly lines, they will likely come with big price tags (over $15,000 with batteries). A conversion can be a much more affordable route to EV ownership.

A counter-argument to the third point: Swatch, the Swiss watchmaker, intends to produce an EV for two people, priced around $6,000. This has placed a damper on the demand for converted vehicles. Perhaps the car will be too small for the expectations of many consumers; this is a wait-and-see game.

Advocates of EV conversion point out that conversions save energy and raw materials by recycling existing cars. People who feel comfortable in an existing car model don't have to trade that comfort and familiarity when moving into an environmentally friendly EV. Although many converted EVs are less energy-efficient than "ground-up" vehicles, the comfort factor is sure to make converted EVs attractive alternatives to the economical Swatch EV.

Gail Lucas, founder of the Nevada chapter of the Electric Auto Association, drives a Sebring-Vanguard Citicar and thinks there's a place for an inexpensive "runabout" today: How about low-performance, **low-cost** electric vehicles in the interim? While we wait for the major auto manufacturers to develop high-performance EVs, we can practice driving and maintaining cheaper EVs.

Bob Batson founded the New England chapter of the Electric Auto Association and has helped to build it to be the largest chapter in the country. He adds:
1. There is no reason to wait. Many of the EV conversions have performance goals equal to or greater than the production EVs. *Note: The GM Impact is not a production model and its engineering and design may change.*
2. EV conversions are less expensive. Conversions (including labor and components) can typically be contracted for under $10,000. This is considerably below the $25,000 to $60,000 being suggested by the auto manufacturers.
3. Recycling makes sense! And what better expression of the recycling ethic than to resurrect a car that's still got some good years of driving in it?

The Morality of Electric Vehicles
Dr. Lester Embree, a professor of philosophy at Florida Atlantic University in Boca Raton, Fla., drives a Sebring-Vanguard Citicar. He plans to develop a low-cost EV equipped with appropriate technology, including an "ice-box air conditioner": a 12-volt fan blowing over frozen ice packs can reduce humidity and lower the car's interior temperature. He shares his view of appropriate technology for industrialized nations.

In the grand scheme of things, does it make much difference whether we drive a gasoline car or an electric vehicle? Not every choice we make is of moral significance. For example, it is difficult to see how the color of the socks we wear might affect any living being. Most car owners appear to believe that the type of car one drives is similarly non-moral.

The morality of an action depends not merely on *whether* living beings are affected but also on *how* they are affected. Actions increasing or preserving health are moral and those destroying or decreasing health are immoral. We can quickly conclude that driving an electric vehicle is a higher moral action than driving a gasoline-powered car, since EVs generally produce fewer pollutants and tend to promote the general well-being.

As citizens, we can conclude that it is moral to seek in various ways to support policies favoring the use of electric vehicles. This can include tax advantages for drivers, manufacturers and distributors, battery recycling plants, and charging facilities as well as the outright mandating of EV use in specific percentages and in specific places, such as downtown areas.

Price is the most serious obstacle in the minds of most people who might consider switching to battery power. Since the benefits delivered to society by the EV are not reflected in the marketplace, the initial cost of an electric car is much greater than a similar gasoline-powered car. Why pay more for a car that gives you less performance and shorter range, and requires more time to refuel?

This is where the awareness of the morality of car ownership can help us make difficult political decisions. At some point the full impact of the internal combustion engine must be felt; how soon depends on our commitment to supporting controversial moral actions, such as subsidies for EV purchases and steeper gasoline taxes to discourage gasoline consumption and to reflect the true cost of extracting products from a limited resource like petroleum.

Moral action also extends to the most minor of political activities. Our culture invests much attention in and attaches great importance to sporting events. No harm seems done by fantasies about what one would have done if one had been the coach of a football game. But too often we discuss with less fervor the bigger games played in Washington and state capitals. What error do we make when we merely talk about how the political authorities or the industrial leaders or some other "they" ought to do this or that to protect ourselves and to invest in the well-being of future generations? Since the choice of transportation is a moral matter and one can act politically by at least writing letters and ethically by driving an electric car, does inaction constitute an evasion of moral responsibility?

Who is better qualified to close this chapter than Robert Beaumont, the force behind the mass-produced Citicar (over 2,200 made between May 1974 and Decebmer 1975)? The following was extracted from a six-page **Plan For EV Production Now***.*

During the past ten years, I have sadly and silently observed a marked decline in the fortunes of the embryonic electric vehicle industry.

An improved Citicar EV right now can provide a substantial percentage of personal transportation almost anywhere in the world where there is an electric outlet. Many countries charge $4 or more for a gallon of gasoline, which at twenty miles per gallon works out at 20 cents per mile.

A marketable useful electric car could be produced and sold today for under eight thousand dollars in the U.S. Experience and direct consumer contacts tell us that this new form of transportation must be reasonably priced, able to maintain a speed of forty miles per hour, travel fifty miles or better on a single charge, carry two people and a small amount of cargo, have sufficient acceleration to move out into traffic, be somewhat safe and highly visible, give long and inexpensive service and be contemporary in appearance.

Is that such a tall order? Not at all. But the cobwebs and past judgments must be swept away and the entity which enters this market must accept what can be produced and sold and not what should be created, then marketed. Myths and proclamations from academia must be discarded and the experts who say it cannot be done must be ignored. A clean sheet of paper is absolutely necessary. There should not be much mystique about cars. A motor vehicle is simple: an engine or motor, a supply of fuel, a drive train, four wheels with tires and other readily available components. While a gasoline car may have in excess of 20,000 parts, an electric car can be manufactured with one-tenth that number. Seats are seats, glass is glass, and the rest of what goes into a motor vehicle is very simple.

The world eagerly awaits a new form of transportation because currently there is nothing between a bicycle and a $9,000 stripped gasoline car for personal transportation. At 20 miles per gallon, gasoline at $1.30 costs 6.5 cents per mile while electricity at 9 cents per kilowatt-hour is 3 cents per mile (the EV described here will get 3 miles per kilowatt-hour).

Right now, without expensive tooling and R&D or a vast amount of lead time, an entity could purchase for assembly all the batteries, motors, drive trains, controllers and other components to produce this car within a year.

Large expenditures for advertising and promotion of this new product will not be necessary. The EV fans will follow your every step and herald the approach of the electric car. You will be network news and the 25,000 car dealers who have survived the slaughter of the last decade will be anxious to add your product to their current lineup. The ease with which 10,000 EVs can be merchandised each month will astound you. Simply select one percent of the 25,000 and allot them 40 vehicles a month. They can sell them on a Saturday afternoon at full list price or better.

Servicing the vehicle presents very little training requirements. Every car dealer has an individual or two who understands the complicated wiring in a conventional car and handling the wiring of an electric vehicle is duck soup compared to the morass inherent in our electronic gasoline marvels.

Most who would be auto manufacturers think the Federal regulations are difficult to comply with. This is not so. The only area in which Citicar failed were sun visors that had connecting hardware a fraction too large, seat belts that were missing a fifty-cent retractor, and a windshield missing a ten-cent retaining clip.

A final note: It may be better psychologically to avoid calling this product an "electric car." Just the terminology engenders delusions of two-ton six-seated tanks for driving to the shopping mall. Perhaps "people mover," "urban car" or some other name is more appropriate.

One of 2,200 CitiCars, made in 1975 and still on the road. *Photo courtesy of Electric Auto Association.*

19

Finding Your Electric Car

Five Paths to Owning an EV

For sources: refer to the directory at the end of the book.

Path 1: Build your own. If you are interested in constructing your own electric car, look up "Kits" and "Consultants."

The remaining paths are for people (like the editors) who don't trust themselves with a wrench! Our motto is, "We want to *buy* a car, not build it!"

Path 2: Pay someone to convert a car you own. Mike Brown has published an excellent step-by-step book on how to convert a gasoline car to electric power. It's called *Convert It!* and it is listed in the EV Resources list (see Part III of this book). Other manuals include one offered by Bill Williams, Williams Enterprises, and several of Michael Hackleman's books will set you in the right direction.

Path 3: Buy a converted car. Called an "electric retrofit" by some, a converted electric car begins as a pre-owned vehicle. The gasoline parts are removed (engine, catalytic converter, all the things *Electric cars don't need*, listed in Chapter Six) and an electric motor is attached to the car's transmission.

Path 4: Buy a manufactured car (built from the ground up). Sometimes referred to as a car built by an OEM or an "original equipment manufacturer." The OEM obtains the EV components and then designs "from the ground up" an entirely new vehicle to hold these parts. The principal advantage of a ground-up car versus a converted car is the ability to invest exceptional engineering to handle the battery pack during a crash. However, ground-up engineering is expensive.

Path 5: Buy a manufactured converted car. The word "manufactured" is meant to suggest that the conversion is performed by a company rather than an individual. The "manufactured" conversion takes advantage of batch production and economies of scale: a one-at-a-time conversion shop employing one or two people will probably have a backlog of orders and some difficulty in obtaining discounted prices for parts; a company that has a full-time staff with division of labor allows individual employees to specialize and to create a manufacturing environment.

If you are thinking about purchasing a converted car, the president of Electric Vehicle Associates in Maynard, Mass., offers these tips:

Questions to Ask When Buying A Converted Car
By Bob Batson

The most important question to ask before buying a converted electric vehicle, is "How will I use this vehicle?" If the person tries to use an EV just like an ICE (internal combustion engine) car, he will be unhappy. If he says it is to drive to work and around town with a limited range of 30-50 miles, he is more likely to be a satisfied EV owner.

Here's a checklist to help you through your purchase:

How long has the EV supplier been in business? *Most reputable suppliers have been around for a lot longer than Earth Day 1990.*
Does the salesman own an EV? *Does s/he believe in her/his product?*
Is s/he an authorized dealer? *Call the manufacturers of the EV components and ask.*
How long will the warranty last? What does it cover?
Are spare parts available? *Ask for references.*
How do you get the car serviced?
At what speed is the range determined?
What safety features are incorporated in the design? *Ask to see the fuse or fuses.*
What is the system's voltage?
What is the vehicle's Gross Vehicle Weight Rating (GVWR)? *It should be greater than the current EV weight.*
Does the converted car have power brakes? *Heavier vehicles need the additional assistance in stopping, since they usually have more batteries on board. Larry Foster, a machinist and EV owner living in Rowland Heights, Calif., recommends converting half-ton pickup trucks, since the vehicle is already rated for carrying 1,000 pounds in addition to its passengers.*
Was the conversion neatly done, with wires in tidy looms, or does it look like the work of a mad scientist? *Sloppy, inefficient design will often cause unsatisfactory performance.*
Is there a small amount of space between batteries? *If not, they may swell with age until they cannot be removed without destroying the battery boxes.*
Is the car low-riding, or possibly low in the rear and high in the nose? *The car should maintain its original ride height. These other positions indicate unbalanced placement of batteries and suspension that has not been strengthened adequately.*
How many instruments are available? What kind? *Digital gauges are often not as informative at a quick glance as analog (needle) gauges. Panel meters are not built for the vibrations and stresses of automotive use and may lack accuracy.*
Ask for an independent assessment of the vehicle by an electric vehicle consultant. *The assessment might be obtained over the telephone if you are dealing with a reputable dealer of converted automobiles.*
Ask for calculations of approximate range at various speeds and percent grades. *Typically, 10 horsepower is required for each 2000 pounds in curb weight.*

Bob Batson adds that consumers should be aware of the relationship between voltage and current. The higher the voltage, the lower the current can be. Smaller currents mean the components are less likely to overheat. However, the higher the voltage, the more batteries are required. Typically, I recommend that vehicles that weigh less than 2,000 pounds before conversion can be 72 volts; larger cars (over 2,000 pounds) require 96 to 120 volts. Much depends also on the space available for battery storage.

Finally, people should not be fooled by the amp-hour rating on batteries. EV batteries are rated at the number of minutes that they can provide 75 amps continuously. Most can provide 105 minutes at 75 amps as a minimum. At 20 amps, this same battery has a much greater capacity, because the load is less. In most city driving, at speeds under 40 mph, the loads are much below 75 amps.

No matter which path you take, an experienced EV mechanic has these words of advice for the would-be electric car owner.

Let The Buyer Beware
By Mike Brown, author of **Convert It!**

The electric vehicle industry is experiencing another surge of interest. This means many people who have little background in EVs are suddenly buying cars and components, and many other people with equally little background are suddenly selling them.

I have a special perspective on the EV industry, since I have been in it since 1979. I watched the spurt of interest rise -- and fall -- with the last gasoline crisis. I stayed in the business through the slow years of "cheap" gas when everyone else folded their tents and moved on. I believed the time for EVs would come again and stay. Now I am watching many of the same mistakes being made again that were made last time.

Those of us in the industry have a duty to educate the buying public about possible pitfalls. Whenever someone has a bad experience with an EV or an EV business, it tarnishes us all. With that in mind, I would like to offer the following guidelines for those trying to sort through the various claims and offers of electric vehicles and components.

Get references

Never take the word of a salesperson on its own merit. Check with independent knowledgeable sources in the industry, such as electric vehicle enthusiasts' clubs or alternative energy publications. Is this person or business well-known and established within the industry? How long have they been involved with EVs? Are they reliable, ethical, and competent?

Any industry in a boom phase will attract a swarm of new "businesses." Some will be outright frauds, but may be extremely smooth and convincing. Others are honest and sincere people who simply don't have the technical or business background to deliver what they promise. Dealing with an established, reputable business will insure technical support for the components you buy.

These are some situations that should be examined carefully:

The Instant Expert: Just because assembling an EV is relatively simple, many people think no special expertise is needed to be an expert. This person may claim to have been in the EV business for ten years. On independent research, however, you will find that no one in the industry heard of him before last year. He's been "in business" for ten years -- installing car radios -- and he's had an EV or two that he bought used and tinkered with from time to time. This person knows just enough to cause serious problems.

Rip Van Winkle: He really has been in the EV industry since 1980. In fact, he's *still* in the EV industry...of ten years ago. His components are three generations behind the times, and will not give satisfactory performance. Surprisingly cheap prices are often a warning sign of this situation.

The Hobbyist: Some hobbyists are brilliant, and should be declared national treasures; others should be declared national disasters. Be sure to find out from outside sources which kind you are dealing with.

Also be aware that you may end up with a one-of-a-kind vehicle that is only fully understood by its creator, and is a mystery to anyone else. Such an orphan can be a problem if you ever need to make changes or troubleshoot a malfunction.

Magical New Components: Someone has always "just come out with" a Magic Motor, or a Better Battery, or some other Holy Grail that will give amazing range and power, weighs almost nothing, produces more power than it uses, and cures cancer. On closer inspection, you will find that these fantasy components are in the hand-built laboratory prototype stage. They also have a few little drawbacks, like enormous price tags, 400 degree F. operating temperatures, or a tendency to self-destruct. Someday some of these fairy tales *will* come true, and will benefit us all. In the meantime, it is foolish to base your vehicle on the magic of the future. Your dream coach-and-four will remain a lumpy pumpkin pulled by white mice.

In general, be realistic. An EV built with proven, current production technology can provide completely satisfactory performance for use as a local commute and errand-running car. This represents the largest percentage of American daily mileage, and is the perfect niche for the EV today. Components that are too cheap or too expensive will prove to be unsatisfactory. Take a little time to learn who is established, respected, and experienced in the industry, and you will be treated well. [This article first appeared in the *EAA News*, Feb. 1991.]

To find a reliable source for an electric vehicle and EV components, consult your nearest EV chapter or contact the Electric Vehicle Industry Association, c/o David Goldstein (secretary), 9140 Centerway Road, Gaithersburg, MD 20879, 301-231-3990.

Finding a Mechanic

After you obtain your electric car, you need to decide whether you want to perform the routine maintenance yourself. If not, hunt around for a golf-cart mechanic and ask to see the person's work. If the mechanic shows you a golf cart that is well-assembled (in other words, it could pass the appropriate questions above), then you may have found someone who can learn to perform simple and complex maintenance on your electric car.

Alternative: put your favorite auto mechanic in touch with EV suppliers who offer training programs, such as Electro Automotive (Felton, Calif.). Maintenance of an electric car is easier than routine check-ups of a gasoline-powered automobile. Any competent mechanic can quickly learn to provide adequate EV car care with a little over-the-phone coaching.

California wants you to own an EV!

Confused about how to qualify for the $1,000 tax credit offered by Sacramento? R.R. Rahders describes this history-making legislation, which could become a model for similar programs to encourage EV conversions in other states and countries.

Most environmentally concerned people are familiar with the California clean air legislation that mandates 2% of all California auto sales to be ZEVs (zero emission vehicles) by 1998 and 10% by 2003. That's the stick to motivate the major car manufacturers.

There's also a little-known carrot to go with the stick and it is, for the first time, being held out to actual commuters, taxpayers, our long-suffering drivers and their families: the $1,000 tax credit and sales tax exemption for building or buying a new or converted EV.

The operative legislation (Stats. 1990 ch. 1611; Vuich; and Stats. 1989 ch. 1006; Leonard) became law by January 1, 1991 and emerged from the California Air Resources Board (CARB), the California Energy Commission (CEC), the Bureau of Automotive Repair (BAR), the Franchise Tax Board (FTB), and the Board of Equalization with some regulations completed in October 1991. Although the legislation applies to vehicles which are low emission vehicles and can include internal combustion engine (ICE) vehicles as long as their emissions are lower than the emissions of gasoline-powered ICE vehicles, analysis of such emissions is so complex that no regulations yet exist for anything other than EVs.

As of this writing, the process for a would-be EV owner works like this:

1. The taxpayer gets two forms from either the car seller or the kit seller: the **Application Form** and the **Purchase/Installation Form**.

2. When you have your EV project planned out and ready to go, you file the **Application Form** with the CEC to reserve tax-credit monies for your project. This holds your place in line for 60 days while you build your EV (or have it built).

3. After you complete your EV, you drive in to a BAR smog referee for inspection of your **Certified Kit**, and you file the **Purchase/Installation Form** with the CEC.

4. The CEC sends you a **Tax Credit Certification Determination**, and you keep the form in case the tax people ever want to see it. You use the numbers to fill out your **FTB Form 3554**, which goes in with your tax return on April 15.

The credit must be taken during the year the vehicle is completed (**not** necessarily the year in which the kit was purchased), and cannot be carried over from one year to the next or used to create a "negative tax." The total annual amount of the fund is $750,000, and it sunsets in 1995.

This legislation encourages drivers to follow what may be, at this time, the most environmentally benign, least-cost path for private motorized transportation: the recycling of ICE cars into electrics. With potential costs of less than $10,000, with effective reuse of the 70% of a vehicle which is not ICE components, with range and speed which exceed 90% of U.S. auto use, certified conversions will work well for those drivers who cannot afford the $25,000-30,000 cost which the major car manufacturers are projecting for their new EVs. Conversions will also avoid the tons of trash generated by the completion of each new auto.

Furthermore, the installation forms require kit installers to swear that they have installed the components in accordance with the instructions approved for every kit certification. This means that drivers who buy certified conversions from their local mechanics, keeping their transportation dollars in their local communities, now have assurances that their recycled EVs will be reliable long after the cash back from the state has been recycled by their families.

Richard R. Rahders is a partner in Electro Automotive Information Services L.P. of Felton, Calif. The company produces electric vehicle training classes, videotapes, manuals and other information to complement the components and kit sales of Electro Automotive. Rahders is a graduate of Princeton University and the University of Minnesota School of Law. He commutes to work in an electric Aztec kit-car VW conversion built with certified parts. He composed the legal jargon for the first "certified pure EV Kit" label.

The Return of Bob Beaumont

The creator of the Citicar, a lightweight EV produced from May 1974 through December 1975, is back with a sporty car for the 1990s. Bob Beaumont's *Renaissance Tropica* measures 12 feet long, 6 feet wide, carries two people, and targets the golfers and sailors in the verdant flatlands of Florida.

"It's built for the marine and golf communities who don't mind a little drizzle now and then," Beaumont explains. Like a pleasure boat, the fiberglass shell has drain holes, a small locker for valuables, and no doors. Passengers sit on the rim, spin and drop into the molded seats, which are cushioned with all-weather fabrics. Adjustable pedals adapt to the driver's leg length. The open design appeals to sunseekers that frequent Florida's beaches and fairways, and the $7,500 price tag makes it one of the best deals on the market for a ground-up vehicle.

"I've got three things that I didn't have when I was building the Citicar: time, talent and funding. We've got time to engineer the components, we've got the right people doing the design work, and we have the money we need so we don't rush into production." The marketing strategy for the Renaissance differs markedly from the scatter-shot, wildfire network of dealers who sold Citicars on three continents. Instead of signing up dealers in every state, Renaissance Cars, Inc. has 20 distributors south of Jacksonville, Fla. "The first thousand cars will be sold strictly through our factory-direct dealers. We're going to encourage sales in Florida so we'll be no more than three hours from any of our customers. Our backup warranty service will be incredible. The car sells itself on convenience and design, and we don't plan to focus on the environmental angle. After all, when it comes selling cars, it's one-on-one, your car against the competition. Talking about zero emissions doesn't work if the car isn't fun to drive."

Beaumont claims that there are four "musts" for a car to succeed: it must look great, it must perform, it must have a low price, and it must be safe. Renaissance has the styling, the solid-state controller and the direct-drive system that the Citicar lacked, and provides a with a sporty ground-up design. Welcome back, Bob.

LEFT: The Renaissance line is designed by Jim Muir of Dimension V, who also created the Citicar's distinctive shape. The Tropica's sporty open design doesn't require doors, allowing for lightweight reinforced panels that give passengers added protection against side collisions. Three batteries between the front wheels form the top of a "T" shape, with the rest of the 12 batteries lined up in a "battery backbone" down the center of the car. Options include a canopy for use while driving. **RIGHT:** Jim Muir says he was inspired by the Sundancer's chassis, designed by Bob McKee in 1970 for Electric Storage Battery (ESB). This is generally recognized as the first EV with the "battery backbone," the tunnel of batteries found in modern EVs like General Motors' Impact.

20

Driving An Electric Car

One of the joys of assembling a book on what it's like to own an electric car is meeting D. Richard Neill. He isn't just another globe-trotting consultant who happens to own an EV. He operates a trading company that specializes in technology transfer to Asia and the Pacific, and was instrumental in getting several Chinese students to safety after the massacre in June 1989. One of his projects involves the development of a manufacturing facility for nickel-metal hydride batteries. Dick Neill was the manager of the EV program at the University of Hawaii's Hawaii Natural Energy Institute from 1986 to 1991. He commuted to work for over four years in a converted Ford Escort wagon. Called the "EVcort," the car has nearly 45,000 miles on its odometer and Neill can often coax three miles out of every kilowatt-hour the car consumes.

When a visitor admires Neill's EV, Dick doesn't waste a moment. "Hop in, I'll let you drive it." But first he demonstrates the art of EV driving.

Dick Neill's Tips

1. Know your car. How heavy is your car? A electric car is likely to weigh more than a conventional gasoline car, so learn the smoothest way to stop your EV. Sudden stops should be avoided to save wear-and-tear on brakes.

2. Know your route. Dick has every curve, every hill, every stop sign memorized. He knows where traffic is likely to accumulate, so he can anticipate the need to stop and when the car can coast or build up speed down a hill. *Comment by John Newell: "This sounds like a range-measuring competition. This is a dedicated person's way to conserve energy! Not essential for the average EV owner, but knowing your route will tend to save energy, no matter what kind of car you drive."*

3. Coast, coast, coast. Don't drive an electric car the way you were taught to drive a gasoline car. How do we travel from intersection to intersection in a conventional car? We accelerate to 40 mph, then brake through the last 100 feet. Dick drives his EV like a migrating bird: to conserve energy, he lets the terrain slow him down gradually, and he uses the down slope of hills to gain speed.

4. Don't hurry. The most important quality for the EV driver to cultivate is patience. Whenever possible, let faster cars pass you rather than attempting to increase speed to accommodate their driving needs. In city traffic, most cars that pass you will be caught at the next traffic light. Why rush?

5. Anticipate traffic flow. This is a corollary to number 3. Coast to a stop by anticipating a light change. If the traffic light is green three blocks away, and the DON'T WALK sign is flashing, the yellow light is probably soon to follow. Yet most of us instinctively hit the accelerator, hoping to make it through the intersection before the light changes. Dick Neill doesn't drive like that, and neither should you if you want to get the maximum miles per kilowatt-hour.

6. Don't depend on "regen" to extend your range. Don't depend on regenerative braking ("regen") to extend your range very much. Regenerative braking uses the electric motor to slow down the car, by shifting it to be a generator. The kinetic energy of the EV is then converted into electrical energy to charge the battery, rather than the thermal energy released through the brakes. The regen feature operates down to about 10 or 15 mph, depending on the gear you are using. It is estimated that the range of the EV is increased from 10 to 20 percent. More advanced designs of regen contribute to a longer effective range. You can use regen to slow the car down and save your brake pads, but regenerative brakes don't put back all of the energy that you used to accelerate the car. In other words, a conservative driver who coasts whenever possible will often use less energy than a jack-rabbiting driver with regen who accelerates quickly and uses the regenerative brakes often between traffic lights.

Bob Batson, Electric Vehicles of America, adds: While Dick Neill's tips reflect a cautious driving style, I am concerned that some readers may become wary of owning an EV. They really shouldn't worry. The major difference in driving an EV versus a gasoline-powered car is that your instruments (ammeter and voltmeter) constantly remind you of the energy being consumed. You don't get that kind of feedback from the standard fuel gauge. Therefore, when you are driving an EV, you find ways to minimize energy use by coasting and anticipating traffic flow, as recommended by Dick Neill.

Some gasoline cars have a "mile-per-gallon" meter in the car. This makes the driver more aware of ways to minimize acceleration and to utilize coasting. In reality, this "energy awareness" can be cultivated in any car we drive, no matter how it is powered. Another analogy is a sailor versus a power boater. The sailor plans his course based on wind direction; the power boater gives the wind very little consideration.

Permission to reprint obtained from the Honolulu Advertiser

Advertiser photo by T. Umeda

D. Richard Neill with the University of Hawaii's Ford EVcort. The batteries are in the floor of the wagon's rear entrance, and the electric meter is on the left inner panel.

Photo by R.S. Bloomfield

Advice culled from 80,000 miles on batteries

John Hoke has worked for the National Parks Service in Washington, D.C. since 1970, and he has earned a special distinction among EV owners in North America. He logged 71,000 miles between 1975 and 1988 in a two-passenger Sebring-Vanguard Citicar. His actual mileage with the car was over 80,000 miles, but he kept records of his commuting to and from work for 71,000 miles. A complete description and analysis of his meticulous 13-year effort will appear in *The EV Encyclopedia*.

John offers these additional suggestions:

1. Take advantage of the EV's quick acceleration. "An electric motor delivers tremendous torque when it's just getting started. If you aren't careful and if your electric motor doesn't have a governor, you can take the rear end off your car. In my Citicar, I could outleap a Jaguar up to a certain point, before the gasoline engine had built up speed." Initial acceleration of a small electric car allows you to zoom around gasoline cars that have engines four to six times larger than the 10-to-20-horsepower electric motor found in most electric cars.

Note: it is more "fuel-efficient" to use a moderate rate of acceleration. Stay in the right-hand lane and accelerate slowly. So what if other cars are passing you? You are thinking of our nation's energy situation and you are helping to reduce our dependence on imported oil.

2. Always carry literature. Your car will attract attention if it has the word "ELECTRIC" emblazoned anywhere on the car. Save yourself time by keeping brochures and cards within easy reach so when people stop you at a traffic light, you have something to give them. *Brochures can be obtained from the EV organizations listed in the EV Resources section in Part III of this book.*

3. Watch out for salt. John's car literally fell apart because its aluminum frame could not tolerate more than a decade of harsh and salty winter conditions. Despite cold temperatures, the car's batteries delivered adequate power for the EV to pass over icy hills that conventional cars couldn't climb easily. What he neglected to do was wash the underside of his car at regular intervals to retard the salt (thrown on D.C. bob roads to melt ice) from corroding the chassis. *Note: Solar Car Corp. of Melbourne, Fla., offers an anti-corrosion device for $150.*

John B. Newell, a member of the Electric Auto Association for two decades, has these additional observations, shared in October 1991:

Recently, a group of researchers from the Institute for Transportation Studies at the University of California at Davis interviewed more than 80 EV owners for 20 minutes each. The interviewers report that they now have a "most favorable opinion" about electric cars and their utility. This shows you how influential a group of EV owners can be!

As a driver of a converted 1981 Ford Escort electric car, I'd like to share with you some of my driving experiences. My car's handling is amazingly smooth, quiet, and virtually vibration-free. It works better for me than any car I have driven, and I'm a former Porsche and Oldsmobile owner. My wife expresses the same feeling. My car has a single-charge range of 60 miles. I find that some days I have driven 90 miles: opportunity charging makes this possible. Usually the charging takes place at home between errands at lunch time and occasionally at a remote destination.

My electric car will go several miles after a clear warning that my propulsion energy is running low. In addition, I have another device in my speed controller that alerts me to drive off the road and onto the shoulder if there is a malfunction. Save your money: try an EV. You will be amazed.

*Michael Hackleman, editor of **Alternative Transportation News**, shares the following observations:*

Practice coasting. Most drivers are so accustomed to the "slow down" form of compression braking in a gasoline-powered car that they fail to appreciate and benefit from the EV's coasting effect. Accelerate to a speed you want, add two miles per hour, take your foot off the accelerator, and note how long it takes before the speedometer drops to two miles per hour below the desired speed.

Record your mileage. Most electric cars are underdriven for fear of getting caught out with a dead battery pack. Keep odometer records to determine your EV's safe driving distance and reset (or note) the trip odometer each time you start on a trip. Since there is a direct relationship between speed and the rate of battery pack depletion, use a slower speed to get home, if necessary. Be safe. Use streets where lower speeds occur.

The Solectria Flash, a three-wheeled prototype
commuter/racing vehicle. Solar panels can convert enough
sunlight to electricity to power the car for several miles.
Photo courtesy of NESEA.

21

Today's Batteries

The heart of the electric car is its source of power. Like the human heart, which beats through a cycle of pumping and resting, batteries work through a cycle of discharging and charging.

Batteries are also like devoted sled dogs: when treated with respect, given rest and water, they will serve you well. If you take them too often beyond their designed limits, or if you make them go too many miles without enough "food" and water, you'll shorten their lives and reduce their capacity to work.

The readings in this chapter explain "the care and feeding" of lead-acid batteries. Other technologies are receiving greater attention and research dollars, from high-temperature sodium-sulfur batteries (used in BMW's commuter car unveiled in Frankfurt in September 1991) to the alkaline nickel-iron battery manufactured by Thomas Edison.

Most electric cars today use the lead-acid battery for three reasons: it has a proven record, an infrastructure exists to recycle the battery (from sale to trade-in to smelting to manufacture to sale), and it's affordable for most applications.

About Deep-Cycle Batteries
By Mike Brown, author of Convert It!
Traction vs. Starting Batteries

The traction batteries used to power EVs are designed differently from the starting batteries used in gas-powered cars. A starting battery is only required to deliver energy in short bursts. After that, the alternator takes over and provides the spark to keep the car running, as well as recharging the battery. If the alternator fails and the car is forced to draw power from the battery, that battery will quickly be depleted.

Most EVs use a standard automotive starting battery as an auxiliary battery to power accessories like headlights, turn signals and fans. However, the motive power is provided by a pack made up of "deep discharge" (deep-cycle) traction batteries. These are usually 6-volt batteries connected in series to yield a pack voltage of 36 to 120 volts. A golf or industrial cart may only need 36 to 48 volts. Most street-going cars need a minimum of 72 volts to be practical, and 96 volts gives a significant improvement in performance.

Traction batteries are required to deliver power continuously over a period of time. While a starting battery is rarely discharged more than a small percent, traction batteries are regularly discharged almost completely. This is called "deep cycling." While traction batteries are designed to withstand hundreds of deep discharges, starting batteries are not and will not recharge completely after 15 or so deep cycles and will fail completely after about 75 deep cycles.

Different plate design: The difference between the two types of batteries is in the design of the plates. A starting battery's active plate material is more porous to provide the necessary short bursts of power. A deep discharge or traction battery has a higher density of active material on the plates. This higher density material makes it possible for the traction battery to withstand the stresses of repeated deep cycling without loss of performance. The specially formulated grid alloy in the traction battery increases the adhesion of the active material to the grid, which protects the battery from vibration damage.

Charging: While starting batteries are ready to go when you buy them, traction batteries need a "breaking in" period. They will come to you with about 95 percent of the full charge. Only after the first dozen deep cycles will they attain full charge. Fully discharged batteries will take about 12 hours to recharge.

It is best to use a charger with an automatic shut-off feature. Overcharging will cause batteries to bubble and release hydrogen gas, which shortens the life of the batteries. In case any hydrogen is produced during charging, the charging area should be well-ventilated.

New batteries recharge more quickly than old batteries. For this reason, it is best to replace all the batteries in the pack at the same time, rather than replacing only the worst ones. When old and new batteries are connected and charged together, the new batteries will charge faster than the old ones, and will begin to bubble before the old batteries have finished charging.

Batteries will also lose their charge if they are left unused for too long. For best longevity, they should be cycled, or at least charged, about once a week.

Temperature: Batteries have an optimum temperature range for operating and discharging. The chemical reactions involved seem to occur most efficiently at about 110 degrees F. For this reason, it is a good idea to build a battery enclosure with insulation, or even a heater, especially in colder climates. Ensure that the enclosure is properly ventilated to prevent accumulation of hydrogen gas.

Advice from Michael Brown from his video, Electric Vehicle
Components Primer (available for $35 postpaid)

There are three types of battery terminals: the L-terminal (connecting them with 1/16-inch-thick, one-inch-wide copper straps gives one square inch of contact surface); the regular automotive-post terminal (a slightly tapered round post with good contact area, but making up the cables can get pricey, and automotive posts are often prone to corrosion); and the universal terminal, which has a threaded steel section embedded in the lead post. Avoid universal terminals, even though most golf-cart batteries are made with this style of terminal. It has a half-inch diameter surface to contact your lug against. When you tighten the lug down, the lead tends to "flow" at room temperature under a certain amount of pressure, and the hard steel section will pull out of the soft lead and become loose. Any time you get a loose battery connection, you get resistance and heat, and the battery terminal will melt off. Loose battery connections are a leading cause of EV failure.

Mike Brown (center) instructs students in his ProMech™ certification course.

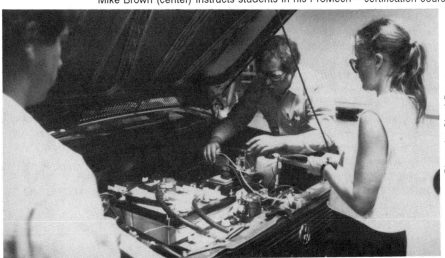

Photo by Shari Prange.

In Praise of 12-Volt Deep Cycle Batteries
By Jim Tervort

Much attention has been focused on the 6-volt golf cart battery, but the 12-volt deep-cycle battery, developed for the electric sweeper, is available thanks to the long-standing commitment of companies like Holt, Pullman, White and Tennant. Trojan battery responded to the market-pull of demand by these companies for reliable 12-volt batteries for their floor cleaners, which are used to clean large enclosed public areas, such as school hallways, shopping centers and malls. These sweepers are either self-propelled or controlled by a driver who walks behind.

A survey of junk batteries taken at random from scrap piles showed that 62.5 percent of the batteries thrown away were not deteriorated from normal use or factory defects. Some were still in good condition; many had been badly abused. Preventative maintenance could have saved many headaches and even more money. From *"Teach Your Customers Protective Battery Maintenance"* by Fred Daniel, product manager, Trojan Battery Co.

How Does The Lead-Acid Battery Work?

First let's discuss the anatomy of a battery. There are two electrodes, where electrons either flow toward the electrode (positive) or away from the electrode (negative). An electrolyte contains molecules that carry away or deposit one or more electrons. In a lead-acid battery, the electrolyte is sulfuric acid, which carries extra electrons to the negative electrode.

The secret to understanding how a battery works is to follow the electrons. When a lead-acid battery is not connected to a circuit, no electrons flow along the wires, so there is no activity in the battery.

Let's examine what happens when you start a conventional gasoline car engine. When you turn the key to start your car's motor, a circuit is formed and electrons flow from the negative electrode to the starter motor. To deliver these electrons, lead in the negative electrode reacts with the sulfate ion (SO_4^{--}) in the electrolyte. Lead (its symbol is Pb) gives up two electrons to make a Pb^{++} ion, which combines with the sulfate ion to form lead sulfate ($PbSO_4$).

The electrons from the lead (in the negative electrode) move along the circuit to the starter motor to start the engine, then flow back to the positive electrode of the battery. There the electrons meet lead dioxide (a lead atom connected to two oxygen atoms, PbO_2), which is a form of lead that lacks four electrons (Pb^{++++}). The lead dioxide molecule uses the two incoming electrons to form a type of lead (Pb^{++}) that combines with a sulfate ion in the electrolyte to create lead sulfate ($PbSO_4$).

When you discharge a lead-acid battery, the battery forms lead sulfate on both electrodes. The negative electrode goes from lead (Pb) to lead that misses two electrons (Pb^{++}), or from lead to lead sulfate. The positive electrode goes from Pb^{++++} to Pb^{++} by accepting two electrons (PbO_2 + 2 electrons + SO_4^{--} makes $PbSO_4$ and $2O^{--}$).

Charging the battery reverses this flow, with the lead sulfate changing from Pb^{++} to lead at the negative electrode (since electrons are being added to the battery) and to lead dioxide at the positive electrode.

A gallon of gasoline has about the same amount of energy as a thousand pounds of lead-acid batteries.
Dr. Michael Seal, Western Washington University, speaking at the NESEA Solar/Electric Vehicle Symposium, Boxborough, Mass., Oct. 27, 1991. This explains the search for a better battery.

Questions Most Often Asked

Answers provided by Fred Daniel, Trojan Battery Co.

What is the minimum level for acid in a cell? The water level should never drop below the top of the separators. If the top of the plates is exposed to air they will deteriorate quickly.

Maximum acid level? Water levels should be 1/2-to-3/4 of an inch above the top of the separators but should not touch the bottom of the vent well. Water levels rise as a battery warms under load, on charge or with normal rises in ambient temperatures.

At one time, overcharge was the biggest cause of battery failure. With the introduction of electronic systems and automatic chargers, this has been greatly reduced. Most battery charging problems occur when the amp hours out (used) are not adequately replaced during recharge. Any depth of discharge greater than 20% should be replaced by charging immediately. Batteries should be charged until they reach the specific gravity suggested by the manufacturer. This is generally a specific gravity of 1.265 on a temperature-corrected hydrometer.

What water is safe for batteries? If the water has an odor, is discolored or tastes funny, it probably should not be used. Many people use distilled water in their batteries. Excessive amounts of calcium, iron, copper or alkali will neutralize electrolyte and eventually ruin any battery.

Should vent plugs be removed during charge? No. Vent plugs should remain in place during charge. Most vent plugs are designed to filter the gassing and retain as much moisture as possible. Vent plugs are usually designed to prevent possible explosions. If vent plugs are removed during the charging, this protection is gone. Vent plugs should only be removed when testing with a hydrometer or when adding water.

How do you clean a battery? A half-cup of baking soda in a quart of water makes a good cleaning solution. It should be brushed on and left for 20 minutes, then rinsed away. Be careful in protecting eyes and clothes when brushing and rinsing. *Editors' note: several EAA members question the wisdom of bringing an alkali solution close to the acidic lead-acid battery. With care, the wash will neutralize any acid on the surface of the battery without affecting the acid inside the battery.*

Do you ever add acid to a battery? Once a battery has been activated, you need never add acid. Only water needs to be added periodically to keep the plates and separators covered.

Why not lift a battery by the post? Battery posts (terminals) are attached by lead burning to the terminal riser in the cell. They are also burned into the cover insert, a lead piece molded into the cover. Lifting by the post can exert enough torque on the lead insert to crack the lead away from the plastic molded around it. This will cause acid leakage and post corrosion. Continued lifting by the post can also break the burned bond to the cell riser. Where this occurs, you have an open circuit and a ruined battery.

Should you dump out acid to store a battery? No. Air will immediately attack the exposed plates and damage them Filling them immediately with water or rinsing with water also does not help. the best way to store a battery is to fully charge it and store it on the coolest place possible. A cool concrete or tile floor will reduce the discharge. *Jim Tervort adds: Place the batteries on a non-conducting material, such as wood, and keep them raised at least three inches off the floor. A sheet of plywood will catch and absorb minor leaks, in case a battery case is cracked. Care should be taken to prevent accidents: a forklift or a heavy tool can puncture the polypropylene side of the battery, spilling sulfuric acid. Take steps to prevent accidental spills and leaks from going down a drain and contaminating your community's waste water.*

Jim also notes: Long-term storage under warm conditions can cause sulfation, where lead sulfate crystals form on the surface of the battery plates if they are not being charged and discharged. This occurs because lead sulfate is not soluble in sulfuric acid. It's nearly impossible to get lead sulfate off the plates once it forms and every square millimeter that is covered by sulfation is lost plate area. We recommend that people keep their batteries on charge as much as possible. If you are going to be away for a month, put the charge on a timer and have it come on a couple hours a day.

Ion tracking: If you don't scrub your batteries clean at least once a month, a slime forms on top of the battery. You can detect "ion tracking" (the leaking of voltage across a battery) with a voltmeter. You can measure the full voltage of the battery between the terminal, but watch what happens when you touch the voltmeter's tips to the surface of the battery where there should be no current flowing. This shows that a certain mount of electricity is leaking across the top of the battery. the "scum" is transferring the charge from one terminal to the other. This is reducing the battery capacity and range of the EV because you have this electrical loss running across the top of your batteries.

The scum comes from the condensation that occurs after charging. The battery's liquid "cooks" a bit after charging and some vapor escapes out of the battery caps. None of the terminals have perfect seal around the posts so there's always a little scum leaking out and condensing on the top of the battery.

The next reading is extracted from a service manual published by the Battery Council International. While some of the advice appears elsewhere in this book, repetition aids learning, and you will extend the lives of many batteries and avoid the need to replace your batteries if you heed this advice.

The reading mentions "specific gravity" and an instrument called a "hydrometer." These are explained in the chapter on Repair and Maintenance.

Charging the EV Battery

An electric vehicle battery should be fully charged every day it is used, even if it is only discharged 25 percent. Do not completely discharge a battery if it can be avoided. The deeper the discharge, the less life you will obtain from the battery. If the batteries are being used more than normal, it is advisable to place them on charge for an hour or two during the day (at lunch time, for example). This reduces the depth of discharge and prolongs battery life. If the vehicle was not used during the work period, do not place the batteries on charge. Over-charging the battery also shortens its life.

Most electric vehicle users have purchased taper rate chargers equipped with timers. This equipment is designed to put back the charge which was taken out of the battery, when the timer is set according to instructions furnished by the charger manufacturer. The charging rate starts high and tapers to a low "finish" rate. They will automatically cover some variation in depth of discharge, but this should be verified with hydrometer readings *(or sensitive digital voltage readings, adds EAA's John Newell)* taken during and after charge.

When taper-rate chargers are used, sometimes they might not recharge the battery 100 percent. Repeated under-charging will shorten battery life. It is recommended that a weekly equalizing charge of three to four hours additional charge be given following the full charge, especially if variation in specific gravity of the electrolyte among the cells is greater than 0.010 or less than the manufacturer's specified full-charge specific gravity.

If the electrolyte level is low, add water near the end of the charge or after taking the battery off charge. Never allow the electrolyte level to drop below the tops of the plates because the exposed portion of the plates will become permanently inactive due to sulfation. Never overfill a battery cell above the level indicator or acid will overflow when the battery is placed on charge. This reduces the capacity of the battery and corrodes metal parts near the battery. If the electrolyte level is below the tops of the plates, add only enough water to cover them before charging. **Add water, if necessary, to bring electrolyte level to the level indicator** *after* **charging or near the end of the charge.**

Electric vehicle batteries should be fully charged and clean if they are to be stored for any length of time. Store in an unheated, dry area. Check the specific gravity of the electrolyte periodically with a hydrometer or give the batteries a boost charge every three months. The colder the storage areas, the slower the battery will self-discharge.

Caution: New electric vehicle batteries do not have their full capacity until they have been cycled several times (somewhere between 5 and 40 cycles). Therefore, they can be excessively discharged early in their vehicular life, thereby shortening their service life. Accordingly, it is advisable to limit operation of new vehicle or older vehicles with new batteries to well below their advertised range for at least the first five cycles and then gradually increase the range.

(Readers should thank the Battery Council International (401 North Michigan Avenue, Chicago, IL 60611) for granting permission to reprint portions of **The Storage Battery Technical Service Manual.***)*

The Difference Between Nickel Cadmium and Lead-Acid Batteries
By Jim Tervort, Sebring Auto-Cycle Inc.

The principal characteristic of the lead-acid battery that distinguishes it from the nickel-cadmium battery is: **the less deeply you discharge a lead-acid battery, the longer it lasts.** For example, if you repeatedly discharge a lead-acid battery no more than 25 or 30 percent, it will last years longer than a battery that is regularly discharged to its maximum of 80-percent level.

Contrast this with the protocol for nickel-cadmium batteries, which are common in portable telephones and video cameras. Many people are familiar with the need to "exercise" ni-cads by discharging them fully before recharging. If you recharge a ni-cad before it is fully discharged, it can develop a memory and its capacity becomes smaller. This is why ni-cad batteries need to be "killed" (drained fully) once in a while to maintain their ability to cycle. **Just remember: what's good for a ni-cad will ruin a deep-cycle lead-acid battery.**

Project EVE: The Emergence of the Gel Cell Battery
By Dave Goldstein, Program Development Associates

The typical EV owner of the '90s is not likely to put up with the maintenance hassles that today's EV hobbyists and enthusiasts routinely endure -- that is, the watering and testing of many dozens of battery cells every two to three weeks, the wiping down of acid mists that build up on battery tops and terminals, and the periodic need to check battery terminal connections for looseness and corrosion.

Breathes there an EV owner anywhere in the country who hasn't at one time or another begged the gods of electricity for a better solution to the drawbacks of today's liquid lead-acid batteries? Yet, realistically, the lead-acid battery is hard to beat for cost and performance, and all the other "magic batteries" that we've been reading about are still years away from practical consumer availability.

That's why millions of dollars are being invested by the major auto manufacturers together with the U.S. Department of Energy (DOE) and the Electric Power Research Institute (EPRI) into the Advanced Battery Consortium (ABC). And that's why, in the **near term**, at least, the lead-acid battery is still likely to remain as a major factor in the EV marketplace.

It's a dilemma that General Motors Corporation has been grappling with for years. In announcing the **Impact** -- the first modern mass-produced *consumer-oriented* EV for the 1990s -- GM wisely chose specially-designed, sealed, no-maintenance gel cell batteries.

Gel cells, also known as *recombinant batteries*, have been around for years, enjoying a near-legendary reputation among yachtsmen and boat owners around the world and serving as the battery of choice in uninterruptible power supplies for computers and for electric wheelchairs. Gel cells **are** lead-acid batteries, but they are completely spill-proof, because the acid is absorbed into a thick, jelly-like substance ("silica gel") that looks like library paste.

You never open up the cells on a gel cell battery, and you never have to add water to it. The battery itself *recombines* the hydrogen and oxygen gases that normally escape from "ordinary" liquid batteries by maintaining a mild internal pressure. Built-in safety valves allow excess pressure to escape if the battery is abused (for example, by severe overcharging.)

Among the many other advantages that gel cells offer:
• There are no hydrogen fumes or acid mists.
• They don't spill acid (even when the case is broken or cracked).
• They can be mounted in any position (even upside-down!).
• They have lower internal resistance (due to the more evenly distributed gel-electrolyte), which, in theory, allows:
• better EV acceleration,
• more energy-efficient recharging, and
• longer battery life.

In tests conducted by EPRI and DOE, gel traction batteries produced by *Sonnenschein* of Germany have demonstrated almost **twice** the cycle life of liquid lead-acid batteries. Other gel cell manufacturers include: Concorde Battery (West Covina, CA), Douglas Battery (Winston-Salem, NC), East Penn Manufacturing (Lyon Station, PA), Gates Energy Products (Denver, CO), GM/Delco (Muncie,IN), Johnson Controls (Milwaukee, WI), Matsushita/Panasonic (Japan), Varta (Germany), and Yuasa (Japan). Some of these companies do not build gel cells large enough for EVs; others use an *absorbed mat* design -- a slightly different class of recombinant battery than a gel cell, but having the same operating characteristics.

The *disadvantages* of gel cells are relatively few, but they are significant: limited availability in EV/golf cart sizes; nonstandard dimensions; high cost (two to four times more expensive in limited quantities, partially offset by longer life); special charging requirements (you must use a special "gel type" battery charger that limits the charge voltage according to temperature).

For practical purposes, this means that you must replace your existing battery charger if you decide to upgrade to gel cells. This is cost-prohibitive for most EV owners, but to some (and especially to EV fleet operators), the promise of a "near-zero" maintenance EV may well be worth the price.

The issue came to a head recently when our consulting firm, Program Development Associates, acquired a special edition EV -- a 1982 Jet Industries *Electrica* (Mercury Lynx) which was displayed at the U.S. Pavilion at the World's Fair in Knoxville, Tennessee. The car featured a custom six-color paint job, factory air-conditioning and AM-FM stereo radio, and had been in storage for almost nine years, with less than 1,500 miles on the odometer.

The car appeared to be **brand new**, except for the fact that the lead-acid batteries had long since died and the early-design PMC transistor controller had been removed. "Why not upgrade this car to today's specifications?" I thought.

Thus began **Project EVE**, which stands for "Electric Vehicle, Enhanced." The basic idea was to take a good design (the hundreds of Jet EV conversions produced for the DOE program in the early 1980s are considered by many to be among the best EVs ever built) and to upgrade it for greater reliability and performance – with the emphasis upon **reliability**.

Gel cells were a natural consideration. I selected the *Sonnenschein 6V-160 "Traction Block,"* imported from Germany by East Penn Manufacturing Company and available in both "DIN" (European) and "SAE" (US) specifications. However, only the SAE spec will fit in the existing steel battery compartments of the Jet *Electrica*.

Project EVE is continuing, with efforts underway to upgrade the main power cables and to improve the reliability of battery terminal connections, with the expectation that we will have further information about the benefits of gel cell-powered EVs by the time that this book is published. In January 1992, East Penn Manufacturing was planning to break ground for a new gel cell manufacturing plant in Lyon Station, Pennsylvania, under license from Sonnenschein of Germany. For further information, Program Development Associates may be reached by dialing (301) 231-3990.

Tim Cutforth, a member of the Denver Electric Vehicle Council, has accumulated some valuable experience with "bringing back the dead." He shares with us here his voodoo magic, which resuscitated the aged batteries in his 1965 Corvair conversion.

Although I believe that batteries shouldn't be abused by over-discharging them early in their life, I have found that when the range starts dropping to unusable levels, a super-deep cycle or two can bring them back up again. When I bought the used batteries several years back, the car wouldn't make twenty miles on a charge. After that, I discharged the batteries on a low 10-amp load until I got them down to under 50 volts on the 20-battery series pack (nominally rated at 120 volts, or 6 volts each), then gave them a long slow charge. The next cycle went 35 miles. After about three more deep cycles, the range got up to the original 70-mile region again and this held until the batteries were recently replaced. I plan to do at least one deep cycle each year as preventive maintenance. Rather than give up on a pack, give them a deep cycle and the cells will either come back or dead short. Either way, there is nothing to lose and quite a bit to gain. I also found that when one cell would boil dry much quicker than the others, the key was to add electrolyte instead of water to that cell. The next time the water was checked, the cell usually was even with the others around it. Because I have never used a

regulated charger but just a diode, a limit resistor and a line cord, I have had to add quite a bit of water sometimes. Because twenty batteries can use five gallons of water at a time, I have reverted to garden hose water, but given the high purity of Denver's water, this is probably of minor significance.

Tim Cutforth's 1965 Corvair.

22

Motors and Other EV Parts

One of the prime advantages of switching away from an internal combustion engine to an electric car is "there's only one moving part" (aside from the transmission, wheels and steering wheel). However, even after owning an electric car and hanging around electric car converters and enthusiasts for more than a year, I still get the **rotor**, *the* **armature** *and the* **commutator** *mixed up. The following description of an electric motor will help the new EV owner to begin building a new vocabulary.*

The electric motor works because Hans Christian Oersted, a Danish scientist, first noticed in 1820 that electricity creates a magnetic field when it moves through a wire. If you put the wire next to a magnet, the wire will "leap" toward or away from the magnet when electricity runs through the wire. The wire is attracted to the magnet if its magnetic pole is opposite to the pole on the magnet (the "north" pole is attracted to the "south" pole, as in "opposites attract"). The wire moves away from the magnet if their poles are the same. This "leaping" can be used to turn a shaft, and that's the essence of an electric motor: move electricity through a piece of metal that is near a magnet, and the metal moves.

A simple electric motor creates the magnet by wrapping the wire as a coil around a metal bar. When current flows through the coiled wire, the metal bar becomes a magnet (this is called "induction," because the wire is inducing or forcing the metal bar to become a magnet). Because electricity is used to make the magnet, the metal bar with the coiled wire is called an "electromagnet."

The simple direct current (DC) electric motor has one stationary magnet (the **field structure**) and one magnet that moves (the **armature**). To make the second magnet move, the DC motor has a **commutator** (think of a commuter, who has to move from home to work and back to home), which switches the direction of flow of electricity in the moving magnet (in the armature). This switching reverses the magnetic poles in the armature. When the north pole in the armature is attracted to the south pole in the field structure, the shaft turns. When it has traveled far enough, the commutator reverses the current's direction, switching the north pole to the south and the armature's south pole moves away from the stationery magnet. The drive-shaft of the electric motor, which is connected to the armature, also turns.

In an alternating current (AC) motor, the names of the stationary and moving magnets are changed: the stationary part, called the **stator** ("stays still"), is the electrically active part, like the armature in a DC motor. The **rotor** moves because current is being induced in it, or because the rotor is a permanent magnet reacting to the armature's current. An **inverter** rotates the magnetic fields around the poles of the armature (changing the battery's electricity from direct current to alternating current), so a commutator is not needed to change the direction of flow.

The British physicist Michael Faraday built a primitive electric motor in 1831 and Zénobe-Théophile Gramme, an electrical engineer, produced a motor for sale in 1873. Nicola Tesla invented the first electric motor to run on alternating current in 1888. So these ideas have been around longer than the gasoline internal-combustion engine for cars.

You now have a basic understanding of how an electric motor works (see a good encyclopedia for diagrams of what has been described, if it isn't altogether clear). Here's an article by Shari Prange (Electro Automotive, Felton, Calif.) which explains the principal parts of an electric car.

An electric car should be much easier to understand than an internal combustion engine car. After all, it has a lot fewer parts. However, each part seems to come in a dozen different flavors and it can be confusing. Some components represent obsolete technology, while others are still experimental. In between are the components that are up-to-date, proven, and readily available. Here is a guide to the pros and cons of the most common items.

Motors: First we can divide motors into alternating current (AC) and direct current (DC). To use an AC motor requires an invertor. Invertors tend to be large, complex, and expensive, and there is always some loss of energy in the transition. *(Editors' note: see below for additional points of view.)*

Next we can divide DC motors into shunt, compound, permanent magnet and series. Shunt and compound motors are built for other uses, but aren't in current production in the size and specification range needed for passenger cars. Many early electric cars used aircraft generators, which were compound motors. They were the best available at that time, but weren't really suited for cars, and have been abandoned by almost everyone today. They were designed to be generators, not traction motors; their revolutions per minute (rpms) were too high, and consequently they required a lot of amperage; and they were intended to run on 24 volts while a car needs at least 72 volts. The shaft has an unusual military spline, which is difficult to match, and the generators lack sufficient internal inductance to be compatible with modern controllers.

Permanent magnet motors can be brush or brushless. While they are popular in ultralight solar race cars, they are not really suited to full-size passengers cars, as they are not large enough. Permanent magnet motors are very efficient, but in a narrow operating band. Since normal driving constantly varies up and down the rpms, the motor would rarely be at its most efficient rate of rotation. Also, the controllers for the brushless motors are large, expensive and not yet developed to a high level of reliability.

The series DC motor is by far the most popular electric car motor. It is in production and available in the necessary size and performance range, and has been debugged and proven reliable over the years. Although GE makes series motors, they are expensive. A relatively new company, Advanced DC Motors, is actively pursuing the electric car market and tailors an affordable motor to suit electric car needs.

Adaptor Plates: The adapter plate is machined from aluminum to allow the electric motor to be mounted to the transmission. It requires precision design and machining to provide an efficient mating that will not put excess stress on motor or transmission. These plates are readily available from experienced EV component suppliers.

Transmission: For many conversions, an electric passenger car needs to retain the manual transmission. .The manual transmission is needed for torque multiplication. Without it, the car would be too sluggish to be safe in traffic. With it, the EV can accelerate and climb hills quite quickly. Direct-drive systems, where the motor is connected directly to the wheel, have the advantage of lighter weight and greater efficiency. However, a direct-drive conversion often requires more labor.

Speed controllers: the first controllers were series-parallel switching systems. The car had two speeds, with a jerky transition from one to the other. These are now found only in old EVs and older golf carts. They were followed by the "chopper" controllers. These control speed by turning the battery voltage on and off very rapidly. They give smooth continuous acceleration. The first choppers were silicon controlled rectifier (SCR) controllers. These are still available, but tend to be large, with their components exposed to the elements, inefficient due to heating, and subject to failures.

SCR controllers were replaced by solid state transistorized pulse-width modulated controllers. These are smaller, completely enclosed and weather proof, making them highly reliable and efficient. Recent improvements include MOSFET technology, which is much more efficient.

Chargers: The electric car is recharged by plugging it into a household outlet for 8 to 10 hours. While 110 volts can be used, usually with at least a 20-amp breaker, faster charging can result when using a charger adapted for 220 volts (the typical outlet for an electric clothes dryer). Modern chargers can sense the level of charge in the batteries and adjust the rate of charge. Too much amperage can damage batteries. Fast charging is being demonstrated and developed by a number of companies, including Nissan.

Solar panels: At this time, solar cells are not efficient enough to allow a car to run entirely on panels. The GM Sunraycer, with the best panels money can buy, could only generate one horsepower. A typical solar race car has a massive expanse of panels, weighs 500 pounds or less, and is designed for optimum aerodynamics and minimum rolling resistance.

DC-DC Converter: Electric cars use a 12-volt battery that is separated from the main battery pack to operate things like headlights, dash lights, horns, fans, etc. The DC-to-DC converter takes over the job of the alternator in a gas car and keeps this auxiliary battery charged. The converter taps a small amount of electricity from the main battery pack and converts it down to 13.5 volts to charge the auxiliary battery. This distributes the load over the entire battery pack so that all the batteries discharge at the same rate rather than tapping only two batteries to run accessories and draining them more quickly than the others. The DC-DC converter can also replace the extra battery, allowing accessories to run directly from 12-volt current generated from the main battery pack.

Batteries: The Magic Battery is the Holy Grail of electric cars. There are always magic batteries "under development" and due on the market "within 3 to 5 years." Unfortunately, the Magic Battery has been just over the horizon for more than ten years now. There are a lot of technologies being studied: zinc-air, aluminum-air, advanced nickel-iron, sodium-sulfur, and hydrogen to menton a few. Some discharge too quickly, some get too hot, some are too expensive, and some just need financing to finish developing and debugging them and get them into production. Someday, some of them will come true.

In the meantime, lead acid batteries are still the reality. These must be 6-volt deep-discharge batteries such as are used in golf carts.

Instrumentation: Many early electric cars built by hobbyists used panel meters for instrumentation because there were no proper gauges available. Panel meters suffered from a lack of backlighting and poor accuracy due to the vibrations, dust and hot sunlight associated with normal driving. There are now electric car gauges available that are built with standard round automotive faces, backlighting and automotive standards for accuracy in spite of vibration, moisture, dust, shock and temperatures.

Traditional analog gauges are preferred to digital ones because it is easier for the mind to interpret at a glance a needle position rather than a number. LED gauges can be impossible to read in bright sunlight.

Regenerative Braking: Regenerative braking applies the energy obtained from braking the car to generate electricity and recharge the batteries. *(EAA member Paul Brasch adds: Regen braking can be used to slow down the EV when the accelerator is not depressed, reducing wear on brakes and allowing the car to mimic the slow down effect of a conventional car. This is especially useful on downslopes.)* It's a wonderful idea, but has some drawbacks in real life. To achieve it requires complicated circuits, or AC power. The return for this investment is slight. Under appropriate conditions, only about 5 to 10 percent of the energy used can be recovered by regenerative braking.

Any electric car will only be as good as the parts and design that went into it. Every compromise will lessen performance, but a well-built electric car will be economical, reliable, carefree and fun.

Note: reviewers of this chapter sent the editors a storm of comments, challenging Mr. Brown's views. **Regenerative braking:** *proponents claim greater recovery of the energy lost during deceleration (more than 10%), and point out that AC drive systems can be adapted more easily than DC systems to handle regen. Alternating current motors are dropping in price, thanks to innovative research. The editors advise the reader to keep an open mind regarding which is "best," DC or AC, and to doublecheck any claims of efficiency. They both have strong advocates with good points on both sides.*

The Use of the Clutch: *Jim Tervort (Sebring, Fla.) points out that a direct-drive system, where the motor is connected directly to the transmission, is preferable to a system that requires a clutch. If the motor is receiving current from the batteries and the clutch is depressed, the motor will spin freely without a load. If the current is not interrupted, the motor could spin so fast that it could explode. That is why direct-drive with fast-response fuses are preferred over a system that requires a clutch.*

Tervort also notes that there is more horsepower in the brake system than in any motor. If an EV is in a runaway situation, the driver can press hard and continuously on the brake. This will force the batteries to send additional current to the motor to overcome the braking resistance, and the fuse will blow. Turning off the "ignition switch" during a runaway situation can sometimes result in locking the steering column (in most modern conversions), making a bad situation worse.

Researcher predicts the cost of AC systems will fall

Dr. C. C. Chan, the founder of the International Research Centre for Electric Vehicles, first worked with electric rail cars in China and eventually made his way to Hong Kong. Since 1983 he has studied AC drive systems for electric road vehicles, and he was one of the earliest researchers to predict that improvements in electronics would make AC systems more efficient *and* affordable than conventional direct current (DC) systems. In a paper on advanced AC propulsion systems for EVs he explained, "Due to the rapid development of microelectronic and power electronic technologies, powerful microcontrollers and high-rating power devices are commercially available at reasonable prices. These changes make variable-speed AC drive systems more competitive among DC drive systems for EV applications." He listed these additional advantages: lower maintenance, greater reliability, lower weight (which extends the EV's range) and efficient regenerative braking can be easily implemented without additional components. Dr. Chan was Chairman of the Tenth Electric Vehicle Symposium (EVS-10) held in 1990.

Dr. C. Chan at the EVS-10 trade show, held in December 1990 in Hong Kong.

AC Motors Are More Efficient Than DC Motors

Since batteries provide direct current (DC), shouldn't the car's motor be DC, too? At first glance, it would appear less efficient to use an AC motor, because the DC has to be converted into alternating current. Jim Worden, explains why AC motors shouldn't be overlooked.

Solectria's line of AC induction motors are typically 90 to 95 percent efficient. This means that for every kilowatt pulled from the battery, 900 to 950 watts are actually used to drive the cars. This translates into a more efficient drive system. From the motor controller to the wheels, high efficiency means the charge in the EV's batteries is not depleted as quickly as in less-efficient DC systems. The battery pack of a car equipped with this motor can be smaller than a car using a DC series-wound motor, which has an efficiency between 70 and 85%.

The key to performance in an EV is to make the vehicle drive as far as possible using a minimum amount of power. Solectria's analysis of efficient drives systems was supported by the California Air Resources Board in June 1991. Solectria's four-seat automatic Force, which uses an AC drive, was able to complete twice as many Federal Urban Driving Cycles as similar vehicles using series-wound motors. The battery packs and weights of vehicles were similar, yet the performance was dramatically different.

Solectria's lightweight (eight pounds) on-board charger provides a 90% efficient mode of recharging. It uses 110-volt outlets. With the cost of AC components dropping, and the need for fewer batteries (a savings that will continue when the batteries need replacing), the total cost of the AC system is becoming more favorable compared to the conventional DC system found in most EVs.

The "plate" of a lead-acid battery is actually a mesh.

23

Make It Safe

Ken Koch, KTA Services (Orange, Calif.) shares insights gained through years of experience as a distributor of EV components and developer of EV instrumentation. For additional information in the evolving area of industry standards, write for Safety Considerations: Guidelines For People Buying An EV Or Wanting To Convert A Conventional Car To Electric, published by the Electric Vehicle Industry Association, c/o EVIA Standards Committee, c/o Bob Batson, Box 59, Maynard, Massachusetts 01754 (please enclose two first-class stamps to help cover postage and reproduction costs).

Integrity of body, brakes, wheel bearings: Most EV conversions wind up being from 400 to 1200 lbs. over stock weight. This represents additional strain on the body, wheel bearings, and brakes. Don't convert any vehicle that has cancer (road rust), because the additional strain eventually could cause structural failure of the body. It's mandatory that a conversion have the best brakes possible. When performing a conversion, always put on brand new brakes; use the best materials available. If the vehicle you're converting has power brakes, be sure to restore vacuum to the brake servo with a vacuum pump system. Also, check wheel bearings for signs of wear; if you have any doubts about them, replace them.

Battery replacement: As much as possible, try to distribute battery weight throughout the vehicle for better handling. Too much weight in the back of the car can cause oversteer with a sensation that the vehicle is too responsive to any change of steering wheel position. If there's too much weight over the front wheels, the understeer created will make you feel like you're driving a snow plow. Also, try to place batteries as close as possible in the center of the car at a low position to lower the vehicle's center of gravity and to avoid the 'dumbbell' effect whereby the vehicle will yaw with each change of steering wheel position.

A vehicle is safer if batteries are kept out of the passenger compartment. If placement outside of the passenger compartment isn't possible, be sure to enclose and secure the batteries inside of a box structure.

Safety components and safe techniques: The power components in an electric vehicle propulsion system can be as simple as a motor, a motor controller, a set of batteries, and some cable to interconnect them. Using only these basic ingredients in the vehicle propulsion system will work and, if you're lucky, you may never need additional components for safety. This reminds me of the time a fellow was proof-testing components in a 2-seater dune buggy with no body. The propulsion system had no safe means of disconnecting battery power from the motor if a problem ever occurred. Sure enough, as Mr. Murphy might have it, the controller shorted out during a test run and the 'test mule' began to run away. Good thing that this fellow had a tool box sitting in the passenger's seat next to him. He was able retrieve a hammer from the tool box, and after two well-placed swings he succeeded in knocking the post off of a nearby battery. This maneuver (at 50 mph and climbing) interrupted power to the motor, and the vehicle was then brought to a stop. Brakes alone were not enough to stop the vehicle, and depressing the clutch would have caused the motor to blow. Fortunately, in this case, the only casualties were a battery with a broken-off post and some underwear that was badly in need of changing! The vehicle could have crashed, or some part of the system could have caught fire. This incident points to the fact that the more safety components you have in a propulsion system, even if some seem redundant, the safer your vehicle will be in the event of some emergency condition.

(1) **Fuses:** A fuse provides an instantaneous automatic interruption of power in event of a malfunction or short-circuit. No fuse is any good unless it is rated at the voltage/current/time characteristics appropriate to its application. Use at least one safety fuse in the main battery pack to protect system power components. An enclosed safety fuse such as the Bussman KAA-400 is best because the fuse element is enclosed in a fire-retardant powder. A fuse link is usable, but with its open construction it can spew molten balls of metal when it blows. If a fuse link is mounted in the open over the top of a battery and it blows, molten balls of metal can burn through a battery case — causing a potential fire or explosion — or, at the minimum, a ruined battery. If your EV has a fuse link, please enclose it in a piece of high-temperature insulated tubing such as phenolic. Also, for maximum safety, any instrumentation line that ties into any part of the propulsion system should be protected with a small fuse of 1-amp or less that is mounted close to the propulsion system tie-in point. This will protect small-gauge wiring from catching on fire if a short ever occurs within the instrumentation circuit.

(2) **Circuit breakers:** While a safety fuse provides instantaneous automatic interruption of propulsion battery power in event of a malfunction, optional use of a circuit breaker can provide a fail-safe manual and/or automatic interruption of battery power in event of a drive-system malfunction. It also can be used to shut off battery power during routine servicing of the system. A circuit breaker is no good unless it is rated at the voltage/current/time characteristics appropriate to its application. Use of a double-pole circuit breaker offers an advantage over a single-pole unit by allowing both sides of a battery pack to be interrupted instead of just one. The circuit breaker should be mounted within easy reach of the EV driver for maximum safety.

(3) **Contactors:** A contactor is used to switch high power remotely by means of a low-level control voltage — such as 12 volts DC supplied from a keyswitch. In an EV propulsion system, high voltage, inductive loads and extremely high current levels are encountered. A contactor should be correctly rated for the high voltage and current characteristics appropriate to its application. Even though a contactor's primary function in most EV systems is to carry current, the type used should be capable of breaking current to an inductive load (motor) in case of a shorted-controller condition. This means that the contactor used should be fitted with magnetic blowouts which extinguish arcing — otherwise, a contactor could weld into a shorted condition if it can't break the arc. Magnetic blowouts work on the principle of Fleming's Left-Hand Rule. At least one main contactor should be used in a propulsion system to apply and remove main battery power to the motor and controller. Contactors used for electrical reversing also should be fitted with magnetic blowouts.

(4) **Wire, cable and terminals:** Wire and cable used in an EV should be sized to safely handle the current being carried without overheating. Undersized wire can get hot or even catch fire. The manufacturer's amp capacity tables should be referred to when deciding which size wire to use. In EV applications, use wire that has thicker insulation to resist abrasion. When running heavy-duty cable underneath a vehicle, protect it from abrasion by enclosing the cable in PVC conduit or rubber heater hose. Put extra covering on wires that are routed through sheet metal with potentially sharp edges. Use copper wire, never aluminum. The debate on whether to crimp or solder terminal lugs onto heavy-duty cable ends may go on forever. Basically speaking, all lugs should be crimped onto wire ends using a proper crimping tool. Solder them too, if you like, but do crimp them. If a cable lug secured to a battery terminal ever becomes loose, it can become hot enough to melt the solder and separate. A crimped lug will hold to the cable because of its mechanical bond. Check and retighten as required all battery terminal hardware at least once a month.

(5) Batteries: Batteries, of course, should be securely fastened from moving around in an EV. The most common type used today for EV applications is the flooded-cell lead-acid battery. These have a liquid electrolyte and are unsealed. During approximately the last 20% of their recharge cycle they will produce a significant amount of hydrogen gas. Allow adequate ventilation for the hydrogen so that it doesn't collect and present an explosion hazard. Hydrogen ventilation can be assisted by using small fans. Never use a DC brush-type fan in this application because commutation sparks can ignite the hydrogen. Always use brushless DC or AC fans. Also, when handling or working around batteries, always: (a) wear heavy-duty shoes to protect your feet, and heavy-duty gloves to protect your hands and fingers; (b) wear a face shield to protect your face and eyes in the event of an explosion; (c) tape the unused ends of wrenches used for removing, installing, and/or tightening battery terminal bolts and nuts; and, (d) place an insulating cover over all batteries that are adjacent to others being installed, removed, or serviced. A sheet of plywood will work fine.

(6) Motors and motor insulation: Use motors that are heavy-duty enough for your application. Don't try to use a 4 HP motor when a 10 HP unit is required. Motors that are undersized for an application will overheat and eventually can burn up. Never use a motor that has an inferior insulation system or is constructed from inferior materials. Insulation systems are rated by 'letter' according to their temperature value. Use motors that are rated class F (155°C), or H (180°C). Better materials may cost more, but the added price is worth it. One formerly popular motor manufacturer used class B (130°C) insulation in his motors to save money. Because of inferior insulation, the armatures in nearly all of his motors eventually overheated and shorted out in electric car applications.

(7) Floating ground system: For maximum safety, no part of the propulsion system should be connected to any part of the vehicle frame. Isolating the propulsion system from the frame will minimize the possibility of being shocked when touching a connection point such as a battery terminal and any part of the body or frame. It also minimizes the chance of having a short circuit to the frame if wire insulation becomes frayed and touches metal.

Bob Batson adds: The DC-to-DC converter takes the battery system's voltage from a higher voltage (such as 72 or 120 volts) down to 12 volts to run headlights and other accessories. This does not mean that the 12-volt battery used to run these accessories in a standard car should be discarded. I recommend that any vehicle equipped with a DC-to-DC converter also carry a smaller 12-volt battery for emergency circumstances. If for some reason the system's circuit is interrupted (a broken terminal or a severed connecting cable can cause this), an EV without a spare 12-volt battery cannot run the emergency flasher lights.

*Larry Alexander, publisher of **Electric Vehicle Progress**, adds:* The big risk opposing widespread acceptance of EVs is bad design and inferior assembly of conversions or ground-up EVs. If junk goes onto the road and fails, it would set back EV growth another ten years. Sellers of EVs must be committed to selling well-designed and well-built EVs; EV buyers must be remember they are ambassadors and commit to maintaining safe vehicles.

EV pioneer Vic Jager.
Photo courtesy of Ken Koch.

24

Repair and Maintenance

With only six moving parts (the motor, the transmission and four wheels), an electric car doesn't need much attention if the batteries are checked regularly. Carl Taylor, an electrical technician from Hollywood, Florida, describes the routine maintenance that every owner of an electric car should perform.

Tools For Every EV Owner
By Carl Taylor

To get the best service from your electric vehicle, you need to routinely check the batteries' ability to hold a charge. If any single cell in a battery is not accepting its full share of a charge, the charger continues to work and the other healthy batteries become overcharged.

Checking a battery's health is simple and any mechanic familiar with batteries can perform the routine checks. However, one way to keep your costs of EV ownership down is to do these checks yourself. Here's what you need:

Hydrometer: To measure the battery's "state of charge," there are three types of hydrometer. The first has three little colored balls, each that float at different levels of charge. This is not accurate enough for the serious EV owner. It's like trusting the air pressure gauges on the air hoses at gasoline stations -- they measure air pressure, but not as accurately as a hand-held pressure gauge recommended by most mechanics.

The second type of hydrometer is the standard mercury float with a gauge for you to read the state of charge. The third type adds a thermometer and a scale so you can adjust your reading according to the temperature of the electrolyte. State of charge is very dependent on temperature. For the serious EV owner, get the third type of hydrometer, available where mechanics shop for their tools.

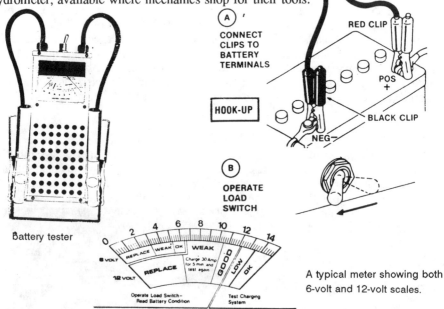

Battery tester

A typical meter showing both 6-volt and 12-volt scales.

Guide to Hydrometer Readings

1.100 to 1.225	Discharged
1.225 to 1.260	Low Charge
1.260 to 1.280	Normal

All cells should read within 50 points of each other: if one cell is 1.175 and another is 1.163, that's 0.012 or 12 points and within the margin expected; if the second cell is 1.120, that's 55 points and should be watched carefully. A difference greater than 50 points may indicate that battery failure is in the near future.

Battery Tester: The Milton Co. makes air hose fittings as its chief product, but the company also makes a sturdy and accurate battery tester. Designed to test both 6-volt and 12-volt batteries, it does everything that the serious EV owner needs: testing a battery's charge, both with and without a load. The Milton battery tester comes with a booklet, "How to Be a Battery Wizard," which is highly recommended.

Testing an individual 6-volt battery under load is achieved by applying the two clamps from the tester to the positive and negative poles of the battery. You don't have to disconnect the battery from the vehicle's other batteries because electricity in a DC battery circuit travels the path of least resistance -- namely from the negative pole to the positive pole of the individual battery.

A healthy battery will maintain its charge under a load, which the Milton battery tester simulates with a small resistor (similar to one found in a toaster). You hold a switch for ten seconds and read the meter. If the needle falls below a certain level, this indicates at least one under-charged cell, and you may need to replace the battery.

Instructions for using a battery tester

1) Always keep your work area well-ventilated. Turn a fan on and open a window or door.
2) Keep flames and cigarettes away from batteries while they are being tested.
3) Keeps hands and other areas of your body away from the vehicle's moving parts.
4) Always wear safety glasses around batteries and when you are testing the batteries.
5) Before testing the batteries and before charging them, put the vehicle in park and apply the parking brake.
6) Always connect the black (negative) pole first, and disconnect it last.
7) Do not test a battery that has a hydrometer reading below 1225. (In other words, test with the hydrometer *first*.) You don't want to place a load on a battery that is discharged.
8) If you are testing a battery after you have been charging the batteries, the state-of-charge might be inaccurate. Chargers often leave a higher "surface charge" shortly after the charging has ended. You can either drive the car around the block or wait for two hours before taking a hydrometer reading -- this will allow time for the electrolyte to mix.

Know Your Charger: Most chargers will give what is called a "leveling" or "finishing" charge after the batteries have been almost fully charged. The current drops to a trickle and will sit at that level for several hours to equalize the charge in all of the batteries.

The theory is that if you let the charger give a slow charge over several hours, all cells in all batteries will return to the same level.

Batteries are not created equal and neither are battery chargers. According to George Gless and Ron Putnam of Denver Electric Vehicle Council, batteries should be carefully matched with the most appropriate charger. Ideally, you should choose your battery type and then select a charger most able to deliver the right charging environment to those batteries. To extend the useful life of your batteries, your charger should be equipped to monitor the level of charge in the batteries being charged. Consult with the battery manufacturer to identify the best charger for the battery's needs. The trick is to make sure the charger is shifting to a trickle charge at the right time to avoid under- or overcharging the battery.

When you test with your hydrometer, you will see a small difference from cell to cell. This is normal -- what you are looking for is a significant difference that will make you want to charge that single battery by itself. If that special charging doesn't bring the weaker battery's state of charge up to normal, you'll have to replace it.

Maintenance Tips

Once every two weeks:
Check the water level in every battery cell.
Once a month:
   Check every cell with the hydrometer. If you see a large difference between cells, you need to check the battery's health with the battery tester.

   Using the battery tester, check every battery with weak cells. Remember to test the battery under load.

   Replace batteries that have permanently weakened cells. By accepting the loss of one battery, you will extend the lives of the remaining batteries by several months. *Note: replace the weakened battery with a used rather than a new battery. Older batteries tend to pull a new battery down to their level.*

   How Often: Start with once a month. If the batteries are checking healthy for three months in a row, scale back your testing to once every two months.

   Therapy for a sick battery: *If one battery lags points behind the rest of the battery set when you test them with the hydrometer, put a small 6-volt/12-volt charger on the slow battery for 30 to 60 minutes. The laggard will often fall in line with the rest of the batteries, and you achieve this without overcharging the entire battery pack (source: Ed Rannberg and Larry Foster).*

   Voltmeter: This device measures the *potential difference* (voltage) between two terminals. A fully charged lead-acid cell holds about 2.1 volts; the cell should not be discharged lower than 1.75 volts. That narrow range of about a half-volt per cell is where your EV gets the energy for driving around. Conventional 6-volt golf-cart batteries have three cells, so the fully charged battery is 6.3 or 6.4 volts and the discharged battery should be no less than 5.25 volts. *Why? The electric motor needs to draw a certain amount of power (watts), which is the product of volts times amps, "pressure" times the "volume" of the electric current. When the "pressure" (voltage)" drops, the current has to increase (a higher amperage) to keep the motor turning. When current rises too high, the delicate circuitry in the EV's components can burn out. That's why it's a good idea not to take the batteries past the 80% depth-of-discharge level and to install quick-acting fuses to protect the components. In the table below, a 96-volt system has a full charge of about 103 volts and drops to 84 volts as the safe minimum. To maintain a cruising speed of 40 mph in a converted Ford Escort (2700 pounds, on flat terrain), you need about 6.3 kilowatts (8.5 horsepower): Volts x amps = 103 x 61 amps = 6.3 kilowatts. When the voltage drops to 84 volts, the amperage has to increase to maintain that 6.3 kilowatts: 84 x 75 amps = 6.3 kilowatts, or 23% more amps.*

   Measuring Voltage Under A Load: Here's a handy guide for estimating state of charge. Always take your measurement after you have driven the car around the block, to ensure proper mixing of the electrolyte. *If your vehicle is equipped with a voltmeter, the state of charge (voltage) will be lower when the EV is moving (under a load).*

Three-wheeled electrathon racers can be constructed
for less than $1,500.

Rated Nominal Voltage	Number of 6-volt Batteries	Fully Charged (volts)	Minimum safe level prior to recharging (volts)
72 V	12	78	63
96 V	16	103	84
108 V	18	116	95
120 V	20	128	105

Open Circuit Voltage 6-volt	12-volt	State of Charge	Hydrometer Reading
6.3	12.6	100%	1.265+
6.2	12.4	75%	1.225
6.1	12.2	50%	1.190
6.0	12.0	25%	1.115

(Source: Battery Council International, 401 N. Michigan Ave., Chicago, IL 60611.)

Testing Amperage "Under A Load"

Jim Tervort offers the following advice based on his hands-on experience with testing batteries: I was test-driving a converted Dodge Colt and it wouldn't go faster than 45 mph. This concerned me because I had calculated a 50-to-52 mph maximum speed. I used a 50-amp battery tester, which places a 50-amp load for ten seconds on the system, and the batteries showed up fine. If there's a dead battery, this test will identify it. However, I also have a 250-amp tester, which is a more realistic simulation of the actual current flow demanded by an electric car. When I put the 250-amp load on the batteries, one at a time, the cause of the problem showed up immediately: a defective battery. It turned out to be a manufacturer's defect, invisible under a 50-amp test, but it revealed itself under the 250-amp test. After I installed a new battery, the car did 52 mph with no problem.

Ken Williams, a transportation manager with Peoples Gas Systems in Miami, Fla., has 10 years of experience with electric vehicles, gained while working with Eastern Airlines. He was directly responsible for over 1,500 vehicles at the Miami Airport and supervised maintenance of 300 EVs, ranging from baggage tractors to forklifts, throughout southeastern U.S. He has these cautionary words: Off-road electric vehicles are definitely a good choice in the short term for heavy-duty constant work. Many of the vehicles I worked with were in motion 12 to 15 hours every day and went through at least two recharging sessions daily. The vehicles worked fine and cost less than gasoline or diesel industrial trucks.

However, after three or four years, the battery chargers and batteries tended to become less efficient. Electricity charging costs went up, the chargers often cooked the batteries and my battery replacement costs soared.

Battery filling procedures were difficult to monitor, causing acid-loss damage to electrical components and higher costs for replacement parts. Many people will fill the batteries with water and then turn the charger on; others will charge first, which is correct, but then they'll look at the charger, see that the batteries are charged, get in the car and start driving without checking the water levels in the batteries.

It is my experience that the care and feeding of electric vehicles tend to increase in cost the longer you own them, and any estimate of the life-cycle cost should include a safety margin to allow for higher operating costs caused by less-efficient battery chargers.

25

Conversion or Ground Up?

By Shari Prange, Electro Automotive, Felton, Calif.

One of the continuing debates involving electric cars focuses on whether they should be converted from existing gasoline-powered cars, or designed from the "ground up" as electrics. I contend that both answers are right, at different times. Let's look at the advantages and disadvantages of each to see what I mean.

The ground-up design makes it possible to provide the best possible platform for an electric. This includes aerodynamics, rolling resistance, curb weight, battery placement, handling, gearing and safety. It certainly sounds like the ideal plan.

However, ground-up engineering takes a lot of time. When Detroit designs a car that is 70 percent new and 30 percent from parts "off the shelf," it takes 3.1 million hours of engineering time. That's just *designing the car,* not getting it into actual production. General Motors announced the Impact in January 1990 and in mid-1991 chose a factory to build it. We may actually see it (or its eventual incarnation) on the showroom floor in 1994 or 1995.

Ground-up engineering is also expensive. Besides the cost of the millions of hours of engineering design time, there is the cost of sourcing new materials and components, retooling, retraining, and shifting the work force and facilities. It is estimated that a ground-up electric, when it reaches the showroom, will be prices in the $20,000 to $30,000 range.

Another factor that is expensive in terms of both time and money is regulatory red tape. The amount of testing and certification required for a ground-up car is so extensive that only a large company has the resources to comply with it. This adds to the delay and expense of introducing the vehicle.

Ground-up designs also inhibit standardization of components and innovation. If each piece is designed to fit into one specific place in one specific vehicle, it becomes difficult to experiment by mixing and matching. Options are limited to the precise package offered by the manufacturer. Since ground-up designs can only be produced economically by a major manufacturer, this essentially shuts small companies completely out of the electric vehicle market – and out of the design and experimentation phase.

Ground-up electrics are a slower way to change the make-up of the automotive population. There are approximately 143 million cars in the U.S. today (1991). Since new car sales run around 10 million cars annually, and only two percent of sales are required to be zero-emissions vehicles in 1998, replacing the gasoline-powered cars with ground-up electrics will be a slow process.

In addition, what kind of pollution does this process generate? The manufacture of each new car generates something on the order of 2 tons of refuse. Each old gasoline car that is retired from service, once stripped of usable parts, leaves 30 percent of its weight as unrecycleable waste. If a substantial portion of the gasoline cars were being retired and replaced, there would be much smaller marker for usable parts form the junkyard, increasing this percentage. Much of this waste ends up in landfills.

Now let's look at conversions. Conversions suffer performance limitations because they are adaptations. Just how serious are these limitations? General Motors claims a projected range for the Impact of 120 miles. Conversions typically can cover 40 to

60 miles in normal commuter driving, and it is not uncommon for the better ones to get more than 80 miles. For comparison, most cars in the U.S. travel less than 30 miles per day, and most household shave more than one car. So conversions can provide 200 percent of the typical daily driving range, while a ground-up electric is expected to provide more than 400 percent. Is this difference significant under actual driving conditions?

• Conversions have tops speeds of 60 miles per hour (or more), and have adequate acceleration and braking. Conversions can be brought to the market more quickly and affordably because they use existing designs. no effort or expense is wasted on designing new bodies, suspensions, steering, braking system or roll-up windows.

Of the "production" electrics built in the past, all of the ones that have adequate streetworthy performance were production conversions based on gasoline-car platforms. So is the G-Van, converted by Conceptor Industries of Canada using a GM Van. Another example of the importance of converted production gasoline cars is GM's use of its Geo Storm for testing the Impact's drive components. The first electric that GM brings to the showroom may be based on an existing platform. Perhaps there is a good reason for this pattern.

• Conversions provide an affordable entry-level electric vehicle. they can be converted for less than $10,000, and are available **today.** They can introduce a large number of people to electrics quickly, and help develop the marketplace.

• Conversions are often more environmentally sound than ground-up cars. They require fewer resources to build and they recycle existing cars that might otherwise be junked.

The fact is that both conversions and ground-up electric cars are needed for the proper evolution of the electric vehicle, each at its own stage. Now is the time for affordable, quickly available conversions to introduce electrics into the market and begin the transition from our dependency on petroleum. The next state is production conversion, which are built on a larger scale using factory-new "gliders" as platforms (using the existing production chassis stripped of the engine, catalytic converter and other internal combustion engine parts). This stage still allows a great deal of experimentation and field testing. The third stage will be ground-up designs from major manufacturers.

Even at the third stage, there will be room for the hobbyist conversion. Just as gasoline car owners swap engines and build kit cars in order to have something a little different from the neighbors, some electric car owners will want to tinker and experiment with conversions.

For everything there is a season.

How much energy does it take to make a car?

Energy required to manufacture a 2500-pound vehicle[1]: **120.7 million Btus**
Energy in one gallon of gasoline: **125,000 Btus**
Amount of gasoline equal to the energy used in manufacturing a 2500-pound vehicle: **965 gallons**
Time taken to consume 965 gallons of gasoline[2]: **1.91 years**
In other words, the average driver can drive for almost two years on the energy saved by converting a car to electric.

Sources: (1) *Indirect Energy Consumption for Transportation Projects,* prepared for the California Department of Transportation by DeLeuw, Cather, October 1975; (2) the average driver consumes 506 gallons per year, *Facts and Figures,* Motor Vehicle Manufacturers Association, 1991, p. 53.

How to bring a converted EV into the classroom

In 1991, a team of high school students from St. Johnsbury, Vt., entered a converted EV in the American Tour de Sol race and won its category. Bruce Burk, an instructor at St. Johnsbury Academy explains how the program started.

Three years ago, a group of my students viewed the beginning of the Tour de Sol in Montpelier, Vt. One of the students asked why we could not build a car and enter the race. There was no reason why we should not. The students went back and began building an electric-powered vehicle for the next year's race.

From the beginning, the electric car was a student-driven event. St. Johnsbury Academy believes that, for authentic learning to take place, the student must have an investment in the education process. The Electric Car Club has developed into a new way of teaching and we received a grant to document this *event-driven curriculum.*

Industry leaders have asked schools to connect the world of the classroom with the world of work. In the event-driven curriculum, all the work students do is focused on contributing to the completion of an event. Students are responsible for all phases of research, design, testing and implementation of technology.

Teachers wanting to introduce an event-driven curriculum into their classrooms should consider the following: selecting the right event, developing an organizational method, designing the organizational components, creating a time table, identifying the sources of information, assessing the viewing audience, identifying the system of support, selecting recording methods and the final project. *For more information, contact Bruce at 802-748-8171 or 802-748-5463 (fax).*

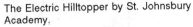

The Electric Hilltopper by St. Johnsbury Academy.

Rep. George Brown, sponsor of the 1976 and 1991 EV bills.

Some hints about converting an old MG into a Zero Pollution Car

When making a change in lifestyle, it's often made easier by hearing how other people made that change. Bob Wing, a member of the EAA board of directors, describes some milestones on the road to becoming an EV owner. He hopes he'll persuade you to make the same journey.

I look back on the great gasoline shortage of 1973, with its long lines at service stations and rising fuel costs, as a positive influence. It motivated me to act on a long-standing desire to have a battery-powered car for local travel.

I didn't want just any electric vehicle. I wanted a rag top, something that did not look like other small sports cars. I stumbled across a promising listing in a trade paper: $100 for a 1959 MGA roadster, or what was left of it after two inoperable MGAs were combined into one. It was just the right car for my conversion plan.

Before I found my optimum system, I went through three motors. The first two were very cheap and had been used in a mechanical experiment (as I found out later). The drive shaft in both motors had twisted off and the seller had welded on new ones, so the motor whined like a police siren when the armature rubbed the stator. As with most things in life, you get what you pay for. Eventually I bought a new 20-horsepower Presolite motor designed for EV application and a solid-state controller. If I had installed these items initially, many hours and dollars would have been saved.

The EV cost $4,500 to complete over a five-year period. In today's market, it could be $8,000 unless you find a used EV for parts. The MGA with gasoline engine weighed 1,995 pounds, while the electric version weighs 2,950 pounds. It gets two miles per kilowatt-hour, which works out to about 8 cents per mile. Occasionally I have to borrow a cup of electricity to get home, but I have never had to grind the valves, install a timing belt, change the oil, or replace a new alternator.

I usually take the MGA to pick up the mail and for other errands. Since we are surrounded by Point Reyes National Seashore, lots of visitors drop in for the day. Some people stop to shop in Inverness and immediately notice the quiet operation of the MGA. At least one person a week tells me, "Nice car. I had one just like that." I have to respond, "No, not just like mine." When they protest, I open the hood.

Bob Wing with his converted 1959 MGA in Inverness, Calif.

Part III

EV Resources

A Directory of Services for Electric Vehicles

Be a considerate consumer.
If you do not heed this advice, you may contribute to the demise of some well-meaning EV entrepreneurs. Many people write to a firm to request information, assuming that the firm has included postage and handling in its annual budget. I have witnessed an EV entrepreneur pick up his mail and seen on returned envelopes the 75-cent postage that must be applied to send people information.

"My board of directors is very annoyed with me," the entrepreneur confided to me. "We made it a policy to send out information only if people help us out with the cost of postage. But I keep sending out our brochure to people who request it, even when they don't send me a self-addressed envelope and a dollar. It probably costs me three bucks when you figure in the cost of typing a label and the literature costs. But what am I going to do? People want information, so I send it to them."

Many of these savvy EV suppliers are not the best business people. I can count a dozen owners of EV businesses who tell me that they are in the business mostly because they feel they are offering a service that people need. "Someone's gotta be there to share this information," they tell me. Although most EV businesses are subsidized by a full-time job or another business under the same roof, their owners can't resist sending out "just ten more" replies to requests for literature. For their own good, don't ask for literature without enclosing adequate postage.

If you provide a service for the EV industry and your company does not appear here, please send your information to the publisher: Editor, South Florida Electric Auto Association, 101 South East 15th Avenue, Ft. Lauderdale, FL 33301. Periodic updates of this book will include the latest information on hand.

Notice to readers: If you would like to receive updates to this directory listing, you are encouraged to send *a self-addressed, stamped envelope (SASE with sufficient first-class postage for a one-ounce update report, plus $2)* to the publisher, South Florida Electric Auto Association. As a public service, SFEAA will mail an update with news of new companies and new products offered by the companies listed in this directory, but only if the SASE is enclosed with the request.

This directory was compiled in October 1991. You are encouraged to consult other directories, such as *The World Electric Vehicle Directory,* available from EV Progress, Alexander Research, #1301, 215 Park Avenue South, New York, NY 10003.

Shari Prange

R.R. Rahder's EV.

Alphabetical Directory

This section brings together in alphabetical order the suppliers of parts, information and vehicles, i.e., the core of the electric vehicle industry. Individuals are listed under their company name and a cross reference will help you connect the person with the company. The alphabetical listing gives some basic information about the service provided by the company.

The companies are then listed **by name only** under the Service Categories, which cover Conversions, Manufacturers, Solar Autos, Kits, Auto-Cycles, Consultants, Electric Car Parts, and Batteries. The remainder of the EV Resources involves listings not mentioned in the Alphabetical Directory, including alphabetical listings of EV Organizations, EV Publications, Other Publications, Related Services and Products, and Bumper Stickers, Etc.

A

Advanced D.C. Motors, Inc.
219 Lamson St, Syracuse, NY 13206
315-434-9303, 315-432-9290 (fax)
Manufacturer of 10 HP and 19 HP DC motors made especially for EV use. Available through authorized dealers.

Aerovironment
Box 5031, Monrovia, CA 91017-7131
818-359-9983/358-1691 (fax)
Design contractor hired by General Motors to develop the Impact.

Alco Battery Co.
2980 Red Hill, Costa Mesa, CA 92626 Battery manufacturer.

Alternative Autos
Box 1249, Parker, CO 80134
303-690-5031 General EV service.

American Council for an Energy Efficient Economy (ACEEE)
1001 Connecticut Ave., #801
Washington, D.C. 20036
202-429-8873 Information about energy-efficient appliances.

American Motion Systems, Inc.
1221 Avenido Acaso, Unit K
Camarillo, CA 93010
805-482-0407, 805-389-1042 (fax)
Electric turbines for EV technology and other transportation applications.

American Public Power Ass'n
2301 M Street, N.W.
Washington, D.C. 202-775-8300

American Public Transit Association (APTA), 202-898-4000
1201 New York Avenue, NW
Washington, DC 20005

Amerigon, 425 E. Huntington Drive
Monrovia, CA 91016 818-305-1100
Developing a commuter EV. Founder Lon Bell played a prominent role in the development of the safety airbag.

Amigo Mobility International
Allan Thiemes, 6693 Dixie Highway
Bridgeport, MI 48722
517-777-0910 Developing a platform mobility aid for less-mobile people.

Arias Research, 13135-C Barton Rd
Whittier, CA 90605 213-944-7975
Developing a sealed bi-polar lead-acid battery for EVs. See Paul Schutte

Arizona Public Service Co.
Box 53999, Phoenix, AZ 85072
Sponsor of the Solar/Electric 500.

Randall Asherlan & Associates
P.O. Box 166, Honokaa, HI 96727
808-775-0301 Compiles EV directory.

ATW, 10 Raiffeisenstrasse
6927 Bad Rappenau, Germany
Commuter EVs, photovoltaic panels.

B

B.A.T., Joseph LaStella
Battery Automated Transportation
2471 South, 2570 West
West Valley City, Utah 84119
801-977-0119, 801-977-0149 (fax)
Advanced battery technology for converted cars.

Baldor Electric Co., 5711 South 7th
Ft. Smith, Ark. 72902
501-646-4711 EV motors.

Batteries Included, Bill Spindler
15174 Kellen Court
Riverside, CA 92506
714-780-6671, 714-369-4997 (fax)
Utility storage, fleet vehicles.

Battery Council International
401 North Michigan Avenue
Chicago, IL 60611 Battery manuals.

Clark Beasley
23725 Oakheath Place
Harbor City, CA 90170
213-539-9223 Supplies electric racer plans and instructions.

Rep. Howard Berman (CA)
137 Cannon House Office Bldg.
Washington, D.C. 20515

202-225-4695, 202/225-9527 (fax)
Staff: Beth Hilliard. Berman
amended the Intermodal Surface
Transportation Efficiency Act (ISTEA)
authorized $12 million for at least 3
consortia (none exceeding $4 million).
Bedford Chloride, United Kingdom
Vehicle: CF4 Heavy Van
Beyond Oil, 415-388-0838
PMC pulse width modulators.
Roger Billings
TechCenter, Suite 1000
26900 East Pink Hill Road
Independence, MO 64057
816-229-3800/229-1000 (fax)
Fuel cell advocate.
Bayerische Motoren Werke BMW
D-8000 München 40 Germany
member of AVERE. Developing a
commuter vehicle expected after
1995, using a drive-train developed by
Unique Mobility of Englewood, CO.
B & M Energy R & D Corp.
P.O. Box 44, Ocala, FL 32678-0044
904-351-3700 EV production planned
in late 1992. Model: Festa Electra
(converted Ford Festiva).
Brasch Labs, 1968 Elden Drive
San Jose, CA 95124-1313
408-371-5969 Instruments for EVs
Rep. George Brown
2188 Rayburn Building
Washington, DC 20515
202-225-6161 Staff: Bob Carey. The
Brown bill (H.R. 1538) – the National
Electric Vehicle Act – provides
funding for EV development,
demonstration and market support,
and infrastructure improvements. The
bill adds electricity to the list of
alternative fuels under the Alternative
Motor Fuels Act of 1988.
Heinrich Bucher, Leichtbau
Industriestrasse 1a
CH-8117 Fällanden, Switzerland
41-1-825-33-22, 41-1-825-34-86 (fax)
Solar autos.

C

California Air Resources Board
Public Information Office
1012 Q Street, P.O. Box 2815
Sacramento, CA 95812
916-322-2990, 916/327-3151
Southern California contact person:
Sylvia Vanderspek, 818-575-6703
California Electric Cars
1669 Del Monte Blvd.

Seaside, CA 93955, 408-899-2012
Model: Monterey, kit car.
California Energy Commission
1516 9th St., Sacramento, CA 95814
916-654-4001 Provides information
about alternative-fuel vehicles. EV
contact: Cece Martin, 916-654-4683
for specific information on EVs.
CAREIRS 1-800-523-2929
Information on renewable energy.
Car-Go Battery Co.
3860 Blake Street
Denver, CO 80205, 303-296-8763
Battery distributor who supports
Denver Electric Vehicle Council.
Chrysler, 12000 Chrysler Drive
Highland Park, MI 48288
313-956-5346 Developing the TEVan,
a minivan conversion.
Citroën International, EV model C15
62 boulevard Victor-Hugo
92200 Neuilly-sur-Seine, France 1-
47-48-56-67 Member of AVERE.
Clean Air Revival, Steve Van Ronk
55 New Montgomery St., #424
San Francisco CA 94608
415-495-0494 Electrathon consultant,
organizer of electrathon racing and
the annual Clean Air Revival.
Clean Air North America, #206
23030 Lake Forest Drive
Laguna Hills, Calif. 92653
714-951-3983 Model: LA 301.
Clean Air Transit
1014 Santa Barbara Street
Santa Barbara, CA 93101
805-564-8986 Battery-powered buses,
in use in Santa Barbara.
Clint Cochran, 817 Arthur Street
Davis CA 916-756-3342
Distributor for mini-el three-wheeler.
Columbia Auto Sales, R. Beaumont
9720 Owen Brown Road
Columbia, MD 21045 301-799-3550
301/799-4572 (fax) Author of a book
on EVs, developing a people-mover.
Commuter Transportation Services,
3550 Wilshire Blvd., #300
Los Angeles, CA 90010 213-365-6803
Ride-sharing programs with literature
and ideas for commuter incentives.
Conceptor Industries, Inc.
A Vehma International Company
521 Newpark Boulevard
Newmarket, Ontario L3Y 4X7
Canada 416-836-4611, 416-836-9784
(fax) Manufactures the Electric
G-Van, built from a GM Vandura/Rally
van "glider." 1991 base prices:

Five-passenger model, $55,179;
Cargo model, $52,737. Conceptor's
close association with GM lends the
appearance of an OEM provider of
electric vans. The converted vans are
sold through GM's dealer network.
Coop Car, 6 Via Principe Tomaso
10125 Turin, Italy
Electric cars with photovoltaic arrays.
Cruising Equipment Co.
6315 Seaview Avenue
Seattle, WA 98107 206-782-8100
206-782-4336 (fax) Offers its **Amp-
Hour+ Meter** for monitoring the state-
of-charge of batteries.
Curtis Instruments
6591 Sierra Lane, Dublin, CA
510-833-8777 (fax) Supplier of
controllers. Also 200 Kisco Ave, Mt.
Kisco NY 10549 914-666-2971
Cushman, 900 North 21st Street
Lincoln, NE 68503 402-475-9581
Makes a 3-wheel electric "parking
enforcement vehicle."

D

Daimler Benz AG, Postfach 600 202
Member of AVERE, developing
hydrogen cars and EVs.
Dolphin Vehicles
Box 110215, Campbell, CA 95011
The **Vortex** is a build-it-yourself 3-
wheeled vehicle designed to accept a
wide variety of power plants, From
electric to high-power motorcycle, the
Vortex provides a high-performance
platform for advanced transportation
visions. The car is not sold as a kit, it
is built from plans.
Doran Motor Company
1728 Bluehaven Drive
Sparks, NV 89431 702-359-6735
Kit and plans for three-wheeled
vehicle from Subaru components.
*Common Questions About The
Doran Three-Wheeler*
*1. Will it flip? For a stable
three-wheeler, two wheels must be in
the front of the vehicle. The front
track should be as wide as practical
with the center of gravity low and
close to the front axle. The vehicle's
handling is similar to any front-wheel
drive car. The tires will lose adhesion
before enough side force can be
developed to flip the vehicle. Further
discussion of this subject and an
engineering analysis is available in a*
*manual (cost: $39.95 plus $4 for
postage and handling).*
*2. What will it cost? This vehicle
will cost from $5,000 to over $10,000,
depending on the amount of labor you
have done by others. Another
variable is the number of parts that
you buy new, rebuilt, or from salvage
yards.*
*3. Where do you get parts? Most
of the Doran's drive-train and
mechanical parts are taken from 1980
to 1989 Subaru hatchbacks with an
1800cc flat-4 engine and a five-speed
transaxle. The front axles and
rack-and-pinion assembly are taken
from a 1986 or newer Subaru sedan,
which has a wider front track than the
hatchback. These parts can be
bought new, bought as rebuilt parts,
or salvaged from wrecking yards.*

E

Eagle-Picher Industries
P.O. Box 47, Joplin, MO 64802
417-623-8000, 417-623-8333 (fax)
Manufacturer of nickel-iron and
nickel-cadmium batteries.
Earthmind, P.O. Box 743, Mariposa,
CA 95338
Michael Hackleman 310-396-1527
Consulting on EV design. Michael
also gives seminars using slides,
videos and overhead projections. He
is the author of *At Home With
Alternative Energy; The Homebuilt,
Wind-Generated Electricity Handbook;
Wind and Windspinners: A nuts 'n'
bolts approach to wind-electric
systems; Electric Vehicles: Design
and build your own; The
Hybrid-Configured Electric Vehicle;
Battery Use Of Utility-Supplied
Electricity and Low-Voltage DC in the
Home and Shop; and Waterworks:
an owner builder guide to rural water
systems.* His production of a video
series, *Hand Made Vehicles,* has
grown to include three programs. He
also edits a magazine on alternative
transportation (ATN) and publishes a
useful bibliography called
Transportation Sources and
References.
Ecotech Autoworks
Jeff Shumway, Box 9262
1524-V Springhill Road
McLean, VA 22102 703-893-3045

He reconditions existing EVs and consults on conversions. For internal combustion engines, he offers fluid filtration systems to eliminate changing of engine oil, anti-freeze and transmission oil. Featured extensively in international media (TV, print, radio), Ecotech identifies itself as "the premier environmentally-conscious auto facility." Ecotech can convert your car into a **planet car**, powered by electricity, propane or ecogas (an overhaul of your conventional gasoline car, including lifetime tune-up and oil changes, recycled tires and high-efficiency components).

El Trans, Haraldsvey 65
8900 Randers, Denmark 41 88 71 (fax) Three-wheeled commuter vehicles (not for highway use).
U.S.: Clint Cochran, 916-756-3342
817 Arthur St, Davis CA

Electric Auto Conversions
4504 W. Alexander Road
North Las Vegas, NV 89030
702-645-2132 Bill Kuehl
"We have been building electric autos since 1979. We can convert any small car with a standard transmission to electric power."

Electric Auto Crafters
2S 643 Nelson Lake Road
Batavia, IL 60510
John Stockberger, 312-879-0207, parts, information and testing for the do-it-yourself EV enthusiast.

Electric Fuel Propulsion Corp.
4747 N. Ocean Drive, #223
Ft. Lauderdale, FL 33308
305-785-2228, Robert R. Aronson (chairman). Working on production of a luxury EV ("Silver Volt") and a tri-polar lead-cobalt battery in China (Shanghai). EFP persuaded Holiday Inn to install six EV rapid-charging stations in motels along 300 miles of Interstate 94, the first electric car expressway. EV motorists were able to travel from Detroit to Chicago. Aronson also supervised the installation of the world's first coin-operated charging station for public use, located at the Los Angeles Airport Marriott Hotel.

Electric Mobility, 591 Mantua Blvd
Sewell, NJ 08080 800-257-7955
Electric bicycles and wheelchairs.

Electric Motor Cars Sales & Service, 4301 Kingfisher

Houston, TX 77035 Ken Bancroft, 713-729-8668 Conversions, parts, maintenance, consultant.

Electric Power Research Institute
3412 Hillview Avenue
Box 10412, Palo Alto, CA 94303
415-855-2580 (technical line). Information on ground-source heat pumps for reducing your electric bill. Washington, D.C.: 202-872-9222

Electric Vehicle Matrix
1088 Bishop Street Suite 911
Honolulu, HI 96813
Ron Richmond 808-521-3122
Seeking to build a commuter EV.

Electric Vehicles of America, Inc.
P.O. Box 59, Maynard, MA 01754
Bob Batson, Registered Professional Engineer, 508-897-9393 Free catalog. EV components, kits, supplier of Advanced D.C. Motors, Curtis controllers, etc., consulting. EVA has a number of technical papers available, including "Selecting a Vehicle for Conversion." EVA makes EV calculations for vehicles to verify estimated performance and range. EVA wants to ensure that people get the performance they want.

Electricars, Ltd.
Carlyon Road, 15, Atherstone
Warwickshire CV9 1LQ, U.K.
Battery-powered industrial trucks.

Electro Automotive
Mike Brown, Shari Prange
P.O. Box 1113, Felton, CA 95018
408-429-1989 Kits, EV components, books and videos, consulting on conversion. He's written a book on how to convert a gasoline-powered car to electric called *Convert It!*

Electromotive Systems, Route 1, Box 88, Lenoir City, TN 37771
615-986-5744 Consultant.

Electric Vehicle Custom Conversion, 1712 Nausika Ave.
Rowland Heights, CA 91748
Larry Foster 818-913-8579
Specialty ICE-to-EV conversions (MG-B, Alfa Romeo, Porsche). Marriage plates/adapters, motor couplings and specialty machining. Report by Larry in August 1991: *My shop has been as busy as I could want it. I have been out every weekend helping do-it-yourselfers. So far we have 2 VW Bugs, a VW square back, an MGB roadster, a Honda CRX, a Rabbit sedan and 2 Rabbit pickups (and two*

more in the works). VW Sciroccos, Chevettes, and Toyota pickups.

Energy Partners, 407-688-0500 1501 Northpoint Parkway, West Palm Beach, FL 33407 Fuel-cell car.

ETAP, Box 8683, Stanford, CA 94309 415-856-2706 415-856-2796 (fax) Stanford University professor Dr. John Reuyl's hybrid EV project, funded in part by the California Energy Commission.

EV Consultants, Ed Campbell 327 Central Park West New York, NY 10025 212-222-0160 Consultant.

EVIA, Electric Vehicle Industry Association, 9140 Centerway Rd. Gaithersburg, MD 20879 David Goldstein 301-231-3990

Eyeball Engineering 16738 Foothill Blvd. Fontana, CA 92336 Ed Rannberg 714-829-2011 Supplies conversion kits. Consultant.

F

FIAT, 200 Corso G. Agnelli Turin, Italy or Stada Torino, 50 10043 Orbassano (Torino) Member of AVERE. Panda Elettra.

Fisher Technology 6045 Upper Straits West Bloomfield, MI 48324 313-363-4847, 313-363-4847 (fax) Automotive brushless DC motors.

Ford Motor Co., The American Road Dearborn, MI 48121 313-322-3000 ETX-II Van, developing the sodium-sulfur battery since 1965.

Fridez Solar AG, Heiligholzstrasse 56 CH-4142 Münchenstein, Switzerland 41-61-46-34-63 Solar-assisted autos. This company's products were featured in a television program which aired on public television in 1990.

G

Gates Energy Corp. See Ovonic Corp.

General Assembly Corp. 117 South Second Avenue West Jefferson, NC 28694 919-246-5143, 919-246-6030 (fax) Printed circuit board assembly, special pricing for electric vehicles.

General Motors, 30200 Mound Road Warren, MI 48090 Impact in 1995.

The Lean Machine: A three-wheeled vehicle with potential as a commuter car or a 150-miles-per-gallon long-distance form of transportation. Developed by General Motors, the concept car is being tested by CALTRANS (the transportation department of the State of California).

Gillas, Lon, 515 W. 25th Street McMinnville, OR 503-684-6026 EV converter (E-motion).

Green Motor Works, 5228 Vineland North Hollywood, CA 91601 William Meurer (Pres.), Jim Lunceford (Conversion Supervisor) 818-766-3800 818-766-3969 (fax) Showroom and conversion shop to sell and service non-polluting vehicles.

H

R. Hahn AG, Curtibergstrasse, 69 CH-8646 Wagen, AVERE.

Bill Hamilton, Box 5025 Santa Barbara, CA 93150 Consult, author of dozens of EV feasibility studies.

Harding Energy Corp. See Ovonic Corp.

Chuck Harrison, 2620 Cool Spring Road, Adelphi MD 20783 301-495-7113, 422-8704 He updates Compuserve's EV listing under **Go Earth**, Energy section. Leave Chuck a message on the bulletin board if you have an update.

Hawaii Pacific Technology and Trade, 98-859 Olena Street Aiea, Hawaii 96701 808-488-8796 Imports electric vehicles from Asia. Cooperates with a Chinese manufacturer of nickel-metal hydride batteries, licensed from Ovonics. Also works with *Hawaii China Asia Energy and Technology (HCA-EAT)* (a not-for-profit organization) to accelerate sustainable rural development in developing nations, based on eco-agriculture and renewable energy sources. Ovonic batteries have long life (1000-plus cycles), no poisonous materials (no cadmium, no lead), no memory effect, and increased tolerance to over-charging and over-discharging. The first test of Ovonic battery packs will be for an electric bicycle, since China has a potential market of well over 100 million electric bicycles that could benefit from this battery and pave the way for its scale up to EVs.

Mr. Cliff Hayden, CMA Limited 4727 Gardner Ave, Everett, WA 98203 Fleet management consultant, 25 years of experience; managed GTE's fleet of 200 alternative-fuel vehicles.

Dr. John Hedger, 505-546-0288 Drawer 1077, Deming, NM 88031 Designer of solar-powered battery charger; holds a patent on a solar tracking apparatus.

HIL Electric Winfield Industrial Park Rowland Gill, Newcastle on Tyne NE39 1EH United Kingdom Manufacturer of electric vans.

Hitney Solar Products EV Products, Gene Hitney 2655 N. Highway 89 Chino Valley, Arizona 86323 602-636-2201 Model: Honda Civics. Contracted by Arizona Department of Commerce to produce EVs.

Höngg, Solar Team, Postfach 3350 8049 Zürich, Switzerland 01 341 77 20 (fax) Makes a three-wheeled aerodynamic solarmobile.

Horlacher AG, P.O. Box 50 Güterstrasse 9, CH-4313 Möhlin Switzerland 41-61-88-21-18 41-61-88-32-00 (fax) This small three-wheeled vehicle appeared in the first issue of M. Hackleman's *ATN*.

L. & J. Huntington Enterprises "Proudly Australian," 2 Broos Rd. Oakville 2765, New South Wales Australia 045-877-371 Model: Mira ECC (Electric Commuter Car) — converted Daihatsu. Conversion kits available. Future: four-seater electric hybrid, all-Australian-built gasoline-electric with all-Australian-made AC 3-phase motor drive.

Hydrocap Corp., 305-696-2504 975 N.W. 95 St, Miami, FL 33150 Profiled in *Home Power #11, July 1989:* "Hydrocaps are a must for lead-acid battery users. They increase the safety of the battery area by reducing explosive hydrogen gas. They are cost-effective by their savings in distilled water alone. They reduce battery maintenance while increasing battery longevity and reliability. They also offer direct tactile feedback regarding the state of charge of the battery's individual cells." — Richard Perez **Directions from Hydrocap:** *Help us make the best Hydrocap for you. A sample vent from your battery shows us how to fit the Hydrocap vent into your battery. Tell us about your battery and your charger by completing our Battery System Information Sheet.*

I

Information Resources 499 S. Capitol Street, S.W. #406 Washington, DC 20003 Newsletters and consultants on alternative fuels. **Instant Auto Heater Co.**, Box 307 Woodside, NY 11377 718-476-1723, 476-2497 (fax) Instaheater for EVs. **Integral Energy Systems**, 109 Argall Nevada City, CA 95959 916-265-8441 800-735-6790 Source of renewable energy devices, including photovoltaic panels. *A portion of all sales is donated to environmental organizations.* **Interesting Transportation** 2362 Southridge Drive Palm Springs, CA 92264 Frank Kelly EV conversions, consultant. **Interstate Batteries** 214-715-6667 Battery manufacturer **IRT Environment**, Ted Flanigan Box 10990, Aspen, CO 81612-9689 303-927-3155/9428 (fax) Global designs for a sustainable environment, publications. **Iveco Bus Division** Corso Lombardia, 20 10099 S. Mauro Torinese Italy, member of AVERE.

J

JDM Products, 543 Bedford Street Concord, MA 01742 Supplies "Taper Ace," a drafting tool. **Johnson Controls**, founded in 1885. 5757 N. Green Bay Avenue Milwaukee, WI 53209 414-228-1200 Battery manufacturer, developing a nickel-hydrogen 30-year battery. **Jordan Energy Institute** 155 Seven Mile Rd, Comstock Park, MI 49321 616-784-7595 Prof. Paul E. Zellar, who spearheaded JEI's entry (*Sunseeker*) in the 1990 GM Sunrayce, describes college's EV program: *To supply the demand for education in the maintenance of EVs, we first contacted EV* *repair facilities to determine the skills needed by their technicians. Employers consistently demand more than technical skills from their employees, namely communications, math and socials skills. This led us, while designing the new program, to concentrate program prerequisites in the first year to allow transfer students who have completed these courses to begin the EV program immediately upon entering JEI. The curriculum consists of Control Systems, Inverters and Battery Chargers, Motors and Generators, Energy Storage, and the Practicum, which allows students to put into practice all the skills required to maintain EVs. We need donations of representative EVs. JEI is a nonprofit organization; all contributions are tax-deductible. We welcome your inquiries.*

K

King Electric Vehicles
Box 514, East Syracuse, NY 13057
Steve Deckard, Kits.
KTA Automotive, Ken Koch
12531 Breezy Way, Orange CA
92669 714-639-9799 EV components, consulting, instruments. Catalog: $4. KTA offers five certified pure-electric vehicle retrofit/conversion kits, which qualify for California's $1,000 tax credit.

L

Larag AG, Nutzfahrzeugwerke
Toggenburgerstrasse, 104
CH-9550 Wil. Switzerland
Models: Larel Elektromobil and Fiat
Panda. Member of AVERE.
Lawrence Livermore National Laboratory, Technology Transfer
7000 East Ave., Livermore, CA 94550
510-422-6416 Seeks collaborators for electromechanical battery R&D.
Lead Industries Association
292 Madison Ave, NY, NY 10017
Information on lead recycling.
Lectric Kar, Robert G. Bucy
Box 28794, Dallas, TX 75228
714-327-7197 Supplier of plans for converting small cars to electric power drive. "The Average do-it-yourselfer can handle the conversion, which may need some welder and machinist help." Plans: $25.
Lightwheels, 49 East Hudson St
NY, NY 10012 EVs in schools
Steve Stollman 212-431-0600

M

W. D. Mitchell, 20 Victoria Drive
Rowlett, TX 75055 214-475-0361
Creates "fancy" EVs.
Ingenieurbüro Muntwyler
Electroingenieur HTL/STV
Zähringerstrasse 53, Postfach 73
CH-3000 Bern 9 Switzerland
41-31-23-15-57 Solar autos.

N

National Association of Fleet Administrators (NAFA)
120 Wood Avenue, South
Iselin, NJ 08830 908-494-8100 Ask for their annual Fleet Reference Book. Learn about fleet administration.
New Concepts Engineering (NCE) Kevin McDonald
2119 N.E. 90th Ave.
Vancouver, WA 98664
206-254-3238, 800-325-3512
4-B SW Monroe Parkway, #168
Lake Oswego, OR 97035
503-781-0270 Kevin has developed a heater for converted EVs that uses the original heater core for heating the EV's interior. NCE has developed a line of digital panel meters as well as standard EV components.
Cap'n Burt Newland, 3317 Maryland Ave, Sebring, FL 33872 813-471-2043
Built a Sines Single-Axle Auto-cycle.
Northeast Sustainable Energy Association (NESEA)
American Tour de Sol
23 Ames St., Greenfield, MA 01301
413-774-6051/774-6053 (fax)
NESEA organizes an annual EV symposium in October. The American Tour de Sol, held in May, educates the public about renewable sources of energy and electric vehicles suited for daily use. First held in 1989, the race has categories for commuter vehicles, photovoltaic racers, and open category for all other battery-powered vehicles. Additional categories, like "innovative storage" (such as hydrogen fuel cells) will be created as needed.

O

OOO7 Triple O Seven Corp.
Box 740, Everson, WA 98247
206-966-7206, 206/966-0362 (fax)

Limited-production sports EV and kits.
Ovonic Corp., 1675 Maple Road
Troy, Mich. 48024 313-280-1900
*Sources for nickel-metal hydride
batteries developed by Ovonic.*
Gates Energy Corp. 904-462-3911
Box 147114, Gainesville, FL 32614
Harding Energy Corp.
826 Washington Street
Grand Haven, MI 49417
616-847-0989, 616-847-1966 (fax)
Real Goods Catalog *(see below
under Related Services and Products)*

P

**Pacific International Center for
High Technology Research
(PICHTR)**, 711 Kapiolani Blvd, #200,
Honolulu, HI 96813 808-539-1571
Palmer Industries, Box 707,
Endicott, NY 13760 800-847-1304
Supplies electric bicycles.
Renton H. Patterson, 618 Glenwood
Drive, Pembroke Ontario Canada
Consultant for educational projects,
directed several high school classes
in constructing EVs and boats.
Performance Speedway, C. Fetzer
2810 Algonquin Ave.
Jacksonville, FL 32210
904-387-9858 Catalog: $5. EV parts
and light vehicles.
Peugeot S.A., Chemin Vicinal 2
F-78140 Velizy-Villacoublay
Also: B.P. 1, 75761 Paris
Telephone (1) 40 665511, member of
AVERE; 205, J5 minicar and Volta 90.
Pfander AG, Fahrzeugbau,
Ifangstrasse 12a, CH-8603
Schwerzenbach, Switzerland
41-1-825-35-25, 41-1-825-06-77 (fax)
Solar autos.
Power Savers, P.O. Box 11389
Honolulu, HI 96828
808-988-9506 Hal Spindel
Longest-running radio talk show on
energy issues: K108, 1080 AM Talk
line: 808-522-5108.
Pro-Electric, Albert Navarro
3440 S. State Road 7
Miramar, FL 33023
305-983-6003 Consultant, EV fleet
management and service.
Progetti Gestioni Ecologische
Via Ippolito Roselini, 1
20124 Milano, Italy
Member of AVERE.
Program Development Associates

9140 Centerway Road
Gaithersburg, MD 20879
David Goldstein 301-231-3990
Consultant, EV programs, marketing
and maintenance, database
administration, end-user support.
Public Service Corp. of Colorado
2701 W. 7th Ave, Denver, CO 80204,
303-571-7511 A utility that offers
"load-shedding": your major
appliances are connected to the utility
via a black box. During peak demand
periods, your appliances may be shut
off for short periods to manage the
system's peak load.
Public Technology Inc.
1301 Pennsylvania Avenue, N.W.
Washington, DC 20004
202-626-2400 Publishes handbooks
for members (funded in part by the
Urban Coalition, including major
metropolitan counties and cities).
Evaluation guides for the purchase of
alternative fuel vehicles.

R

Renault
9 Avenue du 18 Juin 1940
F-92500 Rueil-Malmaison
Member of AVERE.
Russco Engineering, Box 3761
Santa Rosa, CA 95402 707-542-
4151 PWM controllers for EVs.

S

**Sacramento Municipal Utility
District (SMUD)**, Box 15830
Sacramento, CA 95852-1830
916-732-6557 Advocates of
electrified transportation.
SAFT, 251 Industrial Blvd.
Box 7366, Greenville, NC 27835
919-830-1600/752-0057 (fax)
U.S. office of the nickel-iron and
nickel-cadmium battery manufacturer.
Albert J. Sawyer, P.E.
Nevada EAA, Box 19040
Las Vegas, NV 89132
702-438-8294 Consultant
Paul Schutt & Associates
673 Via Del Monte
Palos Verdes Estates, CA 90274
310-373-4063/373-5572 (fax)
Representative for manufacturers who
supply EV components.
S-D-P, 117 Bernstrasse
CH-3613 Steffisburg, Switzerland

Electric car conversions.
Sebring Auto-Cycle
Box 1479, Sebring, FL 33871
813-655-2131, 813-655-0030 (fax)
800-HOT-WATT Conversions for
under $14,000; developing three-
wheeled vehicle ("auto-cycle").
SEER Solar Energy Expo & Rally,
"Tour de Mendo," 239 S. Main St,
Willits, CA 95490 707-459-1256,
459-1360 (fax) In August, the "Solar
Capital of the World" is host to a
showcase of practical renewable
energy systems for transportation,
home and business.
Paul Shipps, 3E Vehicles
Box 19409, San Diego, CA 92119
Publishes EV engineering guides.
Tom Sines, Yvette Chermey
Okeechobee, FL 813-763-0547
They hold patent no. 4,527,648 for
the Single-Axle Auto-Cycle.
SMH Swiss Watchmaking
Box 1185, Faubourg du Lac 6
CH-2501 Bienne, Switzerland
032 22 97 22, fax 032 23 15 95
Working with VW on Swatch car.
Solar Car Corporation
Doug Cobb, Robert Adams
1300 Lake Washington Road
Melbourne, FL 32935 407-254-2997
Model: electric Ford Festiva, electric
Chevy S-10 pick-up truck, solar
options available. Other models
(call). General EV consulting and
energy-efficiency audits. Consulting
services for marine applications,
photovoltaics and the bulk-purchasing
of EV components.
Solar Electric, 116 Fourth Street
Santa Rosa, CA 95401
800-832-1986 Various conversions.
Solar Trike, Box 491, Big Pine Key,
FL 33043 The solar tricycle travels 5
to 17 mph on flat ground and has a
range of 20 to 60 miles, depending on
components and speed.
Solarland, Bruce Meland
63600 Deschutes Road
Bend, OR 97701 503-388-1908
Developer of a solar powered electric
three-wheeler, Bruce provides plans
and a parts list. Publishes an annual
newspaper called "Electrifying Times,"
available in April. The 1992 edition
commemorates the 100th anniversary
of the electric car ($4). Inquire with a
self-addressed, stamped envelope.

Solectria, 27 Jason Street
Arlington, MA 02174 617-894-6670
The Force (converted Geo Metro) and
components. Developer of AC
induction motors, brushless motors,
amp-hour counter, components and
1100-watt air conditioning-heating
systems for EVs.
Soleq, 5969 N. Elston Avenue
Chicago, IL 60646 312-792-3811 Mr.
Obah develops EV electronic
components with advanced
engineering.
Speed of Light, Solar Energy
Education, Box 485, Altadena, CA
91001 800-765-3383 (order line)
EV videos and teacher's guides,
targeted especially for schools.
Spykstall Spykenisse B.V.
Zijlstraat, 9, 3201 CX Spijkenisse
Netherlands, member of AVERE.
Sun-Craft AG, vorm. Solartechnik F.
Plattner, Industriestrasse 6a
CH-6055 Alpnach Dorf, Switz.
41-41-96-29-96 Solar autos.
Suntools, 707-964-9019
1258 N. Main Street, #B2B
Ft. Bragg, CA 95437 Supplier of
parts build your own solar-electric
vehicle. $20 catalog.
Swatch, H.P. Rentch, SMH,
Seevorstadt 6 CH-2501, Bienne,
Switzerland 011 41 32 229722
Planning to produce with Volkswagen
a small EV "in 30 months that will sell
for about $6000" (*The Washington
Post,* August 11, 1991).

T

Carl Taylor, 3871 S.W. 31 Street
Hollywood, FL 33023
305-981-9462 Electrical technician,
EV maintenance and repair.
John Tennyson 808-776-1039
Box 379, Paauilo, HI 96776
Participates in solar car races.
Texas General Land Office
1-800-6-FUEL-99 Information on
alternative-fueled vehicles.
Torpedo, 6 Viale Ghiaie, 24030
Presezzo, Italy Full line of battery-
powered cars, trucks and vans.
Rep. E. Torres, 1740 Longworth
Washington, DC 20515
202-225-5256 Sponsor of Lead
Battery Recycling Incentive Act.
Staff: Fran McPoland California:
310-695-0702, 310/692-6221 (fax).

Toyota Motor Corporation
4-18 Koraku 1-chome
Bunkyo-ku, Tokyo Japan
Jim Treacy, 1508 Swann Street,
N.W., Washington, DC 20009
202-483-1855, 202-483-0073 (fax) EV
expert, consulting and market
research. Targeted direct mailings.
Triple O Seven Corp. See OOO7
Trojan Battery Co., 12380 Clark St.,
Santa Fe Springs, CA 90670
Fred Daniel, product manager
800-423-6569, 213-946-8381
714-521-8215, 213-941-6038 fax
Also: 5194 Minola Drive
Lithonia, GA 30038 404-981-8674
Battery manufacturer.
Tropico Solar, Solar George
Box 417, Big Pine Key, FL 33043
305-872-3976 Catalog: $4. Supplies
EV parts, adds PV panels to EVs.

U

Unique Mobility, 3700 S. Jason
Avenue, Englewood, CO 80110
303-761-2137/761-3218 (fax). Not
currently offering a conversion as of
October 1991. Supplies high-power
drive-train components to a number of
car manufacturers, including BMW's
latest commuter car (designed around
a sodium-sulfur battery). Conversion
of a minivan won the attention of the
judges in the Los Angeles initiative;
lack of "gliders" (the shell of a
minivan) forced Unique to withdraw.
U.S. Batteries, 1675 Sampson Ave,
Corona, CA 91719 714-371-8090
Also: 2750 Raymond Ave., Signal
Hill, CA 90806 Battery manufacturer
UtilityFree™
Box 228, Basalt, CO 81621
303-928-0846, 928-0847 (fax)
Specializing in alkaline battery
technologies. Nickel-cadmium, nickel-
iron, nickel-hydrogen and nickel-
cadmium fiber batteries (new and
reconditioned).

V

Vehicle Development Group
Box 1021, Cambridge MA 02140
617-625-8226 "We prototype the
future." Aerodynamic evaluation,
advanced composites, feasibility
studies, turn-key prototypes, metal
fabrication, safety analysis,
suspension tuning, race support.
Vehma, Inc. (See Conceptor
Industries) 70 Leek Crescent
Richmond Hill, Ont. L4B 1H1
Canada 416-764-5445
Volkswagen, D-3180 Wolfsburg 1
Germany, member of AVERE,
working with Swatch on EV project.

W

W and E Electric Vehicles
Church Lane, Shropshire 5YA 5HS,
United Kingdom
Battery-powered industrial trucks.
Williams Enterprises
Box 1548, Cupertino, CA 95015
Consultant, parts, conversion manual.
Bob Wing, Box 277
Inverness, CA 94937 415-669-7402
EV consultant, has converted two
cars personally and supervised the
conversion of more than 15 others.
Dr. Sumner Wolsky, Ansom
Enterprises, 1900 Coconut Road
Boca Raton, FL 33432 Consultant
407-391-3544/750-1367 (fax)
Victor Wouk Associates
1225 Park Avenue, #5B
New York, NY 10128-1707
212-534-6757 Consultant.

Y

York Technical College
452 South Anderson Road
Rock Hill, SC 29730 803-327-8000
The only two-year technical college
with 17 electric vehicles and Bob
Ferrell, staff consultant who has spent
25 years around EVs and batteries.
One of ten data-gathering Site
Operators for the Department of
Energy.

Larry Foster's converted VW wagon.

CONVERSIONS

Who is converting cars today? Where can you purchase an "electric retrofit"?

Batch Production: The following companies offer a standardized conversion and have issued literature aimed at selling a particular model for conversion.

Battery Automated Transportation
B & M Energy R & D Corp.
California Electric Cars
Hitney Solar Products
L. & J. Huntington Enterprises
Sebring Auto-Cycle
Solar Car Corporation

Solar Electric
Solectria
Unique Mobility*
*Not offering a conversion (as of October 1991). Working with a variety of manufacturers.

THE GRASSROOTS: One-at-a-time conversions and rehabilitations

The following companies offer customized advice and conversion services. Generally, these services are provided by entrepreneurs with small staffs and limited work space. Their overhead is low, but there may be a waiting list for their clients.

WEST COAST
Ken Koch, KTA Services
Orange, CA
EV Custom Conversion
Rowland Heights, CA
Michael Hackleman, Venice, CA
Ron Gillas, McMinnville, OR
EAST COAST
Bob Batson, Electric Vehicles of
America, Maynard, MA
Jeff Shumway, Ecotech Autoworks,
McLean, VA
Albert Navarro, Pro-Electric
Miramar, FL

MIDWEST
John Stockberger, Batavia, IL
MOUNTAIN STATES
Electric Motor Cars, Houston, TX
Alternative Autos, Parker, CO
W. D. Mitchell, Rowlett, TX
ALSO: Contact Electro-Automotive
(408-429-1989) for names of
technicians who have completed the
Pro-Mech Program.

What does it cost to convert a car or pick-up truck?

Most conversions: $8,000-12,000. This price is a general ballpark figure for parts ($6,000) and labor. You supply the vehicle, and the convertor will install standard parts. (Pricing is subject to change — special driving conditions may require more expensive components.) Batteries cost about $75 each, so a 96-volt, 16-battery system would run another $1,200.

Do-it-yourself conversions can cost much less (depending on what conveniences the driver is willing to live without). Some EV owners have used surplus parts and assembled a functioning EV for under $3,000. However, such low-cost vehicles are often neither adequate nor economically sound, since they use a lot of amps and many cannot climb hills (when an inappropriate motor type is used).

SOLAR AUTOS

Switzerland is home to the Tour de Sol and a number of electric vehicle innovators. The country's commercial office has a directory with a special section called "Solar Autos." It is provided here for the reader's reference. When dialing from the U.S., press "011", then the country code (41, given as the first two digits of each phone number below) and the number.

Heinrich Bucher
Fridez Solar AG
Horlacher AG
Ingenieurbüro Muntwyler
Pfander AG
Sun-Craft AG

The U.S. Dept. of Energy reminds you to go 45-55 mph to reduce oil imports.

MANUFACTURERS

Who is making a car from the ground up? This category includes OEM conversions (Original Equipment Manufacturers): for example, when the General Motors Impact components are placed in a Geo Storm, it becomes an OEM conversion. The OEM puts all the components together and sells it as a unit.

Bedford Chloride
BMW
Chrysler
Citroën
Clean Air Technology
Clean Air Transit
Columbia Auto Sales
Conceptor Industries Inc.
Cushman
El-Trans A/S
Ford Motor Co.

General Motors
(ready in January 1995 according to Ken Baker, program manager)
Horlacher
Peugeot
Renaissance Cars
Sebring Auto-Cycle
Solar Car Corp.
Solectria, Inc.
Swatch/Volkswagen
TEVan

KITS

Clark Beasley
Doran Motor Co. (plans)
Electric Vehicles of America, Inc.
Electro Automotive
Eyeball Engineering
King Electric Vehicles
KTA Services
Lectric Kar
Solar Car Corp.
Solar Electric

The complete kit of everything you need for converting an S-10 pickup (batteries not shown). The large box (right) is the charger. *Photo courtesy of Solar Car Corp.*

AUTO-CYCLES

(three-wheelers for the highway)

The auto-cycle is a new generation of vehicle which is legally classified as a motorcycle, but which is perceived, used and driven with many of the functions normally associated with an automobile. The vehicle is a hybrid of a cycle and an automobile. It embodies the best advantages of both types of vehicle.

Auto-cycles can significantly decrease the amount of energy needed for personal transportation, because they are smaller, lighter, and experience less rolling resistance because they lack the fourth wheel. The auto-cycle that we started in Sebring will probably become a generic for whole new mode of transportation. (Jim Tervort) Sebring Auto-Cycle, Inc.

Production of the three-wheeled Zzipper was suspended in February 1992.
Plans For 3-Wheeler: Doran Motor Co
Plans for the Vortex: Dolphin Vehicles
"The Lean Machine": General Motors

The Isetta, one of the early auto-cycles, is a popular conversion.

CONSULTANTS

The following individuals are available for consulting on electric car projects, large and small:

Randall Asherlan & Associates
Clean Air Revival
Earthmind
Ecotech Autoworks
Electric Auto Crafters
Electric Fuel Propulsion Corp.
Electric Vehicles of America
Electric Vehicle Matrix
Electric Motor Cars Sales
Electro Automotive
Electromotive Systems
EV Consultants (Ed Campbell)
EV Custom Conversion
Eyeball Engineering
Interesting Transportation
KTA Services
Newland, Burt
Pacific Int'l Center (PICHTR)
Patterson, Renton
Program Development Associates
Sawyer, Albert
Schutte, Paul & Associates
Sebring Auto-Cycle, Inc.
Sines, Tom and Yvette Chermey
Solar Car Corp.
Solarland
Wing, Bob
Wouk Associates

Attention EV consultants: If you handle inquiries about EV construction projects and your name does not appear here, please send your information to the publisher. Periodic updates of this book will include your latest information.

Typical Consulting Services
Most consultants can offer the following range of services or can recommend where you can obtain these services.

Strategic Planning for the promotion and use of EVs by environmental groups, electric utilities, and environmentally conscious corporations.

EV Components and advice on how to maintain an EV.
EV Calculations
Your consultant can help you select an EV for your conversion by providing calculations for horsepower requirements, current requirements, and estimated range for various speeds and percent grades.

Information
Here's a sample of what two consultants offer:

"I'll take any phone call and consult over the phone. I'm willing to do what it takes to get more EVs on the road. And, since I supply parts, I hope you'll purchase some of your needs from me.

"For example, someone who works at a utility called me the other day and said his company is thinking about buying an electrified van for $50,000. I told him that I converted my pickup truck for under $10,000. He couldn't say anything for a full half-minute, and then said, 'Let's assume I buy a new truck for $15,000 and bring it to you. For another $10,000, you'll give me an electric pickup truck that has the same range, the same top speed as a $50,000 van?' He just couldn't believe it."
(Bob Batson)

Electro-Automotive's philosophy:
"If someone has a used EV and wants to know what should be put in to bring it up-to-date; if someone wants an expert's opinion on the condition of a converted EV; if someone has a straight-forward question, we can often help over the phone. If it's not possible to examine the car, we can give you advice and recommend EV clubs in your area, where you can look for additional guidance. If you give us a list of the equipment that is in the vehicle, we can give you our assessment over the phone. For example, if the EV has an SCR controller, it will need to be updated. Also, if you want an opinion about a dealer of EVs, we can tell you whether or not we've heard of the company and share with you what we know about the person's work. Always ask for references and call around to other EV clubs to see if anyone has heard of the dealer.
"We consider much of this to be

part of customer service. Even if you aren't a customer now, we figure that you'll be needing parts eventually and we'd like to be your supplier. If you have a specific project that you are working on, such as a car you are wanting to build or a car you are hiring a mechanic to assemble for you, you can send a check for $60 and Electro Automotive will analyze your project. You must complete the Project Review form found in our catalog. The $60 can be applied to purchases made within 60 days."
(Mike Brown)

AUSTRIA
Steyr Daimler Puch AG
8010 Graz 0316/404-2215
Fa. Ettlinger, 07483/234
Offiz. Nissan Vertretung
3281 Oberndorf an der Melk
Osterreichischer Automobil
Motorrad–undTouring club
Leberstrasse 56-60
Wien 222 74 16 23/74 16 28 (fax)
Asea Brown Boveri AG
Pernerstorferg. 94
1010 Wien 60109/0
Solarstromtechnik GmbH
Schlossstrasse 13
4111 Walding 07234/3892

ELECTRIC CAR PARTS

The following companies offer components. Several have provided self-descriptions which appear in the main alphabetical listing. Some firms also supply smaller vehicles (bicycles, mopeds).

Advanced D.C. Motors, Inc.
American Motion Systems, Inc.
Beyond Oil
Cruising Equipment Co.
Electric Auto Crafters
Electric Vehicle Associates
Electric Mobility
Electric Vehicle Custom Conversion
Electric Vehicles of America, Inc.
Electro Automotive
Fisher Technology
General Assembly Corp.
Green Motor Works
Hawaii Pacific Technology and Trade
JDM Products
King Electric Vehicles
KTA Services
New Concepts Engineering
Palmer Industries
Performance Speedway
Performance Speedway
Solar Car Corp.
Soleq
Suntools
Williams Enterprises

BATTERIES

Alco Battery Co.
Trojan Battery Co.
U.S. Batteries
Avenue
Interstate Batteries
Hydrocap Corp.
Batteries Included
Car-Go Battery Co.
Reconditioned Ni-Cad Batteries
UtilityFree
Eagle-Picher
Ovonic Corp.
Gates Energy Corp.
Harding Energy Corp.
Real Goods Catalog
Lead Industries Association

Students at Seminole Middle School (Plantation, Fla.) express interest in the EV donated by the editor. The Comuta-Van is one of 367 made for the U.S. Post Office in 1980-81. If you own an EV, consider showing it to students in nearby schools. *Photo by Dennis Yuzenas.*

Gene Cosmano's EV (Phoenix, Arizona)

EV ORGANIZATIONS

These EV organizations are arranged alphabetically by state, and alphabetically by city within each state. Some of the phone numbers are home numbers, so exercise care and consideration when telephoning. The chapters of the Electric Auto Association have the letters "EAA" in their name. Membership dues of these chapters also support the national EAA's educational and public awareness efforts.

For an "International Directory of the Electrical Vehicle Industry," contact: Clarence Ellers, Electronic Transportation Design, P.O. Box 111, Yachats, Oregon 97498. See also *EV Directories* for additional directories. For up-to-date EV listings on computer bulletin boards, contact Chuck Harrison, 301-495-7113 (work), 301-422-8704 (home). Chapters that issue a newsletter are highlighted with "*."

ARIZONA
Phoenix EAA*
Box 11371, Phoenix, AZ 85061
Lee Clouse 602-943-7950
Tucson EAA
Box 23417, Tucson, AZ 85734
Phil Terpstra 602-822-2030
Solar & Electric Racing Association, 11811 N. Tatum, #3031, Phoenix AZ 602-953-6672
>>> CALIFORNIA <<<
Electric Auto Association (EAA)*
1249 Lane St, Belmont, CA 94002
John Newell 415-591-6698 $25 for membership. Call between 10 a.m. and 5 p.m. for information on how to start an EAA chapter. Send a self-addressed, stamped envelope for a free copy of *Current EVents.*
EVAA* (formerly Electric Vehicle Development Corporation), #440 20823 Stevens Creek Boulevard Cupertino, CA 95014
East Bay EAA
1986 Gouldin Rd., Oakland, CA 94611 Jim Danaher 415-339-1984
Los Angeles EAA
2034 N. Brighton "C"
Burbank, CA 91504
Irv Weiss 818-841-5994
Electric Vehicle Association Of Southern California* (EVAOSC)
12531 Breezy Way
Orange, CA 92669
Ken Koch 714-639-9799
Peninsula EAA, 540 Moana Way
Pacifica, CA 94044
Jean Bardon 415-355-3060
North Bay EAA
Box 277, Inverness, CA 94937
Bob Wing 415-669-7402
San Jose EAA, 5820 Herma
San Jose, CA 95123
Don Gillis 408-225-5446

San Diego EAA*
9011 Los Coches Road
Lakeside, CA 92040
619-443-3017/286-3032
Sacramento EAA
5201 Dover Avenue
Sacramento, CA 95819-3824
Richard Minner 916-454-5524
EV Pioneers*, Sacramento Municipal Utility District (SMUD) P.O. Box 15830, 916-732-6557
Sacramento, CA 95852-1830
Santa Barbara EAA, Box 91327
Santa Barbara, CA 93190
Dale Ross 805-687-3919
Silicon Valley EAA*
1968 Elden Dr., San Jose, CA 95124
Paul Brasch 408-371-5969
Solar Alternative Vehicle Exposition, Box 8827
Stanford, CA 94309-8827
415-497-0861, 415-723-0010 (fax)
Organizers of the SAVE California Drive, a six-day, 760-mile event.
COLORADO
Denver Electric Vehicle Council*
12996 Dexter, Thornton CO 80241
Ron Putnam 303-452-3748
2940 13th St., Boulder CO 80304
George Gless 303-442-6566
DISTRICT OF COLUMBIA
Electric Vehicle Association of Greater Washington, D.C.*
EVA/DC, 9140 Centerway Road
Gaithersburg, MD 20879
301-231-3990 David Goldstein
EV Association of the Americas (EVAA), Edison Electric Institute
701 Pennsylvania Ave., N.W.
Washington, DC 202-508-5000
Organization for auto makers and suppliers of EV components. *EVAA is not set up to handle inquiries from the general public.* Affiliated with the

World Electric Vehicle Association, co-sponsor of the biennial EV Symposium with AVERE and Electric Vehicle Association of Asia.
Electric Transportation Coalition*
1050 Thomas Jefferson Street, N.W., Sixth Floor
Washington, D.C. 20007
202-298-1935, 202-338-2361 (fax)
Lobbyists, helped prepare the National Electric Vehicle Bill, sponsored by Rep. George Brown.
>>> **FLORIDA** <<<
Florida EAA, Box 156
Titusville, FL 32781 Bill Young 407-269-4609 Co-sponsor of Florida SunDay Rally.
>>> **HAWAII** <<<
Electric Vehicles of Hawaii (EVAH)
3620 Alohea, #C
Honolulu, HI 96813
Dave Hill 808-943-2784
David Rezachek 808-548-4080
>>> **ILLINOIS** <<<
Fox Valley EVA
2S 643 Nelson Lake Road
Batavia, IL 60510
John Stockberger 312-879-0207
Fox Valley EAA
1264 Harvest Court
Naperville, IL 60565
312-420-1118
>>> **MASSACHUSETTS** <<<
New England EAA*, Box 59
Maynard, Mass 01754
Bob Batson 508-897-8288
>>> **NEVADA** <<<
Nevada EAA*, P.O. Box 19040
Las Vegas, NV 89132-0040
Gail Lucas 702-736-1910
>>> **NEW JERSEY** <<<
New Jersey EAA, 293 Hudson St.
Hackensack, NJ 07601
Kasimir Wysocki 201-342-3684
>>> **NEW MEXICO** <<<
New Mexico EV Users Group 3213
Lucerne, NE 505-296-8523
Albuquerque, NM 87111
>>> **OREGON** <<<
Oregon EVA*, Box 2116
Lake Orange, OR 97035
Lon Gillas 503-434-4332
>>> **PENNSYLVANIA** <<<
Eastern Electric Vehicle Club*
Box 717, Valley Forge, PA 19482
215-279-4373, 215-696-5615
>>> **TEXAS** <<<
Houston EAA*, 4301 Kingfisher
Houston, TX 77035

Ken Bancroft 713-729-8668
>>> **UTAH** <<<
Utah EAA, 3622 South 4840 West
West Valley City, UT 84120
Harry Van Soolen 801-969-1130
>>> **WASHINGTON** <<<
Seattle EAA, 19547 23rd N.W.
Seattle, WA 98177
Ray Nadreau 206-542-5612
Port Townsend EAA
221 Kennedy Road
Pt. Hadlock, WA 98339
Roderick Erwin 206-385-2962
>>> **CANADA** <<<
EVA of Canada*
395 Matheson Blvd. East
Mississauga, Ontario
33 Mann Avenue, Ottawa, Ont. K1N 6N5 613-564-6818
Electric Vehicle Council of Ottawa (EVCO) 613-820-7400
Box 4044, Station E
Ottawa, Ontario K1S 5B1
Vancouver EVA*
543 Powell St., 604-980-5819
Vancouver, B.C. V6A 1G8
604-987-6188 *Send EV news to Bill Glazier, 3344 Baird Rd, N. Vancouver, B.C., V7K 2G7*
>>> **EUROPE** <<<
AVERE, 34 Blvd de Waterloo
1000-Bruxelles, Belgium
Société Europeène des Electromobiles Rochelaises
Avenue P. Langevin
B.P. 6, 17182 Perigny Cedex
France 46452505, 46447162 (fax)
Registro Italiano Veicoli Elettro Solari, Via Poggibonsi, 14
20146 Milano Italy (F. Maggiolini)
Angelo Siniscalco, Via Ruinacci 3
80046 San Giorgio A Cremano, Naples, Italy (manufacturer's rep.)
Battery Vehicle Society (UK)
44 Heath Road, Market Bosworth
Nuneaton CV13 0NX
Warwichsire, England, U.K.
>>> **PACIFIC** <<<
Australian Electric Vehicle Association, P.O. Box 273
Mitcham, Victoria 3132
Australia 61-3-772-1416
Hong Kong/World EVA
Dr. C.C. Chan
Dept. of Electrical Engineering
International Research Centre for Electric Vehicles, Pokfulam Road
University of Hong Kong, H.K.
5-859-2706, 852-5-598-738 (fax)

Japan Electric Vehicle Association,
2-5-5 Toranomon
Minato-ku, Tokyo, Japan

RELATED ORGANIZATIONS

(dedicated to energy conservation, development of sustainable and alternative energy resources, energy policy, etc.)

American Council for an Energy-Efficient Economy (ACEEE)
1001 Connecticut Avenue, N.W., #801
Washington, D.C. 20036 429-8873

American Solar Energy Society
2400 Central Ave, G-1, Boulder, CO 80301 Advocates of solar power.

Association for Commuter Transportation (ACT)
808 17th Street, N.W., #200
Washington, D.C. 20006
202-223-9669 Working to eliminate the major cause of traffic congestion: employer-subsidized parking. Ask them how to encourage car pools and van pools by charging near-market rates for parking at work.

Association of Science and Technical Centers
1025 Vermont Ave., N.W. #500
Washington, DC 20005
202-783-7200 The association has expressed interest in obtaining electric vehicles (loan or donation) for its member museums to exhibit.

Auto-Free DC, Timothy Lidiak
3637 Fulton Street, N.W.
Washington, DC 20007
202-625-7404 Advocates reduced dependence on automobiles. Affiliated with the Institute for Transportation and Development Policy and "Bikes, Not Bombs."

Auto-Free New York
Transportation Alternatives
494 Broadway, Room 300
NY, NY 10012 212-941-4600 Forum for examining our society's dependence on automobiles.

Center for Sustainable Transportation
Greenhouse Crisis Foundation
1130 17th Street, N.W., #630
Washington, DC 20036
202-466-2823, 202-429-9602 (fax)
Jeremy Rifkin (author of books on global warming) works here.

Center for Appropriate Transportation
49 E. Houston St.
New York, NY 10012
Steve Stollman 212-431-0600

Citizens for Clean Energy
Box 17147, Boulder CO 80308
Steve Clark 303-443-6181

Energy Conservation Coalition
Environmental Action
1525 New Hampshire Ave, N.W.
Washington, DC 20036 202-745-4874

Environmental Solutions International
Box 869, Islamorada, FL 33036
305-664-9796 or 202-547-4315
235 Pennsylvania Avenue, S.E.
Washington, D.C. 20003
Founded in 1990 "to find, develop and implement solutions that reverse centuries of abuse and neglect." Focus: alternative energy, waste reduction, protection of marine life.

Florida Solar Energy Center
300 State Road 401
Cape Canaveral, FL 32920-4029
407-783-0300, 407-783-2571 (fax)
Sponsors of the Sun Day Rally
William Young, Craig Maytrott

Floridians for Safe Energy
7269 S.W. 54th Avenue
S. Miami, FL 33143 305-661-2165
Clearinghouse for information on sustainable sources of energy.

Institute for Transportation Studies,
Mail Code 236-N, 916-752-6572 (fax)
University of California at Davis
Davis, CA 95616 Dan Sperling
The Institute investigates the leading questions: what's more energy-efficient, a gasoline car or an EV, and what kind of electric vehicle? What's the source of electricity? They do the tough data analysis.

International Bicycle Fund, 4887
Columbia Dr S., Seattle, WA 98108
Advocates for the true zero-emissions vehicle. This non-profit organization promotes bicycle transport, economic development and safety education.

Midwest Renewable Energy Ass'n
Box 249, 116 Cross Street
Amherst WI 54406 715-824-5166

Northeast Sustainable Energy Association, 23 Ames Street
Greenfield, Mass 01301
413-774-6051/6053 (fax)
NESEA is a non-profit membership organization which promotes

responsible energy use for a clean environment, in an attempt to move toward a sustainable society. Public education efforts include a quarterly magazine, bookstore and the American Tour de Sol. ATdS promotes the use of practical non-polluting electric and solar-electric vehicles.

Northern California Solar Energy Association, P.O. Box 3008 Berkeley, CA 94703 Valerie Howard 408-371-9122

For information on energy efficiency:
Rocky Mountain Institute (RMI) 1739 Snowmass Creek Road Snowmass, CO 81654-9199 303-927-3851 RMI is a nonprofit policy center founded in 1982 by energy analysts Hunter and Amory Lovins. Its mission is to foster the efficient and sustainable use of resources as a path to global security. RMI conducts interrelated programs covering Energy (including Transportation), Water, Agriculture, Economic Renewal (an innovative approach to local development) and Redefining National Security. It has 35 full-time staff. Its COMPETITEK service provides uniquely current and detailed technical information on electric efficiency to more than 220 utilities, industries, and governments in 34 countries. RMI's new transportation project explores systems issues and technologies, especially for super-efficient light vehicles. *RMI favors hybrid-electric cars over pure EVs are inferior in performance and economics. RMI maintains that hybrids allow the car to be lighter, since it doesn't need as much battery mass as the pure EV. The extra motor is not chiefly a range extender, it's a "horsepower extender," giving the vehicle better performance for cruising. Lovins recommends that the HEV should carry only enough batteries to store about 5 kilowatt-hours, the amount of "one day's on-car photovoltaic input while parked." Lovins regards fuel cells as potentially part of a long-term transportation solution, with hydrogen stored in metal hydrides or methanol.*

Population/Environment Balance 1325 G Street, N.W., Suite 1003 Washington, D.C. 20006 Quarterly

newsletter with focus on population's impact on the environment. Works with Carrying Capacity Network 202-879-3044 "A nonprofit, nonpartisan activist network which facilitates cooperation and information dissemination among organizations working on carrying capacity issues such as environmental protection, population stabilization, growth control and resource conservation. *Carrying Capacity* refers to the number of individuals who can be supported without degrading the physical, ecological, cultural and social environment, i.e., without reducing the ability of the environment to sustain the desired quality of life over the long term."

EV DIRECTORIES

Electric Vehicle Directory Box 23417, Tucson, AZ 85734 602-822-2030 Phil Terpstra
Electric Vehicles Unplugged! Douglas Marsh, Box 94 Batavia, IL 60510
World Electric Vehicle Directory by EV Progress, 212-228-0246 Alexander Research Suite 1310, 212-228-0376 (fax) 215 Park Avenue South New York, NY 10003 *The most comprehensive and up-to-date listing of suppliers of electric vehicles. $25 and worth every penny.*
International Directory of the Electrical Vehicle Industry Clarence Ellers, Electronic Transportation Design Box 111, Yachats, Oregon 97498

PUBLICATIONS

Alternative Transportation News (ATN) (6 issues/year, $20) Earthmind, 310-396-1527, Box 743, Mariposa, CA 95338
Solar Mind (6 issues/year, $25) 759 South State, #81 Ukiah, Calif. 95482 707-468-0878/510-524-6770 (fax)
Electric Vehicle News (monthly) 1911 N. Ft. Myer Drive, #703 Arlington, VA 22209 703-527-1936, 703-524-4093 (fax)

Electric Vehicle Progress
(26 issues/year, industry newsletter)
Alexander Research
Suite 1310, 215 Park Ave South
NY, NY 10003 212-206-7979
Electric Car, Richard Richmond
(industry trade journal)
Box 6854, Vero Beach, FL 32961
407-562-9052, 407-778-9686 (fax)
Electric Grand Prix, Paul Heaney
6 Gateway Circle, 716-889-1229
Rochester, New York 14624
Electric Transportation Coalition
1050 Thomas Jefferson St., N.W.
Wash., D.C. 20007 202-298-1935

OTHER PUBLICATIONS

Backwoods Home Magazine
Box 2630, Ventura, CA 93002
805-647-9341 An alternative energy
magazine, covers electric car issues.
Northern Sun
Northeast Sustainable Energy
Association, 23 Ames Street
Greenfield, Mass 01301
**U.S. Department of Energy
Office of Transportation
Technologies**, Phil Patterson, Ph.D.
CE-30, 1000 Independence Ave, S.W.
Washington, D.C. 20585 202-586-9121
Phil edits the Transportation Energy Data
Book, the most comprehensive and up-to-
date compilation and record on how the
transportation sector uses energy. *If we
purchase more efficient cars and consume
energy prudently, the results will appear in
this annual publication. Dr. Patterson
hopes to include more data related to
alternative fuel vehicles and second, third
and fourth cars of multi-car households in
future editions. Let's give him something
to report on: one million converted EVs!*
Home Power, 916-475-3179
Box 130, Hornbrook, CA 96044
An alternative energy magazine that
reports on "what works." Covers EVs
on a regular basis.
The New Economy (monthly)
National Commission for Economic
Conversion, 1801 18th Street, N.W.
Washington, DC 20009
Has covered EV issues.
PV Network News
2303 Cedros Circle
Santa Fe, NM 87505-5252
505-473-1067 Information on solar
panels, photovoltaic systems and how
to connect them for efficient battery
recharging.
Sunworld
International Solar Energy Society
Box 8364, Santa Fe, NM 87504
Publications: alternative fuels
Clean Energy Research Institute
University of Miami, Box 248294
Coral Gables, FL 33124
Clean Fuels Report
Box 649, Niwot, CO 80544
303-652-2632, 303-652-2772 (fax)
In-depth analysis of alternative fuel
news by Jerry Sinor. Niwot in
Arapaho means "left hand."
Hemisphere Publishing Corp.
79 Madison Ave., NY, NY 10015
Specializes in publishing the
proceedings from conferences on
alternative energy.
**International Association for
Hydrogen Energy**, Box 248266
Coral Gables, FL 33124
Established in 1985, the IAHE
publishes the **International Journal
of Hydrogen Energy.**
IRT Publications
Box 10990, Aspen, CO 81612
Ted Flanigan 303-927-3155
Ted has worked with Rocky Mountain
Institute and other groups to describe
"global designs for a sustainable
environment." Recent publications
include *Hydrogen: The Invisible Fire*
and *Transportation: The Grand
ReDesign,* a survey of "attractive
alternatives to automobile
dependency."
Windpower Monthly
Vrinners Hoved, 45 86 36 54 65
8420 Knebel, Denmark; U.S. contact:
Box 496007, Redding, CA 96099

Peugeot's electric 205 has a plug
located in the front of the car,
convenient for charging at a specially
equipped parking meter. *Photo
provided by Peugeot.*

RELATED SERVICES AND PRODUCTS

*Many of the companies listed here have advertised in **Solar Mind** and **ATN** and other EV-related publications. Give them a chance to quote you some prices: it's a way of thanking them for supporting the EV industry's magazines.*

Active Technology
4808 MacArthur Blvd.
Oakland, CA 94619
415-482-8025 New and used PV modules, industrial batteries, solar-powered stage events, kits for hobbyists, surplus motors and parts.

Alternative Energy Engineering
Box 339, Redway, CA 95560
1-800-777-6609
"Solar Electric Stuff." Send $3 for 105-page catalog.

Atlantic Solar Products
9351 J Philadelphia Road
Box 70060, Baltimore, MD 21237
301-686-2500, 301-686-6221 (fax)
Solar electric products and systems.

Auto Ad Quarterly
John H. Huth 703-521-3985
Queen Street Associates
2403 South Queen Street
Arlington, VA 22202
Publication that serves buyers and sellers of old automobile advertisements. John has some great T-shirts with color reproductions of Baker Electric ads: great gift for the EV enthusiast in your life ($25).

Balanced Energy Systems
Ample Power Co, 1150 NW 52nd St
Seattle, WA 98107
206-789-4743, 206-789-9003 (fax)
Source for a range of instruments and information on getting "off the grid."

Earth Energy Association
1701 K Street, N.W. #400
Washington, DC 20006
202-223-1606, 202-223-1393 (fax)
"The voice of the passive geothermal industry." Fact sheets on geothermal systems (heat pumps). Find out how many closed loop geothermal systems have been installed in residences (200,000) and industry (15,000).

Earth Lab Energy Systems
358 S. Main St, Willits, CA 95482
707-459-6272 Systems for solar electricity. Installation, mail order.

General Cryogenics Inc.
3328 Hawthorne Avenue
Dallas, TX 75219 Patrick Martin 214-528-1666 Supplier of refrigerator systems for trucks, based on non-CFC (chloro- fluoro-carbon)

technology. Could be adapted for an EV or alternative fuels van(?).

Geothermal Power
International Ground Source Heat Pump Association, 405-744-5175.
Learn how to reduce your electric bill with a heat pump (and save enough to eventually buy an EV!).

Harris Hydroelectric
632 Swanton Rd, Davenport, CA
95017 408-425-7652
Hydropower for home use.

Kansas Wind Power
Route 1 B, Holton, KS 66436
913-364-4407 Efficient propane refrigerators, freezers, tankless water heaters, windmills. Electric garden tractors (36-volt) and mowers. Supplier of wind, hydro, solar electric systems, water stills. Catalog: $3.

Mendocino Power 707-468-9663
3001 South State St., Ukiah, CA
95482 Solar systems, low-flush toilets, window quilts, water pumping.

Missouri Department of Natural Resources, Division of Energy
205 Jefferson Street, Box 176
Jefferson City, MO 65102
800-334-6946 Information on ground source heat pumps.

Photocomm, 800-223-9580
7681 E. Gray Rd, Scottsdale, AZ
85260 Source for Kyocera solar electric modules. Catalog: $5.

Real Goods, 966 Mazzoni St.
Ukiah, CA 95482 707-468-9214
800-762-7325, 707-468-0301 (fax)
Renewable energy catalog. "Building a Sustainable Solar Future." Send $10 (applied to first order) for 320-page Sourcebook.

RyeNovators, Doug Rye & Associates, 3 Anthony Lane
Mablevale, AR 72103
501-455-2305 Consultant for energy-efficient building and retro-fit.

Sparky Marine Electrics
Schoonmaker Building, #160
Sausalito, CA Dennis 415-332-6726
Solar panels, inverters, energy efficient lighting, 12 Volts DC and 110 Volts AC, etc.

Tropico Solar
Box 417, Solar George
Big Pine Key, FL 33043
305-872-3976 Catalog: $4. Supplies
PV parts and EV supplies.
Transient Voltage Protector
(a device to reduce voltage
fluctuations and to provide some
protection from lighting strikes)
Hal Spindell (distributor)
Power Savers Inc., 808-988-9506
Box 11389, Honolulu, HI 96828

BUMPER STICKERS, ETC.

EcoSource
9051 Mill Station Road
Sebastopol, CA 95472
The Greenpeace Catalog
Box 77048, San Francisco, CA
94107 800-456-4029 Stuff to make
you feel good about being a
consumer. Guilt-free materialism.
Northern Sun Merchandising
2916 East Lake Street
Minneapolis, MN 55406
Peace Resource
Box 1122, Arcata, CA 95521
707-822-4229 Posters, shirts,
bumper stickers and buttons with
sustainable energy themes.
Seventh Generation
49 Hercules Dr., Colchester, VT
05446-1672 800-456-1177/802-655-
2700 (fax) Over 300 top-quality
products for a healthy planet,
including classic natural cotton
clothing, gentle lotios and shampoos,
baby items, environmentally safe
cleaners, 100% recycled toilet paper,
water-saving products. Full-color
catalog: $2. Publishes a booklet
listing over 100 non-profit
organizations that are improving the
world and fostering sustainable
patterns of living. The company's
name comes from this quotation from
the Great Law of the Hau de no
saunee: In our every deliberation, we
must consider the impact of our
decisions on the next seven
generations.
American Hydrogen Association
219 South Siesta Lane, #101
Tempe, AZ 85281

Audubon Society
950 Third Ave, NY, NY 10022
Join the Solar Brigade: *Ten seconds
a month can help save the planet.*
Environmental Youth Alliance
Box 34097, Station D
Vancouver, BC V6J 4MI CANADA
604-737-2258, 739-8064 (fax)
Organizing students.
Public Citizen
215 Pennsylvania Avenue, S.E.
Washington, DC 20003
202-546-4996 Sponsor of Sun Day
1992, the campaign for a sustainable
energy future.
Save The Planet, Box 45, Pitkin, CO
81241 303-641-5035 Roger Cox
Software on climate change.
Addresses for all members of
Congress, handy for badgering your
Senator about passing S. 398, the
lead-battery recycling bill co-
sponsored by the late John Heinz.

Become a star!
Anyone who sends proof of owning
an electric car will be mentioned in
the next book, *The EV Encyclopedia:
A Guide to Electric Cars.* Send a
photo and a description of your EV,
explain why you purchased it, and
you'll be acknowledged for your
"environmental patriotism." The car
must be in running order, and used at
least 10 miles a week (past
registrations shuld show a difference
of at least 500 miles per year). If
your photo and description arrive after
the book has gone to press, we'll
include you in a supplement.

**Libraires with the first editon of
Why Wait For Detroit?**
Kalamazoo Public Libray (Michigan)
Univesity of Michigan, Dearborn
School District of Flint, Michigan

GERMANY
Staatliche Gewerbeschule
Alfredstrasse 3
2000 Hamburg 76 06/040/24 88 25 43
W & S AG, Hinterdorferstr. 27
5032 Rohr 05/064/22 08 06

Index

Additions

The index on page 158 should have these additions:

AC motors 123, 124
American Tour de Sol 134, 153-154
Bancroft, Ken 45
batteries, effects of aging 131
battery charger 129
Beyond Oil (inside front cover)
Clean Air Day 6
Cobb, Doug **16**
contactors 126
Cosmano, Gene **150**
cost per mile 56-59
energy efficiency 42-45
energy needed to make a car 133

gross vehicle weight rating 103
Gulick, Lew 50
ICE Age, end of the 6
obstacles to EV development 6
petroleum fractions 25
Phoenix 500 **37**
Solar George **43**
Symons, Dr. Michael 52
vehicles per household 38
voltage, measuring (under load) 130
voltmeter 130, 131
Wing, Bob 135

Corrections

Back cover: the ISBN (International Standard Book Number) should read 1-879857-02-2.
page 2: in the Acknowledgements, add: George Skarpelos and Gary C. Marshall for their help with the cover; Murray Tuchman and Gus Gonzales for expediting the printing.
page 64: the figures in the diagram, totaling 1.45 million pounds, should drop the last three zeros. The last paragraph should read: In 1990, 1.45 million pounds of lead went into the atmosphere in the U.S. and 588,000 pounds came from the burning of used oil.
page 101: the larger photo's caption: The Tropica by Renaissance Cars, Inc.
page 102: the photo shows electric cars on display at SEER 1991 in Willits, Calif.
page 107: the price shown in the second paragraph should read: the under-$10,000 price tag... *The last line should read:* and provides the driver a reliable car with a sporty ground-up design. *In the caption,* the boldface **RIGHT** should read: **ABOVE**.
page 126: the reader should note that any particular product, in this case the Bussman fuse, is named only as an example of the type of device to look for. Check with an EV consultant before making any purchases.
page 131: in the upper table, the fourth column should read: Minimum safe level prior to recharging.
page 145: Sebring Auto-Cycle has a new phone number: 813-471-0424, located at 1601 Highlands Avenue, Sebring, FL 33870. Conversions of Dodge Colts to make a ZEV.
page 152: the hometown of the Oregon EVA should read: Lake Oswego.
page 158: eletrathon should read: electrathon
Indexed references to page numbers above 120 are accurate to within 4 pages. For example, James Worden has a reference on page 120 but the article appears on page 124. *(Other corrections include various typographical errors, such as Decebmer on page 100).*

For a copy of "Guidelines for Converting Gasoline-Powered Cars To Electric," send two first-class stamps to: EVIA, Box 59, Maynard, Mass. 01754

- -

CLIP THIS VALUABLE COUPON

The only way to handle lead is to recycle it

By the Hon. Esteban E. Torres, Member of Congress, and sponsor of the Lead Battery Recycling Incentives Act (H.R. 870), which would support greater domestic recycling of lead-acid batteries, thereby averting improper disposal.

Lead is a highly toxic substance and it is ubiquitous in our society. the most significant use of lead today is in lead-acid batteries. it is critical to remember, as we are advancing into the era of the electric vehicle, that 85 percent of the lead used in manufacturing is consumed by the production of automotive batteries. Since there is no economically or technically viable substitute for lead in batteries, as the electric automobile industry develops, battery production and therefore, lead use, will increase dramatically.

More than 70 million batteries are taken out of commission every year. Since each battery contains approximately 20 pounds of lead, the result is that 1.4 billion pounds of lead are available for recycling.

Used batteries are a resource. the lead that comes from lead acid batteries is highly recyclable. Unfortunately, lead recycling is simply a function of market forces. If the price of virgin lead is high, the battery manufacture will use recycled lead. IF the price of virgin lead is low, then recycled lead is less appealing.

Lead that is not recycled may wind up in landfills or municipal waste incinerators. In either event, it has the potential of contaminating our air or water supplies or severely polluting our land.

Is the battery problem simply a matter of doing better at collecting batteries or is it a matter of how much value is place on a spent battery. A clear grasp of the economics of the lead recycling industry strongly suggests that any effective approach to increasing the rate of lead acid battery recycling must treat lead battery recovery as a demand problem rather than a supply problem. In other words, the supply of lead available for recycling is high but the demand for secondary lead is low. Collecting more batteries, though necessary, will not increase demand, only supply. We need to concentrate our efforts on putting in place a market system that will increase the demand for used batteries.

The Lead Battery Recycling Incentives Act (H.R. 870) requires battery manufacturers to take responsibility for the products that they produce. Battery manufacturers would be required to use an annually increasing percentage of secondary lead. If the manufacture uses more lead than required, the manufacturer would be entitled to sell the "rights" to the excess to those manufacturers or importers who use less than the required amount. The excess rights are called "recycling credits" and would follow the same model of the highly successful EPA phase-out of lead from gasoline.

The Lead Battery Recycling Incentives Act creates a system of incentives, a mix of carrots and sticks, that will make the lead battery recycling infrastructure work for our environment and our economy, not against it.

Rep. Esteban Torres

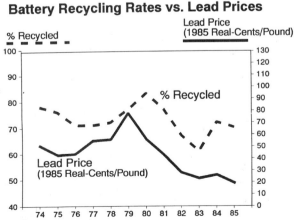

Battery Recycling Rates vs. Lead Prices

Energy Institute

Education to Create a Sustainable Future

Jordan Energy Institute (JEI) offers coursework and field experience in a variety of programs featuring independent power production, energy conservation, applied appropriate technology, and energy and environmental policy coupled with business administration and computer applications.

JEI has one of the most complete alternative energy libraries in the United States. We offer students an exceptional amount of interaction with faculty in the classroom, field, and through independent study. We provide excellent contacts with industry through work-study internships and job placement.

JEI offers itself as a resource for projects aimed at creating or enhancing alternative energy use and awareness in developing countries. We encourage our upper-level students to apply their knowledge and experience in these independent study programs which create goodwill while building a sustainable future for us all.

Jordan Energy Institute offers 1,2, & 4 year degrees in:

Renewable Energy
The renewable energy engineering technology program offers a four-year B.S. degree in the renewable energy field without neglecting the broad spectrum of engineering design philosophy and general education.

Applied Environmental Technology
This four-year B.S. program allows students to focus on the relationship of renewable energy and related technologies to environmental concerns.

Energy Management Technology
This two-year program is concerned with the known energy resources, the availability and cost of the various forms of energy, and the efficient conversion and use of these resources. A one-year certificate in Solar Retrofit Technology is also offered.

Energy and Construction Management
This two-year program trains students in blueprinting, energy efficiency, modern and appropriate construction materials, on-site construction techniques and business methods. A one-year certificate is also offered.

Electric Vehicle Technology
This two-year program offers practical, hands-on study of the motors, controls, and accessories used in modern electrically-powered vehicles.

Degrees are also offered in several fields related to Business Administration and Computer Applications.